MATERIALITIES IN ANTHROPOLOGY AND ARCHAEOLOGY

EARTHY MATTERS

MATERIALITIES IN ANTHROPOLOGY AND ARCHAEOLOGY

SERIES EDITORS

Luci Attala and Louise Steel
University of Wales Trinity Saint David

SERIES EDITORIAL BOARD

Dr Nicole Boivin
Director of the Max Planck Institute for the Science of Human History

Professor Samantha Hurn
University of Exeter

Dr Oliver Harris
University of Leicester

Professor David Howes
Concordia Centre for Interdisciplinary Studies in Society and Culture

Dr Elizabeth Rahman
University of Oxford

MATERIALITIES IN ANTHROPOLOGY AND ARCHAEOLOGY

EARTHY MATTERS

EXPLORING HUMAN INTERACTIONS WITH EARTH, SOIL AND CLAY

Edited by
LOUISE STEEL
and LUCI ATTALA

UNIVERSITY OF WALES PRESS
2024

© The Contributors, 2024

All rights reserved. No part of this book may be reproduced in any material form (including photocopying or storing it in any medium by electronic means and whether or not transiently or incidentally to some other use of this publication) without the written permission of the copyright owner except in accordance with the provisions of the Copyright, Designs and Patents Act 1988. Applications for the copyright owner's written permission to reproduce any part of this publication should be addressed to the University of Wales Press, University Registry, King Edward VII Avenue, Cardiff CF10 3NS.

www.uwp.co.uk

British Library Cataloguing-in-Publication Data
A catalogue record for this book is available from the British Library.

ISBN 978-1-83772-135-1
eISBN 978-1-83772-136-8

The rights of The Contributors to be identified as authors of this work have been asserted in accordance with sections 77 and 79 of the Copyright, Designs and Patents Act 1988.

Typeset by Marie Doherty
Printed and bound by CPI Group (UK) Ltd, Croydon, CR0 4YY

CONTENTS

LIST OF FIGURES

ACKNOWLEDGEMENTS

We would like to thank the many people who have helped us bring this book to fruition. First and foremost, we are grateful to Sarah Lewis, who commissioned the *Materialities in Anthropology and Archaeology* series for the University of Wales Press. We greatly appreciate her enthusiasm and help in establishing this series and for her patience and guidance throughout the editing process. We would also like to thank our contributors for their lively and stimulating chapters, which variously attend to earthy matter, and in particular their enthusiasm for the ideas and theories underpinning this volume and the wider *Materialities* series. Thank you also to our two reviewers for their support and insightful comments, and to Eiluned Rees for her advice on indexing.

Louise would like particularly to thank Steve Thomas, not least because of his own interest in soils and earth, but also for his help in organising student activities working with plaster in class. As always, Steve has been a reliable sounding board, providing an objective view of our writing and ideas. We would also like to acknowledge the role that our wonderful students have played in shaping this volume, most particularly their enthusiasm for working with and learning from clay, lime plaster and plastics in various modules. This book has grown out of your challenging questions, which have honed our own thinking about the liveliness of these substances.

Luci would like to thank every person who is occupied with seeking solutions to our current environmental problems. She would also like to thank her family, friends and neighbours. To those alive – particularly her siblings, children and grandchildren – in all their colourful excitability, enthusiasm and general craziness, without you I couldn't have done this. To those dead – you thought you could get away – well think again, you are still actively influencing and shaping us, and we will all come and join you in the soil (and air) soon enough!

LIST OF CONTRIBUTORS

Benjamin Alberti received his PhD from Southampton University, where he studied gender and the artwork of Bronze Age Knossos from a feminist perspective. He has since gone on to publish widely on this topic, as well as on the ceramics of north-west Argentina and the Archaic rock art of northern New Mexico, where he also co-directs projects. Teaching what he loves, Benjamin incorporates archaeology, anthropology, art and materiality into many of his classes. In addition, queer theory, feminism, studies of masculinity and social theory all feature prominently. During the summer, Benjamin teaches on the graduate anthropology programme at Universidad Nacional de Cordoba, Argentina.

Luci Attala is an award-winning anthropologist who has published ethnographic work on environmental issues connected to water with communities in Wales, Colombia, Kenya and Spain. She is currently Director of the UNESCO-MOST BRIDGES humanities-driven transdisciplinary sustainability science programme in the UK and works as an Associate Professor at the University of Wales, where she has a record of innovation in research and championing alternative pedagogical methods. Luci also works with the Educere Alliance at the University of Oxford. She was awarded the first EAUC International Green Gown for teaching that furnished graduates with the skills to respond to the conditions associated with the climate changing. In addition, Luci is a Fellow of the World Academy of Arts and Sciences and is a UNESCO inclusive policy lab expert.

Natalie Boyd is a PhD student in archaeology, history and anthropology at the University of Wales Trinity Saint David. Her research focuses on the archaeology of the Near East, particularly its material culture. She has worked in commercial archaeology in the United Kingdom since completing her MA in 2011, and is currently archives manager and project officer for South West Archaeology Ltd.

Joanne Clarke is professor in the School of Art Media and American studies at the University of East Anglia. She is an archaeologist with extensive fieldwork experience in Cyprus, the Near East and north Africa. Joanne currently directs excavations at two prehistoric sites in Kalavasos, Cyprus and co-directs a programme of archaeological and environmental research in western Sahara. Her principal research interest is human adaptation to, and exploitation of, rapid changes in climate and environment in the early and middle Holocene. Joanne's key interest are the social changes that took place during the late Neolithic (the 8.2 Kyr event) and the Chalcolithic (the 5.9–5.1 Kyr event). She recently led a research network funded by the Arts and Humanities Research Council's Landscape and Environment Programme, *Environmental Change in Prehistory*.

Eloise Govier is an artist who has recently been awarded a PhD in social archaeology at University of Wales Trinity Saint David. She is interested in human and material interactions, while making and using contemporary art practices (including her own) to understand the material remains of the past. Eloise teaches theoretical approaches to material culture in both archaeology and cultural anthropology and has specialist knowledge of Anatolian Neolithic creative practices. Eloise's PGCert HE research focused on multisensory, collaborative and experiential learning – these learning strategies inform both her teaching and her creative practice.

Simone Sambento works at the intersection of Anthropology and Science and Technology Studies (STS), mainly in environmental fields and policy. She is currently finishing her PhD in Multidisciplinary Collaborations in Cave and Karst Environments with the University of Edinburgh. Her academic interests focus on the democratisation of knowledge, participatory research, multi-stakeholder collaborations, and policy development. She is a member of the Centre for Science, Knowledge and Policy at Edinburgh (SKAPE) and does consultancy work for environmental projects and for social and gender equality issues in sports and science fields. In her spare time, she can be found practising speleology, sailing the west coast of Scotland and writing crime-fiction stories. She is an operational member of the Scottish Cave Rescue Organisation (SCRO).

Alexander Scott is researcher and assistant curator for National Museums Liverpool and lecturer in modern history at the University of Wales Trinity Saint David. His research focuses on the histories of cities, museums and colonialism, and his publications include an article on animal exhibitions for the *Journal of Victorian Culture* (2020) and a chapter exploring access to museums in *Museums and the Working Class* (Routledge, 2022). He is currently helping to develop new exhibits at the International Slavery Museum, Liverpool.

Louise Steel is professor of Near Eastern archaeology at the University of Wales Trinity Saint David. She has worked extensively in Cyprus, focusing her research on the consumption of late Bronze Age pottery, and has directed excavations at al-Moghraqa (Gaza) and Arediou (Cyprus). Louise is the author of *Materiality and Consumption in the Bronze Age Mediterranean* (Routledge, 2013), which explores the interaction of objects in peoples' social worlds. More recently she has been exploring the vital materiality of earthy matters and how these have been entangled in peoples' lives, including a podcast, *Interactions with Clay: The Creation of Settled Communities in the Near East* in the Earth and World Series, Camden Arts Centre. Louise is also *Materialities in Anthropology and Archaeology* series editor for the University of Wales Press, and associate director of the UNESCO-MOST BRIDGES UK hub.

Alexander Wasse is a lecturer in the department of anthropology at Yeditepe University in Istanbul. His work focuses on the late neolithic periods of eastern Jordan and Cyprus. He is interested in early pastoralism and zooarchaeology, the correlation of archaeological with climatic records, and cycles of economic intensification/deintensification in prehistory.

PREFACE

This book is one of a series that contributes to what is broadly termed the 'new material turn in the social sciences'. The underpinning intention that coheres the numerous interdisciplinary moves that participate and feed into this flourishing body of literature, is to challenge anthropocentricism (Connolly 2013). This series dethrones the human by drawing in materials. Positioned under the broad umbrella heading of the 'new materialisms' or 'new materialities', the series aims to draw in the non-human as agent with a view to both recognise and advocate for the other-than-human entities that prevail and engage in our lives.

In recognition of the fact that these terms are somewhat slippery to grasp, we have outlined the following distinctions to put clear water between the terms and to demonstrate how we are using them.

Distinctions between Materiality and Matter

The term 'materiality' describes the quality or character of the material that a thing is made of – its 'materialness', if you like. On the other hand, the term 'matter' is used to describe physical items that occupy space (mass). Traditional theories of materiality explore how the objects (made of matter (different materials)) shape people's lives. New materialities attends to the materials (matter) that objects are made of and how those materials influence human behaviour.

Materiality and material culture studies have tended to focus their attention on *things* or *objects* (cf. Banerjee and Miller 2008; Miller and Woodward 2010), especially the things that people make. Scholarship has been less concerned with how materials behave in favour of looking at how people use materials. Materiality studies, therefore, demonstrates a connection between humanity and the things that humans make and use. In other words, it explores how items reflect their makers and owners and therefore embody meanings.

The new materialities turn moves away from objects and attends to the materials that the objects are fashioned from. Turning attention to the materials allows a new dimension to open up, whereby the substance that a thing is made out of becomes significant. Bringing materials to the foreground not only shows that materials are instrumental in providing the character and meaning of an item, but also that the materials themselves are determining – even actively responsible – for the final shape and manner by which the finished article can manifest. Thus, how a material behaves predicates how it can be used (see Drazin and Küchler 2015) and in turn how we understand it. This perspective, following Latour (1993), gives materials a type of agency that is both inherently present while also in relationship to other materials (see Barad's concept inter-relationality, 2007). Indeed, using this perspective, it is how materials interact or engage that becomes the place of relationship, creativity and attention. Therefore, new materialities draw the materials that things are made of into focus and by attending to the behaviours and characteristics of those substances, asks the question: 'how do the materials (substances) that we make things out of, shape our lives?'

References

Banerjee, M., and Miller, D., 2008. *The Sari: Styles, Patterns, History, Techniques*. London: Berg.

Barad, K., 2007. *Meeting the Universe Halfway: Quantum Physics and the Entanglement of Matter and Meaning*. Durham NC and London: Duke University Press.

Connolly, W. E., 2013. 'The "New Materialism" and the Fragility of Things', *Millennium: Journal of International Studies*, 41(3), 399–412.

Drazin, A., and Küchler, S. (eds), 2015. *The Social life of Materials: Studies in Materials and Society*. London: Bloomsbury Publishing.

Latour, B., 1993. *We Have Never Been Modern*. Cambridge MA: Harvard University Press.

Miller, D., and Woodward, S. (eds), 2010. *Global Denim*. London: Berg.

1 INTRODUCTION

The Quivering Potential of Earthy Matter

Louise Steel and Luci Attala

This book explores human relationships with earthy matter – sediments, soils and clay – examining how these are embedded within, and responsible for, eco-cultural practices. It draws attention to the importance of understanding how we humans are *of the earth* by highlighting our profound and physical entanglement with all earthy materials. Through the distinct capacities of these substances, which both provoke and constrain how we interact and engage with them, we show how the substances we walk on have co-produced our daily activities and experiences of being in the world – and, indeed, continue to do so. *Earthy Matters: Exploring Human Interactions with Earth, Soil and Clay*, therefore, seeks to situate humans in relationship with a wider landscape of materials emerging underfoot (see also Attala and Steel 2019; 2023).

'Earthy matter' refers to the very sediments and rocks that make up our world: a mix of mineral materials broken down over millennia of geological processes, commingled with the matter of living beings – mineralised and crumbling carbon deposits from the skeletons and shells of long-dead animals, decomposed plant matter (Attala, this volume), crumbling charcoal and the dust that separates from human and non-human bodies (Coard 2019). The materials that form the ground are in a constant state of change based on local geological and ecological features. Increasingly, these earthy matters are shifting to incorporate particles of microplastics (Carrington 2019a; 2019b; 2019c; B. Katz 2019; Govier, this volume), the by-product of human interactions with the environment, artificial materials intra-acting and becoming-with (Haraway 2008) the matter of the Earth.

As the fourth book in this *New Materialities* series, *Earthy Matters* focuses its sights on a number of case studies from the Palaeolithic to the present day, with a wide geographic reach from southern Africa to northern Europe, and from the eastern Mediterranean to South America. Each contribution has been chosen for its unique perspective on the diversity of human engagements with these substances in radically contrasting cultural and temporal contexts, which range from the creation of symbolic worlds to the construction of the built environment, and from continuing interactions with the soils above ground to explorations beneath the surface of the planet. They demonstrate how people worldwide and over the millennia have been transformed by the matter of the world in multiple astonishing ways. Thus, avoiding the typical anthropocentric lens, with a focus on how people manipulate and represent the world around them, here we have sought to illustrate how people are in relationship with these materials, and not only co-create but are fundamentally shaped by them. Steel explores how some of the earliest documented modern humans in southern Africa related with ochre to create new social worlds. Clarke and Wasse investigate how ancient peoples formed relationships with plaster, while Boyd and Alberti examine miniature clay worlds in Cyprus and South America respectively, to illustrate the role that clay played in bringing ideas and relationships to life. In contrast, Scott considers the built environment of modern urban communities in the north of England, while Govier traces the devastating effects of the modern throw-away plastic culture to demonstrate how human and material worlds are inextricably entwined. Sambento explores the ironically less intrusive interactions of speleologists who, through penetrating the surface of the Earth, are altered, and Attala looks at how on the fragile coating of soil covering our planet is physically incorporated into and comprised of bodies. By shifting the lens to the new materialities (Attala 2019; Attala and Steel 2019; 2023) and 'rethink[ing] matter as interaction and correlations' (Rovelli 2021, 148), each of these contributions seeks to draw attention to the very materiality of being human and thus to highlight how we share our physicality with the other entities of the world.

Earthy Matters brings together a number of different accounts of humans' ongoing material entanglements with earthy matter to perhaps suggest ways in which we might better attend to the world around us and to recognise that we are simply one of its many matterings. While Attala, Govier and Scott highlight the uncomfortable relationships – or monsters (Swanson et al. 2017) – emerging in the twenty-first century, several chapters (Alberti, Boyd, Clark and Wasse, and Steel) engage with ancient entanglements of human-earthy matters. These help to draw attention to the 'ecophobic dynamic associated with the rise of agricultural civilization' disrupting 'humanity's most successful and sustainable way of living on earth' (Hartman and Degeorges 2019, 458); indeed, some of these early interactions might be considered humanity's first steps towards the Anthropocene (see below) and are thus relevant to current environmental concerns. The new materialist perspective adopted in the chapters problematises the notion that agency is the sole preserve of humanity (see Barad 2007, 177) and focuses on relationality, blurring boundaries between 'supposedly passive objects (de-animated matter) and the agency of (human) subjects' (Hartman and Degeorges 2019, 463; see, e.g., Attala and Sambento). As Bennett (2010, 13) observes, '[i]f matter is itself lively, then not only is the difference between subjects and objects minimized, but the status of the shared materiality of all things is elevated'. Relationality is explored through a variety of new materialist theoretical lenses: Latour's networks (2005; Scott), Deleuzian assemblages – the ongoing, open-ended flux and flow of entities into and out of relationship (Bennett 2010, 23–4; Boyd) – and intra-actions – an approach that questions the ontological priority of things and instead describes how entities (or things-in-phenomena) emerge from the agency of matter (Barad 2003; 2007; see also Rovelli 2021; Alberti, Attala, Steel). Sambento and Attala draw attention to consequent blurring of boundaries (e.g., Averett 2020) between the matters of the world. In so doing, the new materialities encourage a radical recalibration of our understanding of being in and *of* the world and are perhaps more in-tune with the ontologies of many of the world's indigenous communities (see, e.g., Lamb 2000; Rahman 2015; Fayers-Kerr 2019; Ereira and Attala 2021). Exploring the myriad ways in which humans engage with the matter of the world and attending to our own ongoing material entanglements will, we hope, encourage us all to focus on better ways of living in and as part of the worlding world. The following discussion highlights some of the key themes and concepts that have emerged in our chapters, in our individual explorations of the vitality of earthy matters and how these have shaped human experiences of being in the world.

'Don't Panic!': Rethinking (E)earth in the Anthropocene

> [C]ivilization's progress in its confused war on nature has made the world uninhabitable in so many ways, and in so many places.
>
> (Hartman and Degeorges 2019, 465)

Our engagement with earthy substances is all the more resonant as we grapple with the material effects of the Anthropocene and seek to adapt or find solutions to being in an increasingly turbulent world (see Steffen et al. 2015; Ellis et al. 2016; Blaser and de la Cadena 2018; Hartman and Degeorges 2019; Boivin and Crowther 2021). It is now indisputably clear that human actions and material engagements are transforming the physical world around us. With regard to soils specifically, intensive farming, deforestation and the removal of plant cover, along with widespread use of chemical fertilisers and pesticides that disrupt the delicate microbalance of organisms, have resulted in the loss of around half the topsoil of the planet over the past 150 years (WWF 2022; see Attala, this volume). A loss of around one-third of the world's arable land through erosion over the past half a century contrasts dramatically with the staggeringly long time necessary for new soils to replenish – estimated at 300–600 years to generate a mere centimetre (Fouke 2011, 150; see below). Meanwhile, as industrial processes scar the Earth's surface with huge quarries for the extraction of mineral resources (see Figure 1.1), a coating of concrete, tarmac (Fouke 2011, 151; Ingold 2011; Swanson et al. 2017, M7; Krznaric 2020, 103, 114) and, increasingly, plastics (Gan et al. 2017, G4; see Govier, this volume) is covering it. This 'hard surfacing of the earth actually blocks the very intermingling of substances with the medium that is essential to life, growth and habitation' (Ingold 2011, 124), effectively creating concrete, paved and tarmacked deserts and restricting growth to cracks and crevices. The urgency with which we need to shift our understanding of our relationship with the matter of the world and take account of the impact of our actions on the environment is all the more pressing as we write these words during the hottest summer on record in the United Kingdom and with global record-breaking heatwaves affecting our planet (Earthobservatory 2022). Indeed, scientists are now warning of a catastrophic climate endgame and potential human extinction (Carrington 2022a; see also Hartman

Figure 1.1 Red Lake near Mitsero, Cyprus. The crater from an abandoned copper mine.

and Degeorges 2019, 457–8), the inevitable result of Euro-American ontologies that view the planet as an inert resource waiting to be exploited and controlled by humans (see Clarke and Wasse).

Other voices, while not denying the enormity of the impact of the Anthropocene, instead encourage us to seek solutions. There is an increasing awareness that we must listen to and learn from local and Indigenous knowledges of being in the world (Krznaric 2020; Bridges-Earth 2023; The Fifth Element 2023), enabling us to discover stories that might allow a 'livable [*sic*] future' (Solnit 2023) where we can change our relationship with the world, of which we are just one small element. There is an urgency to recognise that humans do not inhabit the world 'as an individual, biological body but self-consciously and historically *as the Earth*' (Hartman and Degeorges 2019, 466–7), not living on and exploiting the planet but co-creating with it 'in a mutually beneficial relationship with the Earth and as the Earth' (Hartman and Degeorges 2019, 467). Such possibilities reveal 'a new world, full of disruption … yet mercifully short of true climate apocalypse' (Wallace-Wells 2022, n.p.; see also Krznaric 2020 for examples of alternative future thinking).

The Vitality of Earth, Clays and Soils

> It is materiality – the very physicality of matter – that gives things agency.
> (Boivin 2008, 129)

The genesis of this book was a series of experiential seminars with our undergraduate students, working primarily with clay, but also exploring lime plaster, soils and other substances. It was while we were working with clay in particular that the 'curious ability of inanimate things to animate, act, to produce effects dramatic and subtle' (Bennett 2010, 6) became apparent. We discovered that, despite its malleability, more often than not we did not impose *our* will on the clay but could only do with it what it *allowed* us to do (cf. Ingold 2013). The vibrancy and unique properties of the clay, as much as our differing levels of skill, provoked, enabled and constrained how we were able to work with it, resulting in very different material outcomes. While some students moulded complex ceramic designs (see Figure 1.2) others simply gave into the tactile, plastic pleasure of the substance, perhaps rolling it into balls, or into long strips to coil into spirals. We became aware that working with clay is not an intellectual process, whereby a person decides what the clay might become and makes it happen. Working with clay is a relational exercise, an essentially haptic and co-creative process in which the location of agency between our hands and the clay is blurred, permeable and fluid (Malafouris 2013), and where the outcome depends on how both the clay *and* the person are able to behave together. In other words, the clay equally determines outcome. Indeed, as we have previously noted:

> materials are instrumental in providing the character and meaning of an item, but also that the materials themselves are determining – even actively responsible – for the final shape and manner by which the finished article can manifest. (Attala and Steel 2019, xviii)

Unsurprisingly therefore, in many cultures, clay is perceived to be alive and permeated with 'a spiritual energy and life-force' (Boivin 2012, 2). The Hidatsa of North Dakota for example, recognise their pottery as beings with souls, acquiring their spiritual essence as the vessel is

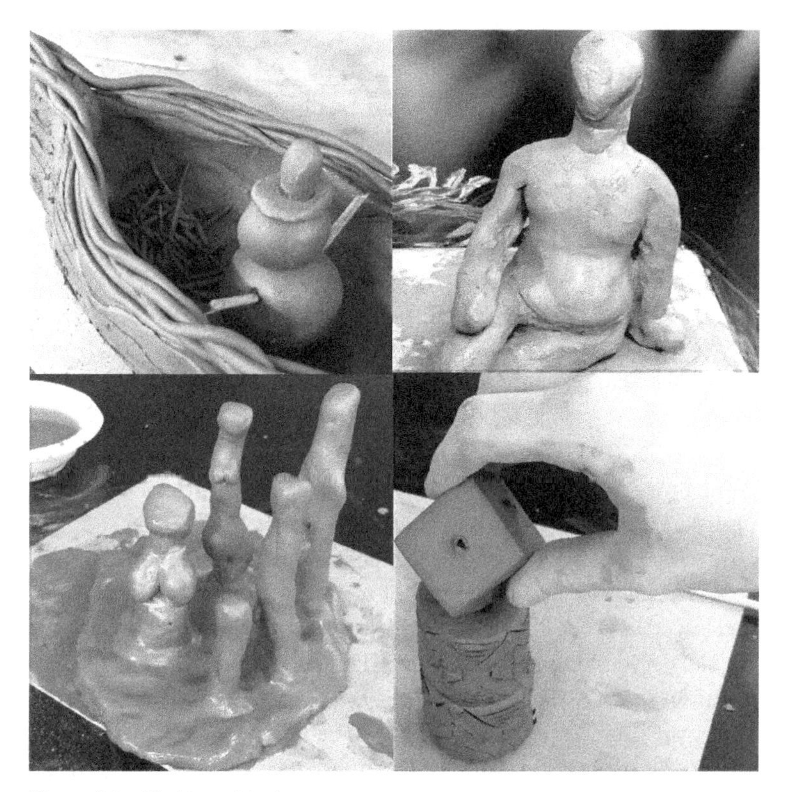

Figure 1.2 Working with clay.

shaped, even before being fired (Lévi-Strauss 1985, 47). The animation of clay is similarly illustrated by Emma Rabalago of the Transvaal Ndebele, who described the mixing of dry clay with water to make pottery as the union of man (the water) and woman (the clay). She describes how the clay sleeps during the night and that 'if the clay is good and the water is strong the clay will take the water in and the union will be fruitful' (Emma Rabalago, quoted by Krause 1985, 68).

Numerous ethnographic studies have drawn attention to the vitality of a range of earthy substances that provoke humans to engage with them in a variety of ways. Kate Fayers-Kerr, for example, notes how among the Mun of Ethiopia:

> older boys and men develop a compulsion to sample earths as they come across them, rarely passing an outcrop of pigmented

> soil without stopping to rub some on their face, head and/or body. Indeed, throughout the landscape there are places where earthy materials seem to beckon them to stop and enter into a relationship. (Fayers-Kerr 2019, 116)

They respond to the vital properties of these substances. Eloise Govier (2017; 2019, 26–7) explores similar interactions with colourful earthy substances, such as cinnabar, at Neolithic Çatalhöyük. She demonstrates a variety of ways that cinnabar was used at the site, suggesting its specific properties were valued for different purposes. The bright vermillion pigment, mixed with liquids, was applied to lime plaster to decorate the built environment, while its preservative qualities might explain its incorporation within burials. Possibly its hallucinogenic properties were also highly valued – people 'may have actively desired ... the feelings associated with sedation or altered states of consciousness' (Govier 2019, 27). Steel (this volume) posits a comparable visceral response to the vibrant matter of ochres in the landscape and how these were incorporated in social practices, stretching back to human's earliest demonstrably recorded interactions with earthy matter in southern Africa. Sambento (this volume) explores the material vitality and agency of caves and how the intense experiences of the vital forces of the underworld spaces provoke co-creative engagements from parietal art to contemporary songs, prose and poetry. In part, this is a response to the liveliness of limestone. Indeed, as Macfarlane comments (2020, 32), the 'dance of death and life that goes into limestone's creation is what makes it without doubt, the liveliest, queerest rock I know', reflecting the 'vibrancies and the multispecies makings that have brought limestone into being'. But, for Sambento, this concerns the effects of rock and human coming together and the intimate relationships that cavers have with the cold, slippery physicality under the Earth's surface.

Making Miniature People

> [T]he giving of form to clay and its transformations through fire, has a primeval quality.
>
> (Barley 1994, 47)

The complex ways in which earthy matter appears animate is evident in the many examples of clay figurines – human and animal – worldwide, as well as the practice of reshaping the facial form in plaster over human skulls characteristic of the Neolithic in the Levant and Anatolia, interpreted as a way to re-flesh and perhaps even revitalise the deceased (Casella and Croucher 2014, 100; Clarke and Wasse, this volume). For Clarke and Wasse, this intimate relationship between plaster and skull illustrates how for Neolithic communities of the Near East, the living and the dead, the quotidian and the sacred, were in relationship (see also Steel 2019). The malleability of clay (and plaster) and its perceived similarities to human flesh, therefore, have frequently elided in what might be described (following Saunders 1999, 246) as 'an act of transformative creation'.

Shaping people from clay is an ancient practice (see Boyd and Alberti, this volume) and also one that is attested across the continents. The earliest documented figurine production, dating to around 26,000 BP,[1] is represented by largely fragmentary material recovered from four sites in the Czech Republic, most famously at Dolni Věstonice (Vandier et al. 1989). These represent the first clearly evidenced examples of the transformation of the very materiality of a substance through human-material interactions – mixing coarse loess soil with water, working this by hand as well as with bone and flint tools and heating the moulded shapes with fire (Vandier et al. 1989, 1003–4), thereby altering a malleable substance into something durable. Perhaps the most famous of the loess figures is the so-called 'Venus of Dolni Věstonice' (see Figure 1.3), moulded in the form of a mature woman with pendulous breasts, wide hips, a slightly rounded belly and, perhaps the most evocative, the delicately sculpted clavicles. This figurine stands at the beginning of a long tradition of forming miniature humans from clay (see Boyd, this volume).

Frequently viewed as mimetic representations, these clay sculptures illustrate a cross-cultural understanding of the similarities between clay and human flesh (Barley 1994; Gosselain 1999; Boivin 2012, 7). Lamb (2000, 207) for example, notes how women of Mangaldihi, India, are thought to be malleable like clay and should be shaped by the husband (conceptualised as a potter) into the form of his choice, while in Judeo-Christian thought it was a man that was first created from 'the dust of the ground' (Genesis 2:7) and activated

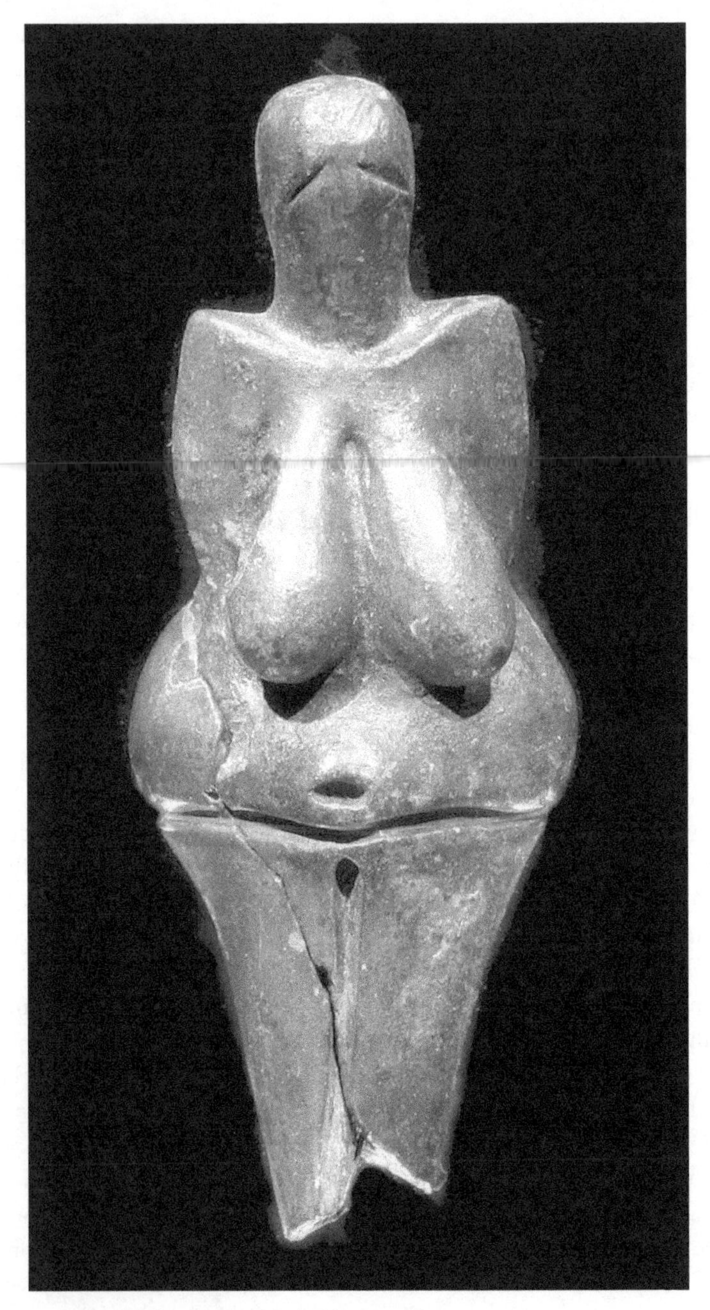

Figure 1.3 Clay figurine from Dolni Věstonice.

by the breath of God. Indeed, earth, soil, mud and clay are recounted in numerous creation stories worldwide, from ancient Egypt and Mesopotamia, Greece, India, Africa and the Americas (Leeming 2010, 312–13). Together with the countless clay figurines recovered from Neolithic and Bronze Age sites around the world, these stories demonstrate the close relationship between people and earth or clay, but likewise embody humanity's tendency to represent the world (see Govier and Steel 2021, 304–6) and to view matter as something inert, awaiting human (or divine) agency to shape it and to imbue it with life and meaning. A new materialist perspective, however, problematises this anthropocentric tendency and encourages us to move away from the 'doctrines of representation' (Haraway 1992, 313) that serve to separate us from the world. Instead, it highlights that sculpting in clay is part of the ongoing process of co-constituting the world (as explored by Alberti, Boyd). Moreover, the new materialities remind us that fashioning people out of the very substance of the world and '[t]he supposition that humans were made from clay makes us *literally products of the earth*' (Leeming 2010, 313, our emphasis, see also Attala, this volume).

Shaping Earthy Worlds

> [A] change of focus, from the 'objectness' of things to material flows and formative processes wherein they come into being.
>
> (Ingold 2012, 431)

Alberti, Boyd, Steel, Clarke and Wasse draw attention to lively interactions between people and earthy materials through the creation of portable objects frequently embedded within symbolic worlds. Indeed, the unique properties of earthy matter and its role in the construction of social and symbolic worlds have long been recognised by archaeologists. Nicole Boivin (2008, 129–38), for example, explores the materiality of clay in the construction of Neolithic lifeways at Catalhöyük (see also Doherty 2020, 19–22). Amy Richardson (2014) discusses how the easy accessibility and malleability of clay allowed this substance to be manipulated into abstract representations – figurines and tokens – imbued with symbolic content by the Neolithic communities of the central Zagros. The capacities of earthy matter likewise enabled the development of the distinctive social and material worlds of southern Mesopotamia in the later fourth-third millennium BCE, not simply pots and pans, but also clay administrative paraphernalia, comprising tokens, bullae[2] and tablets (Schmandt-Besserat 1992; Steel 2021).

The use of clay in modern traditional communities usually focuses on ceramic production (Gosselain 1999). Evans-Pritchard (1940, 86, fig. 12) extends this picture by describing a culture reliant on clay in his ethnography among the Nuer, who live in a land of heavy clay that lacks good stone. The Nuer household is crafted from local earthy matters found in the surrounding landscape: the houses they construct, as well as their pots, grain bins and hearthstones, are formed from a combination of clay, mud and sand, and even their grindstones are made from baked marsh mud mixed with ground-up pot sherds. Children play with miniature cattle in kraals modelled from mud (Evans-Pritchard 1940, 38, fig. 7). Being in the traditional Nuer world, therefore, is negotiated through day-to-day interactions with malleable earthy substances to hand, which have enabled an effective way of life within a difficult landscape. It also provides an example of how the physical properties of a place co-develop the character of culture and tradition.

Although most studies of clay objects past and present have focused on either their functionality or inherent symbolism, Boyd and Alberti (this volume) challenge these anthropocentric approaches, instead encouraging us to focus on relationality. Boyd examines a ceramic model of a building, miniature ceramic stool and associated clay figures from Chalcolithic Cyprus. At first glance, this group of objects resembles the miniature kraals and cattle played with by the Nuer children, and indeed it has been viewed as a mimetic teaching aid associated with childbirth (Bolger 1992). Boyd, however, discusses it as an assemblage, exploring the flow of human-non-human relationships involved in its creation, use and ultimate disposal. Alberti investigates the elaborate Candelaria pottery from Argentina, in particular those that draw on plant imagery, as a lens on human-plant relationships. Rather than creating accurate replicas of various plant-forms, he explores these vessels as agentive beings within ceramic-plant-human entanglements (following Barad 2007).

Scott examines the different properties of fired brick and concrete and how these materials were political tools in the populations' experiences of living in the urban community of Liverpool in the nineteenth and twentieth centuries. He considers not only the physical properties of brick and concrete and how they became associated with specific types of building, but equally how the choice of building material was symbolically charged and affective. He focuses on the promise and consequences of building with concrete for modernity and explores how brick and concrete did more than provide dwellings. Using the earth to fashion homes is an ancient and worldwide practice. Clay, mud and plaster have been used as building materials since the Neolithic in the Near East and southeast Europe (Stevanović 1997; Boivin 2008, 134–5; see also Clarke and Wasse, this volume). Clarke and Wasse explore how building materials in the Neolithic Near East, in particular plastered floors, co-existed and indeed interacted (e.g., with plastered skulls) in a relationship of vibrant matter. The early urban landscapes of southern Mesopotamia – temples, houses, city walls – were also built from mud (Hnaihen 2020; Steel 2021). The layering of mud house upon mud house over generations resulted in the distinctive tell sites that shaped the landscapes of the region. Various earthy substances continue to feature as co-creative partners in the architecture of communities worldwide, from the adobe houses making up the pueblo villages of the south-west United States (Markovich et al. 2015) to the clom houses of rural Wales (Alfrey 2008) and the mud and plaster houses of Rajasthan (Boivin 2008, 130–4). Perhaps among the more impressive built environments crafted from earth are the tall conical domed houses of the Musgum of north Cameroon, built from sundried mudbrick. These stand up to 9 metres high and are covered in a distinctive ribbed decorative pattern that not only allows the rain to drain off the buildings but effectively provides an in-built scaffolding during construction and equally allows the Musgum to climb the buildings for regular maintenance and recoating of the surface (Chin 2010). Djamila (2016, 825) highlights the efficiency of the construction, the domed form supporting the maximum weight using the least mud. The skills inherent in the construction of these houses illustrate how the Musgum's 'intense intimacy with their material' (mud mixed with water), knowing what it can *do* enables them to 'collaborate … productively with it' (Bennett 2010, 60). Moreover, it also illustrates how the material properties of different substances have determined the types of skill and expertise that humanity has been able to develop in different regions. This shift in perspective – away from the human as exclusive agent to a relational perspective – provides a picture of how all physical entities are implicated in the formation or configuration of each other. These architectural structures are certainly evidence of humanity's creativity, memory and attentiveness, but they also demonstrate how physicality and substances' capacities have played a significant role in moulding people (see Drazin 2015).

What it is to be there

> Creatures live *in* the land and not *on* it. There could be no life in a world where medium and substances do not mix, or where the earth is locked inside – and the sky locked out – of a solid sphere. (Ingold 2011, 120, emphasis in original)

In the urbanised areas of the world, where people claim to feel separated from fully experiencing what is known as 'the natural environment', people are increasingly coming to appreciate experiencing earths and soils directly – through our fingers and bare feet – and are finding ways of being within spaces less constructed (Miller 2022; see Attala, this volume). Scientific research (Chevalier et al. 2012; Menigoz et al. 2020) has drawn attention to the very real health benefits of earthing (or grounding); literally walking barefoot on the ground. Direct physical contact with the Earth's surface allows our bodies to absorb negative ions which intra-act (cf. Barad 2003; 2007) and become-with with our bodies, stabilising our internal electrical balance and neutralising free radicals – the positive molecules produced in our cells on a daily basis. Earthing, therefore, increases antioxidants in our bodies, reducing stress and improving our mental and physical health. That this is integral to *being* human is embedded in our language: people talk of having their feet on the ground, being well grounded and describe someone reliable as being the salt of the earth. Similarly, the Welsh refer to *halen y ddear* ('salt of the earth') and describe the process of returning to our roots (or to reality) as *mynd nôl i'm coed* ('return to my trees'), referring to the solidity and connectedness of a tree with its roots in the soil.

Medical geology examines the relationship between human health and earthy materials (Sing and Sing 2010), highlighting in particular the health benefits of consuming soil. Research demonstrates the importance of geophagy (the ingestion of soils), which is attested in many cultures worldwide, for its medicinal properties, as well as to supplement nutrient-poor diets and detoxification of plant materials (e.g., Johns and Duquette 1991), and suggest that these practices stretch back into the distant human past (Sing and Sing 2010; Blum et al. 2019). These studies have highlighted a complex relationship between soil and human intestinal microbiomes, which is believed to have evolved over the millennia of human evolution and which is still developing (Blum et al. 2019). The pathogens in the soil microbiome and humans intra-act and 'replenish each other with inoculants, genes and growth-sustaining molecules' becoming 'superorganisms' (Blum et al. 2019), all of which contribute to an effective immune system (Wall et al. 2015). Alarmingly, however, research has demonstrated that the human gut microbiome in industrialised, urbanised communities is being transformed with the loss of beneficial microbes, due to multiple anthropogenic interventions – including increased hygiene and 'cleanliness', ingestion of processed foods, use of antibiotics and the loss of plant and soil biodiversity from rigorous soil management (see below) – and this is resulting in an increase in lifestyle diseases related to the human intestinal microbiome.

Indigenous knowledges further reiterate the importance of the earth, land, soils and clays to our health and wellbeing, our being in the world. Country (the land) is integral to the knowledge of Indigenous Australians (Blair 2019; Steffensen 2019), who recognise that when people become disconnected from and neglect the land, it (and we) becomes sick, but 'when we heal the land we heal ourselves' (Steffensen 2019, 235; see also Ereira and Attala 2021, discussing the Kogi of Colombia). Kate Fayers-Kerr draws attention to the healing properties of soils and clays and how among the Mun of Ethiopia regular body painting, smearing the face, head and bodies with earthy substances, is believed to be 'part of a daily cultivation of a healthy self' (Fayers-Kerr 2019, 116). She describes how young men smear themselves with moist clay and pigmented soils to renew (*sudê rrê*) the body. Fayers-Kerr demonstrates that the practice of body painting is more than a simple cosmetic adornment of self, but instead encourages us to think about how people and earthy matter are active participants in relationship with each other and how specific substances are seen to have healing and generative properties. Likewise, the active properties of ochre – both as an insect repellent and as a sunscreen – might plausibly have played a role in early humans' interaction with this substance (Rifkin 2015; Rifkin et al. 2015; see also Steel, this volume). In a similar vein, artist Helen Acklam has explored the emotional healing properties of earthy matter through her art project *What it is to be there* (2022), looking at her own somatic relationship with soils and clays from the relict coal-mining landscape of Garw Valley, south Wales. She focused specifically on memory and how her body's sensual, experiential connection with the valley is corporeal, rekindled and known through touch. The act of putting skin and clay together reminded her of how she is embedded into this place. Acklam (2022) comments that 'thinking with my body about "what it is to be there" has made me realise that there's a bridge between narrative enquiry, autoethnography and creative arts practice'. Her haptic engagement with the soils of her home valley have been both a healing process and have also elucidated how memory and events are materially embedded and experienced physically, through body, matter and place.

Subtle Soils

> Soil is the earth's fragile skin that anchors all life on Earth. It is comprised of countless species that create a dynamic and complex ecosystem and is among the most precious *resources* to humans.
>
> (WWF 2022, our emphasis)

The importance of soil to sustaining life on the surface of the planet cannot be overemphasised; nonetheless, the perception that this is another of Earth's finite resources awaiting human interaction reiterates a tendency to view the world from an anthropocentric perspective. A more-than-human approach serves to trouble this asymmetrical relationship between people (particularly of the industrialised world) and soils, instead suggesting that people need to find ways to participate in soil's being (Given 2018, 134–5). Fouke (2011, 148) draws attention to an 'alarming disproportion between the seriousness of environmental problems and the level of moral concern these evoke', noting in particular how current human activity is effectively destroying the soils on which our very existence depends. This, he suggests results from a misconception that soil is an inert substance 'improved' by nutrients added from chemical fertilisers and that 'anchors' plants (2011, 148). Moreover, soil as it coheres to our bodies and encroaches on our built environment, in many parts of the global north, is reconceived as dirt, or, as Douglas (1966) so eloquently describes it, as matter out of place (see also Coard 2019). Soil, however, is more than the earth or ground outside in which we grow plants, or the dirt that gets under our nails and is trodden underfoot onto our floors as we come inside from the garden. It is not merely inert farmland, needing human intervention – fertilisers, pesticides and planting of monocultured seeds – to allow essential food crops to grow. Rather, it is a lively vibrant assemblage (cf. Bennett 2010; Sing and Sing 2010; Fouke 2011; Given 2018; Miller 2022; see also Attala, this volume) abounding with a wide diversity of life, active participants ranging from the microscopic (bacteria) to the more substantial (such as fungi, worms, ants and moles) that aerate and mix the fabric of the soil, often symbiotically. Indeed, Given (2018, 130) draws attention to the *conviviality* of soils, 'a "living together" … vitality through symbiosis" (Given 2018, 130).

Macfarlane (2020, 88–91; see also Sheldrake 2021) draws attention to the interconnectedness of soil by highlighting the work of mycorrhizal fungi, micro-organisms, minerals, gases and the plants they support. Humans (and, of course, other animals) are inseparable from this vast rhizomic assemblage, literally becoming one with the earth by consuming the plants nourished in these soils and returning to the ground in death. Attala highlights how, over time, watching this connectivity blurs the confines of what can be successfully separated as soil, plant or flesh. Consequently, soil is more than a layer of dirt, dust and mud, but instead is the place where a vital commingling of multiple shifting matters co-develop – matters that develop into people and then back to soil. Attala, thus, invites us to think about the more-than-human politics of what one expects from, conceives of and how one treats, the soil, recognising the ongoing relationships between bodies and the soils that envelop our planet. She proposes the concept of *re*-placing, as a mechanism to think about the values inherent in practices such as composting, or adding artificial fertilisers in association with the brute fact that we re-assemble and commingle with the matter of the earth in death (Macfarlane 2020, 31). Ongoing depletion of the Earth's soils threatens the very biosphere, and as Morton so eloquently reminds us, the 'end of the biosphere as we know it is also the end of the "world" as a normative and useful concept' (Morton 2016, 46). To address the ongoing pollution and erosion of this lively symbiotic ecosystem requires a political project (cf. Bennett 2010, viii; Given 2018, 130), a humanities-driven ecology of practice (cf. The Fifth Element 2023) that recognises both the positive and negative impact of people depending on how they choose to exist and work with soils. Recognising that humans are part of the 'biochemical process [of life] that unfold[s] across the surface of the Earth' (Rovelli 2021, 142) encourages us to think more responsibly about our actions and how these impact on the world.

The Plastocene: Becoming(-with) Plastic

> [T]he debris of capitalist waste, the unspectacular lives of discarded things.
>
> (Gan et al. 2017, G3)

Govier's chapter also gives a sense of urgency for our understanding of human relationships with earthy matter and why we need to take responsibility for our part within the ongoing matterings of the world. She draws particular attention to the effects of plastic on our environment, a phenomenon that is being increasingly discussed in the geosciences. Modern plastic waste is becoming part of the planet, being sedimented as a new earthy layer covering the globe and embedded as a geological horizon marking the boundary between the Holocene and the Anthropocene (Skinner 2019), even being formed into rocks, termed 'plastiglomerates', which have been identified on Kamilo Beach, Hawaii (see Figure 1.4) (Corcoran et al. 2014; Skinner 2019). Plastic clogs our landfills (McCormick 2020), pollutes our soil (Plastic Planet 2021), is present in our water systems (Dunn 2019) and oceans (Fava 2022), falls as rain (Christensen 2019; Singh 2019; Imster 2020) and has even been detected at both Earth poles (C. Katz 2019; Carrington 2022c). Indeed, the disastrous impact of increased plastic waste on our oceans and aquatic life as a result of the Covid pandemic is already being documented (Peng et al. 2021). Ultimately our transformation of substances into plastics is impacting on the ecosystem,

Figure 1.4 Plastiglomerate from Kamilo Beach, Hawaii, displayed at Museon in The Hague, The Netherlands.

human and non-human. 'While we gain plastic gyres and parking lots, we lose rainforests and coral reefs' (Gan et al. 2017, G4).

Humanity, too, is becoming-with plastic as we inhale and ingest it (Carrington 2019c); it is sedimented in our bodies, detected in our blood and deep in our lungs (Carrington 2022b; Osborne 2022; Rosane 2022). This recalls the ways in which humans have become with other earthy matters, evident in the skeletal remains of Neolithic burials at Çatalhöyük – the ochre and cinnabar painted onto the fleshy body parts and the carbon deposits found on rib bones, interpreted as the residue of smoke inhalation (Andrews et al. 2005). As with the ancient earthy matters, modern plastics might be viewed as 'proximal, quasi-agents, that exist in polluted air, [to] become key and debilitating agents when nestled in the lungs, and make humans co-creating life-matter' (Govier 2019, 32).

Final Remarks

> [The Earth] is made up of individuals who interact with what surrounds them, formed by structures and processes that are self-regulating, maintaining a dynamic equilibrium that persists over time.
>
> (Rovelli 2021, 142)

Our intention with this book has been to expose some of the ways that the materials of the ground physically influence people's actions and shape cultural activities. But it is also concerned to show how soils are objectively implicated in how humanity is able to be. This pursuit fits under the overarching objective of the new materialities move – specifically, to encourage an alternative ontology that recognises that people are part of the physical world, not users of it. Following this, this collection of chapters illustrates the complexities, ambiguities and effects associated with how the world underfoot is represented and known, while attempting to illustrate how these materials are constant companions – even kin (Haraway 2016) – that co-create the bodies we temporarily form and claim to be.

We and our contributors have sought throughout *Earthy Matters* to attend to the 'strange and wonderful as well as the terrible and terrifying' (Swanson et al. 2017, M7) of innumerable human interactions with the soils, sediments and clays of the Earth. Encouraging us to fall into the chthonic, Sambento draws attention to the dripping, smooth, mysterious and enchanting properties of the vibrant matters under the surface, while Govier and Scott take us out of the unfamiliar darkness to shine a bright light on two of what are being characterised as modernity's monsters: plastic and concrete. Other contributions (namely, Alberti, Boyd, Steel, Clarke and Wasse) reveal how the ghosts of past lifeways and ecosystems (Gan et al. 2017) have actively formed what being human means today. Attala, focusing more on the contemporary, encourages a more proactive and conscious engagement with the soil so that people can embrace their role in becoming the ground for future generations. According to Swanson et al. (2017, M7), we need to 'repurpose the tools of modernity against the terrors of Progress to make visible the other worlds it has ignored and damaged'.

In most parts of the world, farming practices, the cultivation of the soil and development of permanent, fixed settlements have effectively anchored people to place (Boivin 2008, 137). These daily entanglements of humans, non-humans and earthy materials have irrevocably marked the landscape: ongoing deforestation to provide new lands to cultivate or minerals to exploit, depletion of earthy resources to provide building materials (see Scott), extinction of multiple ecosystems and littering of the surface of the planet with objects of daily life (once shaped from clay, now increasingly made from plastic; see Govier). The concept that the matter of the earth is there to be extracted, used, manipulated, discarded, at will – that this is a resource that humans own – is the lifeblood of capitalist ontologies. Modern industrialised attitudes prioritise the concept of land *ownership*, emphasising *control* not only over other social groups but also over other non-human beings with whom we share the world. The land has become a resource and its exploitation to meet the needs of humans has shaped ongoing relationships between humans and other beings. Understanding ancient as well as modern material entanglements and their diverse impact on the planet is, we argue, of relevance to our current preoccupation with the detritus of the Anthropocene and the mark that humans leave/have left on the world. *Earthy Matters* has variously emphasised the vibrancy and agency of earthy materials (Sambento and Steel) and, challenging ontologies of boundedness, individuality and the separateness of humans from the rest of the world, we have likewise explored how these earthy substances are in multiple overlapping and shifting relationships with other matter, both human and non-human (Alberti). Following Swanson et al. (2017), we hope that *Earthy Matters* encourages attentiveness to and curiosity about the earthy matter of the world. 'Living in a time of planetary catastrophe thus begins with a practice at once humble and difficult: *noticing* the worlds around us' (Swanson et al. 2017, M7, our emphasis).

Notes

1. BP stands for Before Present and is used by archaeologists to date events relative to the introduction of radiocarbon dating. By convention present is 1950 CE.
2. Clay formed into a ball around tokens (of bone, stone or clay) identifying quantities of goods and commodities. The surface of the bulla would be stamped to prevent tampering.

References

Acklam, H., 2022. 'What it is to be there'. *www.helenacklam.com/projects/what-it-is-to-be-there/* (accessed 24 August 2022).

Alfrey, J., 2008. '"The habitations of wretchedness"? Clom buildings in Wales', *Vernacular Architecture*, 39(1), 71–7.

Andrews, P., Molleson, T., and Boz, B., 2005. 'The human burials at Çatalhöyük', in *Inhabiting Çatalhöyük: Reports from the 1995–1999 Seasons*, ed. I. Hodder. Cambridge and London: British Institute of Archaeology at Ankara; McDonald. Institute for Archaeological Research, Cambridge, pp. 261–78.

Attala, L., 2019. *How Water Makes Us Human: Engagement with the Materiality of Water*. Cardiff: University of Wales Press.

Attala, L., and Steel, L. (eds), 2019. *Body Matters: Exploring the Materiality of the Human Body*. Cardiff: University of Wales Press.

Attala, L., and Steel, L. (eds), 2023. *Plants Matter: Exploring the Becomings of Plants and People*. Cardiff: University of Wales Press.

Averett, E. W., 2020. 'Blurred boundaries: Zoomorphic masking rituals and the human-animal relationship in ancient Cyprus', *World Archaeology*, 52, 724–45. *https://doi.org/10.1080/00438243.2021.1900903*.

Barad, K., 2003. 'Posthumanist performativity: Toward an understanding of how matter comes to matter', *Signs: Journal of Women in Culture and Society*, 28(3), 801–31.

Barad, K., 2007. *Meeting the Universe Halfway: Quantum Physics and the Entanglement of Matter and Meaning*. Durham NC and London: Duke University Press.

Barley, N., 1994. *Smashing Pots: Feats of Clay from Africa*. London: British Museum.

Bennett, J., 2010. *Vibrant Matter: A Political Ecology of Things*. Durham NC and London: Duke University Press.

Blair, N., 2019. 'Lilyology as a transformative framework for decolonizing ethical spaces within the Academy', in *Decolonizing Research: Indigenous Storywork as Methodology*, ed. J-Archibald Q'um Q'um Xiiem, J. B. J. Lee-Morgan and J. de Santolo. London, New York NY and Dublin: Zed Books, pp. 203–23.

Blaser, M., and de la Cadena, M., 2018. 'Introduction. Pluriverse', in *A World of Many Worlds*, ed. M. de la Cadena and M. Blaser, Durham NC: Duke University Press, pp. 1–22.

Blum, W. E. H., Zechmeister-Boltenstern, S., and Keiblinger, K. M., 2019. 'Does soil contribute to the human gut microbiome?', *Microorganisms*, 7, 287. *https://doi.org/10.3390/microorganisms7090287* (accessed 30 November 2023).

Boivin, N., 2008. *Material Cultures, Material Minds: The Impact of Things on Human Thought, Society, and Evolution*. Cambridge: Cambridge University Press.

Boivin, N., 2012. 'From veneration to exploitation: Human engagement with the mineral world', in *Soils, Stones and Symbols: Cultural*

Perceptions of the Mineral World, ed. N. Boivin and M. A. Owoc. London and New York NY: Routledge (2nd edn), pp. 1–29.

Boivin, N., and Crowther, A., 2021. 'Mobilizing the past to shape a better Anthropocene', *Nature, Ecology and Evolution*, 5, 273–84. *https://doi.org/10.1038/s41559-020-01361-4* (accessed 30 November 2023).

Bolger, D. L., 1992. 'The archaeology of fertility and birth: A ritual deposit from Chalcolithic Cyprus', *Journal of Anthropological Research*, 48(2), 145–64.

Bridges-Earth, 2023. 'Humanities-driven Sustainability Science'. *https://bridges.earth/* (accessed 1 June 2023).

Carrington, D., 2019a. 'Microplastic pollution in soil spells trouble for food safety', *Canada's National Observer*, 15 December 2021. *www.nationalobserver.com/2021/12/15/news/microplastic-pollution-soil-spells-trouble-food-safety* (accessed 14 March 2022).

Carrington, D., 2019b. 'Microplastics "significantly contaminating the air", scientists warn', *Guardian*, 14 August 2019. *www.theguardian.com/environment/2019/aug/14/microplastics-found-at-profuse-levels-in-snow-from-arctic-to-alps-contamination* (accessed 16 August 2019).

Carrington, D., 2019c. 'People eat at least 50,000 plastic particles a year, study finds', *Guardian*, 5 June 2019. *www.theguardian.com/environment/2019/jun/05/people-eat-at-least-50000-plastic-particles-a-year-study-finds* (accessed 11 April 2022).

Carrington, D., 2022a. 'Climate endgame: Risk of human extinction "dangerously underexplored"', *Guardian*, 1 August 2022. *www.theguardian.com/environment/2022/aug/01/climate-endgame-risk-human-extinction-scientists-global-heating-catastrophe* (accessed 5 August 2022).

Carrington, D., 2022b. 'Microplastics found in human blood for first time', *Guardian*, 24 March 2022. *www.theguardian.com/environment/2022/mar/24/microplastics-found-in-human-blood-for-first-time* (accessed 24 March 2022).

Carrington, D., 2022c. 'Nanoplastic pollution found at both of Earth's poles for first time', Guardian, 21 January 2022. *www.theguardian.com/environment/2022/jan/21/nanoplastic-pollution-found-at-both-of-earths-poles-for-first-time* (accessed 20 April 2022).

Casella, E. C., and Croucher, K., 2014. 'Decay, temporality and the politics of conservation: An archaeological approach to material studies', in *Objects and Materials: A Routledge Companion*, ed. P. Harvey, E. C. Casella, G. Evans, H. Knox, C. McLean, E. B. Silva, N. Thoburn and K. Woodward. London: Routledge, pp. 92–103.

Chevalier, G., Sinatra, S. T., Oschman, J. L., Sokal, K., and Sokal, P., 2012. 'Earthing: Health implications of reconnecting the human body to the Earth's surface electrons', *Journal of Environmental Public Health*, 291541. *https://doi.org/10.1155/2012/291541* (accessed 30 November 2023).

Chin, A., 2010. 'Musgum earth architecture', *Designboom*. *www.designboom.com/architecture/musgum-earth-architecture/* (accessed 22 April 2022).

Christensen, J., 2019. '"It is raining plastic": Scientists find colorful microplastic in rain', *CNN*. *https://edition.cnn.com/2019/08/14/health/plastic-rain-colorado-trnd/index.html* (accessed 11 April 2022).

Coard, R., 2019. 'Dead and dusted: Exploring the mutable boundaries of the body', in *Body Matters: Exploring the Materiality of the Human Body*, ed. L. Attala and L. Steel. Cardiff: University of Wales Press, pp.157–72.

Corcoran, P. L., Moore, C. J., and Jazvac, K., 2014. 'An anthropogenic marker horizon in the future rock record', *The Geological Society of America Today*, 24(6), 4–8. *https://doi.org/10.1130/GSAT-G198A.1* (accessed 30 November 2023).

Djamila, H., 2016. 'Sustainable development: Learning from nature', *Journal of Engineering and Applied Sciences*, 11(4), 822–7.

Doherty, C., 2020. *The Clay, World of Çatalhöyük*. BAR International Series 2981. Oxford: BAR Publishing.

Douglas, M., 1966. *Purity and Danger: An Analysis of the Concepts of Pollution and Taboo*. London and New York NY: Routledge.

Drazin, A., 2015. 'To live in a material world', in *The Social Life of Materials: Studies in Materials and Society*, ed. A. Drazin and S. Küchler. London: Bloomsbury, pp. 3–28.

Dunn, C., 2019. 'Microplastic pollution widespread in British lakes and rivers – new study', University of Bangor Press release. *www.bangor.ac.uk/news/archive/microplastic-pollution-widespread-in-british-lakes-and-rivers-new-study-40043* (accessed 5 September 2022).

Earthobservatory, 2022. 'Heatwaves and fires scorch Europe, Africa, and Asia'. *https://earthobservatory.nasa.gov/images/150083/heatwaves-and-fires-scorch-europe-africa-and-asia* (accessed 5 August 2022).

Ellis, E., Maslin, M., Boivin, N., and Bauer, A., 2016. 'Involve social scientists in defining the Anthropocene', *Nature*, 540, 192–3. *https://doi.org/10.1038/540192a*.

Ereira, A. and Attala, L., 2021. 'Zhigoneshi: A culture of connectedness', *Ecocene: Cappadocia Journal of Environmental Humanities*, 2(1), 7–22. *https://doi.org/10.46863/ecocene.18*.

Evans-Pritchard, E. E., 1940. *The Nuer: A Description of the Modes of Livelihood and Political Institutions of a Nilotic People*. Oxford: Clarendon Press.

Fayers-Kerr, K. N., 2019. 'Becoming a community of substance: The Mun, the mud and the therapeutic art of body painting', in *Body Matters: Exploring the Materiality of the Human Body*, ed. L. Attala and L. Steel. Cardiff: University of Wales Press, pp. 109–33.

Fava, M., 2022. 'Ocean plastic pollution an overview: Data and statistics', *Ocean Literacy Portal*. *https://oceanliteracy.unesco.org/plastic-pollution-ocean/* (accessed 5 September 2022).

Fouke, D. C., 2011. 'Humans and the soil', *Environmental Ethics*, 33(2), 147–61.

Gan, E., Tsing, A., Swanson, H., and Bubandt, N., 2017. 'Introduction: Haunted landscapes of the Anthropocene', in *Arts of Living on a Damaged Planet*, ed. A. Tsing, H. Swanson, E. Gan and N. Bubandt. Minneapolis MN and London: University of Minnesota Press, pp. G1–G14.

Given, M., 2018. 'Conviviality and the life of soil', *Cambridge Archaeological Journal* 28(1), 127–43.

Gosselain, O. P., 1999. 'In pots we trust: The processing of clay and symbols in sub-Saharan Africa', *Journal of Material Culture*, 42(2), 205–30.

Govier, E., 2017. 'Creative practices: How Communities were "made" at Çatalhöyük', (unpublished PhD thesis, University of Wales Trinity Saint David).

Govier, E., 2019. 'Bodies that co-create: The residues and intimacies of vital materials', in *Body Matters: Exploring the Materiality of the Human Body*, ed. L. Attala and L. Steel. Cardiff: University of Wales Press, pp. 19–37.

Govier, E., and Steel, L., 2021. 'Beyond the "thingification" of worlds: Archaeology and the New Materialisms', *Journal of Material Culture*, 26(3), 298–317. *https://doi.org/10.1177/13591835211025559*.

Haraway, D., 1992. 'The promises of monsters: A regenerative politics for inappropriate/d others', in *Cultural Studies*, ed. E. Grossberg, C. Nelson and P. Treichler. New York NY and Abingdon: Routledge, pp. 295–336.

Haraway, D., 2008. *When Species Meet*. Minneapolis MN: University of Minnesota Press.

Haraway, D., 2016. *Staying with the Trouble: Making Kin in the Chthulucene*. Durham NC: Duke University Press.

Hartman, S., and Degeorges, P., 2019. '"DON'T PANIC": Fear and acceptance in the Anthropocene', *Interdisciplinary Studies in Literature and Environment*, 26(2), 456–72.

Hnaihen, K. H., 2020. 'The appearance of bricks in ancient Mesopotamia', *Athens Journal of History*, 6(1), 73–96.

Imster, E., 2020. 'Plastic rain: More than 1,000 tons of microplastic rain onto western US', *EarthSky*. *https://earthsky.org/earth/microplastic-rain-western-us/#:~:text=EarthHuman%20World-,Plastic%20rain%3A%20More%20than%201%2C000%20tons%20of%20microplastic%20rain%20onto,the%20western%20U.S.%20each%20year* (accessed 20 April 2022).

Ingold, T., 2011. 'Earth, sky, wind and weather', *Being Alive: Essays on Movement, Knowledge and Description*. London and New York NY: Routledge, pp. 115–25.

Ingold, T., 2012. 'Towards an ecology of materials', *Annual Review of Anthropology*, 41, 427–42.

Ingold, T., 2013. *Making: Anthropology, Archaeology, Art and Architecture*. Abingdon and New York NY: Routledge.

Johns T., and Duquette M., 1991. 'Detoxification and mineral supplementation as functions of geophagy', *American Journal of Clinical Nutrition*, 53(2), 448–56. *https://doi.org/10.1093/ajcn/53.2.448*.

Katz, B., 2019. 'Americans may be ingesting thousands of microplastics every year', *Smithsonian Magazine*, 6 June 2019. *www.smithsonianmag.com/smart-news/americans-may-be-ingesting-thousands-microplastics-every-year-180972370/* (accessed 1 December 2023).

Katz, C., 2019. 'Tiny pieces of plastic found in Arctic snow', *National Geographic*. *www.nationalgeographic.com/environment/2019/08/microplastics-found-in-arctic-snow/* (accessed 16 August 2019).

Krause, R. A., 1985. *The Clay Sleeps: An Ethnoarchaeological Study of Three African Potters*. Tuscaloosa AL: University of Alabama Press.

Krznaric, R., 2020. *The Good Ancestor: How to Think Long Term in a Short-Term World*. London: Penguin Random House.

Lamb, S., 2000. *White Saris and Sweet Mangoes: Aging, Gender, and Body in North India*. Berkeley CA, Los Angeles CA and London: University of California Press.

Latour, B., 2005. *Reassembling the Social: An Introduction to Actor-Network-Theory*. Oxford: Oxford University Press.

Leeming, D. A., 2010. *Creation Myths of the World: An Encyclopedia*. Santa Barbara CA, Denver CO and Oxford: ABC Clio.

Lévi-Strauss, C., 1985. *La Potière Jalouse*. Paris: Plon.

Macfarlane, R., 2020. *Underland. A Deep Time Journey*. London: Penguin Random House.

Malafouris, L., 2013. *How Things Shape the Mind: A Theory of Material Engagement*. Cambridge MA: MIT Press.

Markovich, N. C., Preiser, W. F. E., and Sturm, F.G. (eds), 2015. *Pueblo Style and Regional Architecture*. Abingdon and New York NY: Routledge.

McCormick, E., 2020. 'America's "recycled" plastic waste is clogging landfills, survey finds', *Guardian*, 18 February 2020. *www.theguardian.com/us-news/2020/feb/18/americas-recycled-plastic-waste-is-clogging-landfills-survey-finds* (accessed 20 April 2022).

Menigoz, W., Latz, T. T., Ely, R. A., Kamei, C., Melvin, G., and Sinatra, D., 2020. 'Integrative and lifestyle medicine strategies should include Earthing (grounding): Review of research evidence and clinical observations', *Explore*, 16(3), 152–60, *https://doi.org/10.1016/j.explore.2019.10.005*.

Miller, D., 2022. 'The surprising healing qualities ... of dirt'. *Our World*, United Nations University. *https://ourworld.unu.edu/en/the-surprising-healing-qualities-of-dirt* (accessed 26 August 2022).

Morton, T., 2016. *Dark Ecology: For a Logic of Coexistence*. New York NY: Columbia University Press.

Osborne, M., 2022. 'Microplastics detected in human blood in new study', *Smithsonian Magazine*, 28 March 2022. *www.smithsonianmag.com/smart-news/microplastics-detected-in-human-blood-180979826/* (accessed 28 March 28 2022).

Plastic Planet, 2021. 'Plastic planet: How tiny plastic particles are polluting our soil', UN Environment Programme. *www.unep.org/news-*

and-stories/story/plastic-planet-how-tiny-plastic-particles-are-polluting-our-soil#:~:text=Chlorinated%20plastic%20can%20release%20harmful, species%20that%20drink%20the%20water (accessed 20 April 2022).

Peng, Y., Wy, P., Schartup, A. T., and Zhang, Y., 2021. 'Plastic waste release caused by COVID-19 and its fate in the global ocean', *PNAS*, 118(47). *https://doi.org/10.1073/pnas.2111530118*.

Rahman E., 2015. 'Hydrocentric infants and their sedimentation: Artfully binding the bodily soul among Xié river dwellers of northwestern Amazonia', *TIPITI, Journal for the Society of Anthropology of Lowland South America*, 13(2), 44–59.

Richardson, A., 2014. 'Early clay technologies: Studies in Early Neolithic clay usage from the Central Zagros', in *Proceedings of the 8th International Congress on the Archaeology of the Ancient Near East*, ed. P. Bieliński, M. Gawlikowski, R. Koliński, D. Ławecka, A. Sołtysiak and Z. Wygnańska. Wiesbaden: Harrassowitz, pp. 41–53.

Rifkin, R. F., 2015. 'Ethnographic and experimental perspectives on the efficacy of ochre as a mosquito repellent', *South African Archaeological Bulletin*, 70(201), 64–75.

Rifkin, R. F., Dayet, L., Queffelec, A., Summers, B., Lategan, M., and d'Errico, F., 2015. 'Evaluating the photoprotective effects of ochre on human skin by *in vivo* SPF assessment: Implications for human evolution, adaptation and dispersal', *PLOSOne*, 10(9). *https://doi.org/10.1371/journal.pone.0136090*.

Rosane, O., 2022. 'Microplastics found in lungs of living people for first time, and deeper than expected', *World Economic Forum*. *www.weforum.org/agenda/2022/04/microplastics-lungs-living-people/#:~:text=A%20total%20of%2039%20microplastics%20were%20found%20in%20all%20regions,people%20studied%2C%20The%20Guardian%20reported* (accessed 11 April 2022).

Rovelli, C., 2021. *Helgoland*. London: Allen Lane.

Saunders, N. J., 1999. 'Biographies of brilliance: Pearls, transformations of matter and being, c.AD 1492', *World Archaeology*, 31, 243–57.

Schmandt-Besserat, D., 1992. *Before Writing, Volume I: From Counting to Cuneiform*. Austin TX: University of Texas Press.

Sheldrake, M., 2021. *Entangled Life: How Fungi Make our Worlds, Change our Minds and Shape our Future*. New York NY: Vintage Books.

Sing D., and Sing C. F., 2010. 'Impact of direct soil exposures from airborne dust and geophagy on human health', *International Journal of Environmental Research and Public Health*, 7, 1205–23. *https://doi.org/10.3390/ijerph7031205*.

Singh, M., 2019. 'It's raining plastic: Microscopic fibers fall from the sky in Rocky Mountains', *Guardian*, 13 August 2019. *www.theguardian.com/us-news/2019/aug/12/raining-plastic-colorado-usgs-microplastics* (accessed 20 April 2022).

Skinner, C., 2019. 'The Plastocene – Plastic in the sedimentary record', *Stratigraphy, Sedimentology and Palaeontology*. *https://blogs.egu.eu/divisions/ssp/2019/01/09/the-plastocene-plastic-in-the-sedimentary-record/* (accessed 21 April 2022).

Solnit, R., 2023. '"If you win the popular imagination, you change the game": why we need new stories on climate', *Guardian*, 12 January 2023. *www.theguardian.com/news/2023/jan/12/rebecca-solnit-climate-crisis-popular-imagination-why-we-need-new-stories* (accessed 25 May 2023).

Steel, L., 2019. 'Embodied encounters with the ancestors', in *Body Matters: Exploring the Materiality of the Human Body*, ed. L. Attala and L. Steel. Cardiff: University of Wales Press, pp. 89–108.

Steel, L., 2021. 'Interactions with Clay: The creation of settled communities in the Near East', *Earth and World*, Camden Art Audio. *https://soundcloud.com/camden-arts-centre/earth-and-world-interactions-with-clay* (accessed 8 April 2022).

Steffen, W., Broadgate, W., Deutsch, L. Gaffney, O., and Ludwig, C., 2015. 'The trajectory of the Anthropocene: The Great Acceleration', *Anthropocene Review*, 2(1), 814–98.

Steffensen, V., 2019. 'Putting people back into the Country', in *Decolonizing Research: Indigenous Storywork as Methodology*, ed. J.-Archibald Q'um Q'um Xiiem, J. B. J. Lee-Morgan and J. de Santolo. London, New York NY and Dublin: Zed Books, pp. 224–38.

Stevanović, M., 1997. 'The age of clay: The social dynamics of house destruction', *Journal of Anthropological Archaeology*, 16, 334–95.

Swanson, H., Tsing, A., Bubandt, N., and Gan, E., 2017. 'Introduction: Bodies tumbled into bodies', in *Arts of Living on a Damaged Planet*, ed. A. Tsing, H. Swanson, E. Gan and N. Bubandt. Minneapolis MN and London: University of Minnesota Press, pp. M1–M12.

The Fifth Element, 2023. 'Life for learning, learning for life. Background paper', The Club of Rome, *www.the5thelement.earth/_files/ugd/27fe1e_c03601113086 49f9a01ce4bc37b54dfb.pdf* (accessed 25 May 2023).

Vandier, P. B., Soffer, O., Klima, B., and Svoboda, J., 1989. 'The origins of ceramic technology at Dolni Věstonice, Czechoslovakia', *Science*, 246, 1001–8.

Wallace-Wells, D., 2022. 'Beyond catastrophe: A new climate reality is coming into view', *New York Times*, 26 October 2022. *www.nytimes.com/interactive/2022/10/26/magazine/climate-change-warming-world.html* (accessed 1 June 2023).

Wall, D. H., Nielsen U. N., and Six J., 2015. 'Soil biodiversity and human health', *Nature* 528, 69–76. *https://doi.org/10.1038/nature15744*.

WWF, 2022. 'Soil erosion and degradation', *World Wildlife Fund*. *www.worldwildlife.org/threats/soil-erosion-and-degradation* (accessed 5 September 2022).

'active process of materialization of which embodied humans are an integral part, rather than the monstrous repetitions of dead matter from which human subjects are apart' (Coole and Frost 2010, 8).

The approach developed here focuses on the agency of matter, its quivering evanescence and vitality (Bennett 2010, 55). Moving beyond Gell's causal agency (1998), this chapter draws specifically on thing-power, which Bennett (2010, viii) describes as '[t]he capacity of things … to act as quasi agents or forces with trajectories, propensities, or tendencies of their own'. Thing-power refers to what Bennett describes as conative bodies: objects, things and matter that 'strive to enhance their power of activity by forming alliances with other bodies' (2010, x). Seemingly inanimate matter and things have agency by *working together* 'to produce effects dramatic and subtle' (Bennett 2010, 6), and for Bennett this agency is located within a human-non-human group, or assemblage. While Bennett tends to refer to objects as relational entities, each with their own quivering potential and vitality, she also recognises that things such as humans are a 'heterogeneous compound of wonderfully vibrant, dangerously vibrant, matter' (2010, 13). The nature of a thing is in fact contested (see Govier and Steel 2021, 304; Rovelli 2021, 67–8). Deleuze and Guattari (2017, 398–9), like Bennett, draw attention to relationality; they question the matter-form of the world, instead highlighting how the world comes into being through material forces at a molecular level. Likewise, Ingold (2010) focuses on the liveliness of matter and the generative capacity of relationships embedded in the things of the world. His example of the thingness of a tree (see also Rovelli 2021, 155) illustrates how it *is* or *becomes* through its relationships. It is impossible to demarcate where a tree ends and the surrounding matter of the world begins: and here I would draw attention to the material engagements of soil and water providing nutrients and photosynthesis with air and light, as well as air or insects spreading pollen. As such, the tree is a thing that *becomes* through its relationships. For Ingold therefore, things are not bounded entities but are a gathering (see Heidegger 1971) in a network of relationships:

> A thing is a 'going on', or better, a place where several goings on become entwined. To observe a thing is not to be locked out but to be invited in to the gathering. We participate … in the thing thinging in a worlding world. (Ingold 2010, 4)

The concept of thing-power is based in the notion that matter is a source of agency, it can do things and can produce affects. The properties of an entity cannot be separated from the interactions within which these properties become manifest (Rovelli 2021, 69). For Rovelli (2021, 78, my emphasis) 'properties do not reside in objects, they are *bridges* between objects'. From a new materialities perspective, I will be exploring the liveliness of ochre as a substance that derives from the heterogeneity, or alchemy, of matters from which it is composed.

Equally, we might explore this relationality enacted through the agency of matter as intra-acting phenomena (Barad 2003; 2007; Govier 2017; Govier and Steel 2021, 309–11), which draws attention to the material entanglement and ongoing mattering, merging and coalescing of substances, rather than thinking about groupings of 'independent objects with inherent boundaries and properties' (Barad 2003, 815). Jones also explores the ways in which people work with materials to co-create art works as an intra-action, noting that the 'maker follows the forces and flows of the material; they attentively work with it' (2018, 24). He does not however, emphasise the vibrancy or agency of matter but argues, contra Ingold (2007) and Boivin (2008; 2012), that the affect of these artworks does not simply emerge from the materials from which they are made but rather are 'always aided and abetted by the field of intra-actions of which they are a part' (Jones 2018, 25). Jones, moreover, situates intra-actions within a symmetrical 'fluid relationship between matter and human' (2018, 26), seemingly elevating the ontological position of people in the material world. Arguably, such a perspective perpetuates the separation of human-non-human agencies and 'the pervasive positioning of the human agent at the helm, imposing their will upon a passive and inert natural world' (Govier and Steel 2021, 301). Instead, as Rovelli (2021, 67) highlights, quantum theory in fact describes how '*[o]ne part of nature manifests itself to any other single part of nature* ... how any physical entity acts on *any* other physical entity', thus that humans are not separate from the world, observing and acting upon it, but instead 'are all part of nature ... [in] a dense web of interactions' (Rovelli 2021, 67–8, see also 157).

Using Bennett's thing-power, alongside Barad's agential realism (see also Govier 2017, 2019; Govier and Steel 2021, 309–11), I would argue that it is the distinct capacities of ochre, as of other earthy substances, that provokes, enables and similarly constrains human behaviour (see also Steel 2020, looking at clay). This is not a binary relationship but describes relationality and affect between distinct entities (see Alberti, this volume). As Rovelli (2021, 69) comments, 'there are no properties outside of interactions'; consequently everything – including humans and earthy matter such as ochre – exists in relation to how it *affects* something else. Working with earthy matter is essentially tactile and responds to the capabilities of the human agent; however, as much as the painter (also potter, figurine maker, builder with clays and muds) manipulates matter, he or she also works with and responds to the physical properties of the materials (see Boyd, this volume). As Deleuze and Guattari comment 'artisans are those who follow the matter-flow' (2017, 481).

The Ghosts and Shadows of Material Entanglements

> As humans reshape the landscape, we forget what was there before ... Our newly shaped and ruined landscapes become the new reality ... Forgetting, in itself, remakes landscapes, as we privilege some assemblages over others. Yet ghosts remind us. Ghosts point to our forgetting, showing us how living landscapes are imbued with earlier tracks and traces.
>
> (Gan et al. 2017, G6)

While ethnographic studies reveal much about the countless ways in which humans interact with earthy matter, this chapter investigates how archaeology might contribute to our understanding of how our early ancestors developed their engagements with these substances. Drawing on the concept of *ghosts* developed in *Art of Living on a Damaged Planet* (Tsing et al. 2017) allows us to explore the immaterial, social aspects of past human and non-human lifeways that have long since disappeared from the fragmentary residues of the archaeological record – the 'landscapes, where assemblages of the dead gather together with the living' (Gan et al. 2017, G5). This intellectual lens allows us to consider how '[a]s life-enhancing entanglements disappear from our landscapes, ghosts take their place' (Gan et al. 2017, G4) and that every landscape is haunted by these past lifeways. Indeed, archaeology has two specific strengths for such an exploration: first, the longue durée (see Braudel 1958) – we *can* examine the material and environmental effects of human actions over vast time scales, back indeed to our earliest hominid ancestors – and second, we are intrinsically interested in the materiality of the world (see Jones 2018) – the focus of archaeological enquiry is environments, substances, materials and objects. In the absence of human informants (our ghosts and shadows) who might explain their actions, archaeologists cannot necessarily answer why people acted in specific ways; nonetheless, we can trace the residues of their interactions with the material world, especially with clays, soils and minerals, which leave indelible traces in the archaeological record and thus illustrate the great antiquity of the 'intricate dance' (Bennett 2010, 31) between human and non-human agencies in the co-creation of material worlds.

Painting the World Red: Material Entanglements in the Palaeolithic

> There was never a time when human agency was anything other than an interfolding network of humanity and nonhumanity.
>
> (Bennett 2010, 31)

Arguably, the commingling of people and earthy matter stretches back to a series of material engagements by which our distant ancestors materialised new ways of being in the world. Here, I explore the ghosts and shadows of human-non-human interactions with ochre in the Middle Palaeolithic in southern Africa. Ochre is a mineral pigment containing red and yellow oxides (typically iron oxides derived from iron-rich rocks such as haematite) and that occurs commonly in soils and geological formations (Sajó et al. 2015). It occurs naturally in iron-rich rocks, erodes out into soils and is easily obtainable (Geggel 2018). Human engagement with this substance is of great antiquity and it is arguably through these material interactions that we 'became human'. Certainly, it is through human correspondence (cf. Ingold 2013) with ochre that we have been able to document the development of human cognition and behavioural practices (Henshilwood and d'Errico 2011). Ochre-entanglements weave 'like a red thread through more than 500,000 years' of human activity (Wreschner 1980, 633). Its earliest known use is at Olduvai associated with Homo Erectus; Neandertals were also interacting with ochre as early as 250,000 years ago (Roebroeks et al. 2012). While these appear simply to be lumps of ochre, there is more evidence that early modern humans were using the substance in deliberate, culturally meaningful ways in combination with other things. It was used to pigment marine shells at the Mousterian site of Qafzeh, Israel 90,000 years ago (Bar-Yosef Mayer et al. 2009). Red ochre is consistently identified in Upper Palaeolithic burials across Europe, typically associated with shell beads (Sommer 2007; Trinkaus et al. 2014, 29–30; Ronchitelli et al. 2015), and it frequently occurs as a pigment in combination with stone tools, seashell pendants and bone artefacts associated with parietal art in western Europe (Lewis-Williams 2008, 224, 252, 254, 263).

While people's early interactions with ochre have received attention (see Wreschner 1980), these have largely been explored as evidence for the development of human cognitive skills and symbolic behaviours; namely, the origins of art, language and religion (Hovers et al. 2003; Lewis-Williams 2008; 2010, 11–15; Bar-Yosef Mayer et al. 2009; Henshilwood et al. 2009; 2011; 2018; Henshilwood and d'Errico 2011; Tarlach 2018). There is some understanding in the literature that the red hue of ochre might have been perceived as mimetic, symbolising blood (Wreschner 1980, 633). Ethnographic accounts reveal other uses for this substance, including an effective sunscreen and insect repellent, medicinal properties, an adhesive for hafting tools and weapons, preserving foodstuffs and tanning hides (Lombard 2007; Henshilwood et al. 2009, 29; Rifkin 2011; 2015; Roebroeks et al. 2012, 1889; Macintyre and Dobson 2018). Rather than necessarily trying to assign symbolic meaning and to discern the cultural uses of ochre, the following discussion instead draws attention to the capacities and properties of ochre and how these shaped people's collaboration with the mineral, enabling and provoking particular practices; these material entanglements are explored as phenomena (following Barad 2003; 2007). I will be looking at some of the earliest known examples of ochry engagements from Blombos Cave, South Africa. These have been the focus of rigorous microscopic and chemical analyses supported by experimental studies (Rifkin 2012; Henshilwood et al. 2018) that have thrown considerable light on the properties of the materials, their specific combinations and the associated anthropogenic practices.

Blombos Cave is a Middle Palaeolithic site on the southern tip of the Cape of South Africa; the well stratified remains reveal four main phases of use from 100,000 to 73,000 years ago (Henshilwood et al. 2018, 115–16). M1 and M2 upper, date to around 77,000–73,000 years, M2 lower is a low intensity occupation horizon dating to around 85,000–82,000 years, and M3 dates to around 100,000–94,000 years. Blombos Cave stands out, in comparison with other southern African Middle Palaeolithic sites, for its abundance of natural and worked ochre finds. For the most part, ochre was worked with grinding stones or scraped with marine shells (Henshilwood et al. 2009, 30) to produce a powder for use in various ways that we can only conjecture. The source of the ochre has been identified as outcrops of the Bokkevold deposits, probably procured from the coastal zone some 3–5 kilometres from the site (Henshilwood et al. 2009, 29). Excavations at Blombos Cave have also documented the repeated combination of ochre with other materials in intricate ways that seemingly illustrate the origins of modern human behaviours, most importantly perhaps demonstrating how working with materials enabled the creation of complex social worlds. For the excavators these ochry occurrences are evidence of our ancestors (among the earliest anatomically modern humans) developing their technological and conceptual abilities, sourcing, working with, combining and storing different substances, and ultimately creating symbolic worlds (Henshilwood et al. 2004; 2009; 2011; 2018; Henshilwood and d'Errico 2011). Alternatively, we might consider this comingling of human-non-human matter to be more than the agency of human participants. Rather than simply an interaction of people and things, which 'implies action between two *fixed and discrete bodies*' (Jones 2018, 24, my emphasis), I explore these various ochry combinations as materials in-phenomena, emerging in intriguing ways through intra-actions with other materials and substances (including embodied humans) between 100,000 and 73,000 years ago. Such a change of focus, thinking about the vitality of ochre and allowing it 'to actively matter' (Barad 2003, 809) will demonstrate how the cultural and technological knowledges of these early communities were equally the result of material forces as of intentional human agency.

The earliest documented material engagements with ochre at Blombos Cave include two toolkits from the lower M3 layer, c.100,000 years ago (Henshilwood et al. 2011). The toolkits each comprise an abalone shell containing an ochre-based compound. Toolkit

1 was associated with a group of artefacts. A quartzite cobble, which had been used to grind ochre, was packed tightly inside the shell and beneath the shell there were three quartz flakes, used as grinders, the ulna of a dog, with ochre residue on its broken tip, and a seal scapula with traces of ochre on the surface: the bones were possibly used to mix and apply the ochre-mixture and as a palette, respectively. The compound found in both shells comprised two types of ochre, charcoal fragments and the crushed and burnt spongy part of animal bone, which had probably been treated to extract the marrow fat as a binding agent. Micro-flakes of quartzite, some with ochre on the striking platform, and quartz grains covered with ochre powder are likely the by-products of the grinding process. Striations marked the nacreous inner surface of Toolkit 2; these were made by ochre grains and quartz grits when the mixture was stirred, a shadowy ghost of the production process and human participants. The close proximity of the two toolkits, which were found some 16 centimetres (cm) apart, suggests these belonged to contemporary work events, perhaps a workshop or taskscape (Ingold 1993, 158) where people worked together collaborating with the ochre and other materials to produce an ointment that they perhaps applied to each other or to other surfaces such as hides – the shadows of long-disappeared painting practices. The toolkits, therefore, might be viewed as the residues or 'tracks and traces' (Gan et al. 2017, G6) of making events, where humans collaborated with diverse materials and produced shared knowledges to create new social worlds. Rather than looking at these as discrete bounded objects that happen to occur together within the same archaeological stratum, I would view the Blombos Cave toolkit assemblage[2] as an event in the flow of material substances (Harris 2014, 331–2), or as intra-acting materials in-phenomena.

Two deliberately engraved rectangular pieces of ochre (between 5.36cm and 7.58cm in length) were identified in layer M1 at the site, dating to around 75,000 years ago (see Figure 2.1) (Henshilwood et al. 2002; 2009, 27) and have been heralded as the earliest known human-made art (Lewis-Williams 2008, 98), or at least of symbolically mediated behaviour. The flat surface of one ochre piece was prepared by grinding and scraping and both are decorated with a cross-hatched engraved patterns; the more complex of the two designs is framed by parallel lines, with a third parallel line scored across the middle of

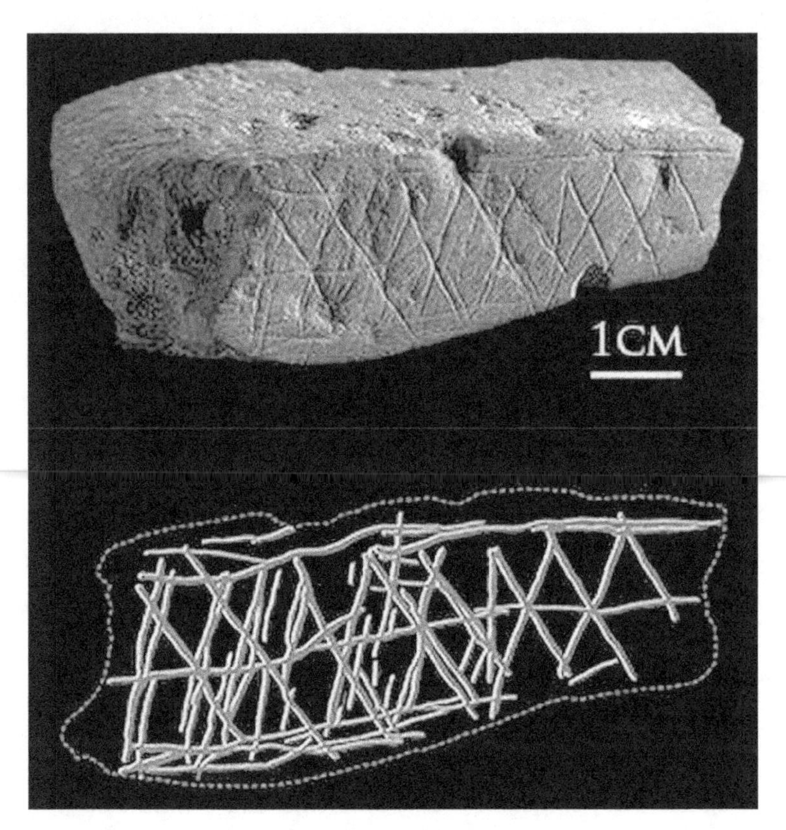

Figure 2.1 Engraved ochre from Blombos Cave.

the pattern. Microscopic observation (Henshilwood et al. 2002, 1279) reveals that the cross-hatches were made first in one direction and then in the other and both pieces reveal precise and careful application of tools to work the ochre surface and a deliberate sequence of choices made by the craftsman. Microscopic analysis of a further thirteen pieces (Henshilwood et al. 2009) from all levels provides more evidence for the practice of inscribing ochre with cross-hatched designs at Blombos Cave. There was unequivocal evidence for engraving on eight pieces, in some cases dating back 100,000 years (Henshilwood et al. 2009, 41), which demonstrates ability to conceptualise an abstract design and the focused attention and dextrous skills to control pressure and engrave lines to an even depth. An abstract drawing of a similar cross-hatched design, made with ochre on the smoothed surface of a silcrete flake, was also found in level M1, *c*.73,000 years ago (Henshilwood et al. 2018, figs 2–3). Residue analyses reveal that this was the flake from a grindstone – an early example perhaps of an object with a biography, changing careers (cf. Kopytoff 1986) and being repurposed when the original grindstone was broken. Experiments in replicating the drawing on silcrete suggest the original had been drawn with a pointed ochre crayon; moreover, much of the loose powder that constituted the painted line had been lost through the intra-actions with the surrounding matrix in the taphonomic process (Henshilwood et al. 2018, 116). Only ephemeral traces of these ancient actions persist.

A group of thirty-nine perforated tick shells (*Nassarius kraussianus*) – found in pairs or in groups of up to seventeen shells – were found in the M1 levels dating to *c*.75,000 years (see Figure 2.2) (Henshilwood et al. 2004); an additional two shells, possibly intrusive, were found in the underlying M2 level. These have been interpreted as beads, probably strung and worn around the neck,

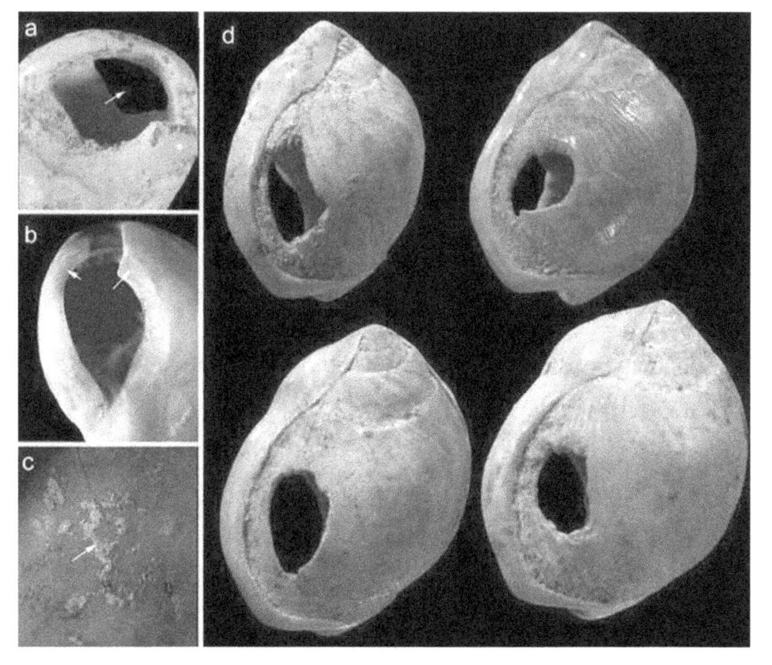

Figure 2.2 Shell beads stained with ochre, from Blombos Cave.

wrist or ankles. Microscopic analysis reveals the beads to be stained with ochre; rather than deliberate pigmentation, this appears to be incidental, perhaps the residue from ochre-based body paint rubbing off against the bead surface as they were worn against the skin (Rifkin 2015, 65). The ochre-stained beads reveal the ghosts and shadows of human actors involved in this enactment and document a number of meaningful behaviours: from the sourcing of the shells and ochre, grinding ochre and probably mixing it with some sort of fatty substance (Rifkin 2015, 65; Young 2020, 274, 278) – perhaps similar to the compound identified in the abalone shells (Henshilwood et al. 2011) – before smearing it on their bodies, piercing and stringing the shells and using these to further layer their bodies (Knappett 2006). These actions all suggest group engagements, embodied actions of materially situated people and the communication of skills and practices – effectively a community of practice (Wenger 2007, cf. Govier 2017) as much as of substances (Fayers-Kerr 2019). The ochre-bead phenomenon emerged through the commingling of different substances and materials, including the sweat and skin of the human bodies and likewise illustrates the porosity and blurred boundaries of the human body. Moreover, this was not a deliberate, purposeful staining but an intra-action, or materialisation of matter, quite separate from the intentionality of human agency.

Rather than attempting to discern cultural meanings and functions embedded in these inscribed and painted designs and perforated shells – as, if these existed, they have long since vanished – I would instead draw attention to the thing-power of the ochre. The humans at Blombos Cave were working with the ochre, choosing pieces for their hardness and vibrant red hues and so might be seen as participating in ochre's vital materiality. This draws attention to the efficacy of materials beyond 'the human meanings, designs, or purposes they express or serve' (Bennett 2010, 20). Moreover, I would argue that each individual piece of decorated ochre should not be examined as a separate entity; instead, the material interactions evident in these pieces show them to be in relationship. Thinking about people working with ochre as phenomena in constant intra-action (Barad 2003, 815) reveals this to be an ongoing material process, shadowy ghosts reminding us of the otherwise long forgotten dynamism of the creative process at Blombos Cave.

Seeing Red: The Distinct Capacities of Ochre

> It is *impossible* to separate the properties of the objects from the objects interacting with them in order for these properties to be manifested in the first place.
>
> (Rovelli 2021, 120)

To better understand ochre in-phenomena, we must consider its capacities – what does ochre *do*? – but equally we should recognise that these properties emerge through intra-action. Rather than simply thinking about a world made up of substances and materials with distinct attributes and properties this instead '*forces* us to think about everything in terms of relations' (Rovelli 2021, 120, my emphasis). The redness of ochre therefore becomes significant, and has affect, because of how people engage with it. Archaeologists have drawn attention to diverse capacities that encouraged our early ancestors to work with ochre – its medicinal and preservative properties, and effectiveness as a sunscreen and an adhesive agent (Rifkin 2011; 2015; Rifkin et al. 2015; Macintyre and Dobson 2018). Perhaps though, the primary source of attraction for the humans at Blombos Cave was the chromatic qualities of ochre. Certainly, as anyone who has collected pebbles, shells, feathers or wild flowers will recognise, the visual (and tactile) appeal of colours in the landscape should not be overlooked; these attract our attention and call to us, inviting us to gather, collect and correspond with things (see also Fayers-Kerr 2019, 116). Before modern pigments, ochre, blood (Young 2020, 276) and cinnabar (Govier 2017; 2019, 26–7; Schotsmans et al. 2020, 2021) were the main sources of the colour red available to people.[3] Henshilwood et al. (2009, 29) observes a preference for red ochre with a deeply saturated hue, suggesting that this chromatic quality was particularly valued by the people of Blombos Cave. Even today, high value is attributed to a saturated hue among Indigenous Autralians, who in the past used to walk hundreds of miles to source ochre of the highest quality (Young 2020, 277), while the added sheen derived from mixing the substance with fats, or applying ochre to greased skin, also adds to the value of the colour (Young 2020, 276). April Nowell notes that ochre's 'vibrant color and ability to adhere to surfaces – including the human body – make it an ideal crayon or paint base' (quoted in Geggel 2018).

Additionally, ochre stains the surfaces, from human skin to cave walls (see Sambento, this volume on material engagements with caves), to which it adheres. Indeed, as a mineral substance there is also a sense of permanence; it does not wear off. It can be easily worked as crayons or ground into powders and mixed with liquids to form a paint, as has been documented at Blombos Cave and other Palaeolithic sites (see above). The nature of the ochry entanglements outlined above suggest that people collaborated and co-produced with this substance primarily because of its rich red hue (see also Geggel 2018; Tarlach 2018).

The vibrancy of colour, as well as its ability to stain, lies at heart of the *thing-power* of ochre; these distinctive properties generated the relationships between ochre and people that we can see emerging in the Middle Palaeolithic in southern Africa. Working with the substance, grinding with other harder stones to form a pigment with the ability to stain and colour other materials, allowed humans to develop forms of abstract symbolic communication through their bodies and the objects they made, used and wore. Their 'intense intimacy with their material' (ochre), knowing what it can *do*, enabled the early modern humans at Blombos Cave to 'collaborate … productively with it' (Bennett 2010, 60). Considering the phenomena outlined above as co-creative *making events* – as Eloise Govier (2017, 41; see also discussion of affects-events in Deleuze and Guattari 2017, 475) has done for similar combinations of materials in-phenomena at Neolithic Çatalhöyük – highlights the unique ways in which ochre *mattered* at Blombos Cave. This vibrant pigment enabled multiple shared experiences of collecting and working with this substance (Wreschner 1980), which we might view as an early example of communities of practice (Wenger 2007). The emphasis on collaborative practices draws attention to the relationality of making/doing and working with the material world, recognising how human actions are in direct correspondence with agency of the materials and substances (Ingold 2013; Govier 2017, 165). Moreover, it draws attention to the importance of embodied participation by groups of individuals in these activities, a process by which knowledges and practices are shared, learned and passed down through the generations (Wenger 2007, 7). The ghosts of these ancient engagements and the vibrant affect of the red mineral reveal tantalising glimpses of long-disappeared lifeways.

Becoming-with Earth

> [T]he materials with which social actors interact hold a generative quality
> (Fayers-Kerr 2019, 118)

The finds from Blombos Cave illustrate the great antiquity of human correspondences with earthy matter, but it is impossible for us to fully understand the commingling of ochre and human bodies at the site and how these engagements were socially embedded. Nonetheless, numerous ethnographic studies have emphasised the importance of earths and soils to humans' experiences of being in the world:

> an expansion of our muscles and senses. It is not within ourselves, obviously, but it is not entirely separate from us either; it is the accomplice of our body and that which anchors it to the world. (Descola 2010, xiii).

While such accounts cannot answer how or why the people at Blombos Cave chose to work with ochre, they are instructive as they reveal multiple diverse ways in which soils and earths are integral to cultural lives. Kate Fayers-Kerr (2012; 2019), for example, explores the generativity of earths among the Mun (Mursi) in Ethiopia, noting their '[d]aily intimacy and ease of interaction' with these substances and the 'pervasive and persistent role earth has' (2019, 115–16). The Mun exist as a *community of substances* through their engagement with earths, soils and dung. They recognise these different earths and soils have personalities and through engagement create protective relationships with soils in different locations. They cleanse their bodies with earths and soils, play with these as children, harvest and ingest soils from different locations and engage with earthy matter in ritual contexts. The Mun also recognise the healing properties of mud, clay, ash and earth, which they eat and rub on their skin. Effectively, earths and soils mediate between communities and kin and also embed them in a place; they merge and become consubstantial with earth and the human body *becomes-with* (Haraway 2008) the substances it variously interacts with, consumes or is painted with.

Ethnographies also illustrate the commingling of matter as substances 'leak, forever discharging through the surfaces that form temporarily around them' (Ingold 2010, 4). Fayers-Kerr's accounts of the Mun, for example, recognise how the human body *becomes-with* (Haraway 2008) the substances it variously interacts with, consumes, or is painted with. Lewis-Williams writes about a similar blurring of boundaries between the vibrant matter of *qhang qhang* (the paint used in San rock art) and the rock-face, which allows images of the spirit world to permeate the stone. The combination of glistening haematite and eland blood (Lewis-Williams and Dowson 1990, 14; Lewis-Williams 2008, 159) in correspondence with the properties of the rock-face, allows the paintings to appear to enter and leave through cracks and crevices of the rock surface (Lewis-Williams and Dowson 1990, 5). Moreover, people other than the artist are able to interact and commingle with the vitality of the painted images through touch. Patches of paint might be blurred, smudged and worn away, and while a good person might absorb the potency of the paint, a bad person would adhere to the image, waste away and die (Lewis-Williams and Dowson 1990, 14). The distinct capacities of the materials and the correspondence of artist, rock and paint co-create to enable shamanistic journeys to the spirit world.

The vibrancy of earthy substances and minerals, their animate properties seemingly infused with a life-force or agency, is key to understanding the affect of earthy matters and how they have become embedded in human interactions with the environment over the millennia. Indeed, it is the very liveliness that informs how such earthy matters have become embedded in peoples' cultural lives. Diana Young (2020) discusses how the very essence of the colour red enlivens substances such as ochre for the Aṉangu of the Western Desert, Australia; 'reds are not in but *of* the material' (Young 2020, 270, emphasis in original). Similarly, ethnographic studies in Africa have documented how habitual application of red ochre to hair, body and clothing – for example, among the Hamar of southern Ethiopia (see Figure 2.3) and the Ovahimba of Angola and Namibia, is more than cosmetic and symbolic – but responds equally to its vital properties, such as its vibrant hue and its protective qualities (see above; Rifkin et al. 2015). Similarly, Bubandt examines the agency of the mud volcano Lumpur Sidoarjo in Indonesia, which he describes as 'an earth being with a will

Figure 2.3 Woman of the Hamar tribe, Ethiopia, wearing ochre hair paint.

of its own' (2017, G123–4). He notes how people respond to its raw power, being drawn to its mudflats to collect and polish pebbles 'in an evident labor of love and dedication' (Bubandt 2017, G128). These accounts all reveal the many ways in which humans have responded to the affective pull of earths, soils and minerals around them, from which, I would argue, we might make tentative conclusions about the ghosts of the far more ancient ochry engagements at Blombos Cave.

Conclusion

> [A] spread of biographical events and memories of events and a dispersed category of material objects, traces and leavings.
>
> (Gell 1998, 222)

This chapter explores how ochre as an earthy substance has been inextricably entangled in human interactions with the material world from the Middle Palaeolithic. There has been a tendency to focus on the symbolic content of ochre, how it was manipulated and used, what this means and how it might inform us about the evolution of human cognitive abilities and development of modern human behaviours and cultural practices. Such an approach, I would argue, elevates humans to 'the ontological center' (Bennett 2010, 110), separating us from the material world of which we are a part (cf. Bennett 2010; Coole and Frost 2010; Attala 2019; Attala and Steel 2019; Rovelli 2021).

Here, however, I have chosen to focus on human engagements with ochre from a new materialities perspective, to explore how practices of co-creating with ochre at Blombos Cave were affected by its specific qualities, in particular its vibrant red hue. Such an approach recognises ochre as a participant in these material relationships, as having affect and provoking specific human actions through its unique capacities. Looking at these early ochry entanglements from a vital materialist perspective, that does not place humans at the ontological centre, reveals people at Blombos Cave working with and participating in 'a *particularly rich and complex* collection of materials' (Bennett 2010, 110, emphasis in original), with which they co-created material and social worlds. I have sought to demonstrate how thinking about the capacities of ochre and examining its correspondence with humans and other materials through the lens of Baradian phenomena might result in 'a change of focus, from the "objectness" of things to material flows and formative processes wherein they come into being' (Ingold 2012, 431). These phenomena describe the affect of one part of the natural world on another (Rovelli 2021, 120). Moreover, exploring the material flows evident in the combinations of ochre and other materials at the site, including the ghosts of the long-vanished humans, as intra-actions, emphasises ochre in-phenomena as an event and arguably allows us to envisage the process of making in these shadowy taskscapes as collaborative practice. These ancient phenomena persist – indeed continue intra-acting (see Govier and Steel 2021, 309–11) – in the environment millennia after they first materialised, the phantoms of 'earlier tracks and traces' (Gan et al. 2017, G6) of lifeways that have long since disappeared.

Notes

1. The source of 'In the Red' is Young 2020. Earthy matter is defined here as soils and sediments comprising eroded, crumbling mineral materials mixed with the decayed plant and animal matter.
2. Here I use assemblage in its archaeological rather than new materialist sense; see discussion in Govier and Steel 2021, 306–8.
3. We should not discount the use of vegetable-based dyes.

References

Attala, L., 2019. *How Water Makes Us Human: Engagements with the Materiality of Water*. Cardiff: University of Wales Press.

Attala, L., and Steel, L., 2019. 'Introduction', in *Body Matters: Exploring the Materiality of the Human Body*, ed. L. Attala and L. Steel. Cardiff: University of Wales Press, pp. 1–17.

Barad, K., 2003. 'Posthumanist performativity: Toward an understanding of how matter comes to matter', *Signs: Journal of Women in Culture and Society*, 28(3), 801–31.

Barad, K., 2007. *Meeting the Universe Halfway: Quantum Physics and the Entanglement of Matter and Meaning*, Durham NC: Duke University Press.

Bar-Yosef Mayer, D. E., Vandermeersch, B., and Bar-Yosef, O., 2009. 'Shells and ochre in Middle Palaeolithic Qafzeh Cave, Israel: Indications for modern behavior', *Journal of Human Evolution*, 56(3), 307–14. *https://doi.org/10.1016/j.jhevol.2008.10.005*.

Bawaka Country, Wright, S., Suchet-Pearson, S., Lloyd, K., Burarrwanga, L., Ganambarr, R., Ganambarr-Stubbs, M., Ganambarr, B., and Maymuru, D., 2015. 'Working with and learning from Country: decentring human author-ity', *Cultural Geographies*, 22, 269–83. *https://doi.org/10.1177/1474474014539248*.

Bennett, J., 2010. *Vibrant Matter: A Political Ecology of Things*. Durham NC and London: Duke University Press.

Boivin, N., 2008. *Material Cultures, Material Minds: The Impact of Things on Human Thought, Society, and Evolution*. Cambridge: Cambridge University Press.

Boivin, N., 2012. 'From veneration to exploitation: Human engagement with the mineral world', in *Soils, Stones and Symbols: Cultural Perceptions of the Mineral World*, ed. N. Boivin and M. A. Owoc. London and New York NY: Routledge (2nd edn), pp. 1–29.

Braudel, F., 1958. 'Histoire et sciences sociales: La longue durée', *Annales: Histoire, sciences sociales*, 13(4), 725–53.

Bubandt, N., 2017. 'Haunted geologies: Spirits, stones and the necropolitics of the Anthropocene', in *Arts of Living on a Damaged Planet: Ghosts and Monsters of the Anthropocene*, ed. A. Tsing, H. Swanson, E. Gan and N. Bubandt. Minneapolis MN and London: University of Minnesota Press, pp. G121–G141.

Conneller, C., 2011. *An Archaeology of Materials: Substantial Transformations in Early Prehistoric Europe*. London and New York NY: Routledge.

Coole, D., and Frost, S., 2010. 'Introducing the New Materialisms', in *New Materialisms: Ontology, Agency and Politics*, ed. D. Coole and S. Frost. Durham NC and London: Duke University Press, pp. 1–43.

Deleuze, G., and Guattari, F., 2017. *A Thousand Plateaus: Capitalism and Schizophrenia*. London and New York NY: Bloomsbury Academic (reprint).

Descola, P., 2010. 'Preface', in *Soil and Culture*, ed. C. Feller and E. Lander. Dordrecht and London: Springer, pp. xiii–xv.

Fayers-Kerr, K. N., 2012. 'The "Miranda" and the "cultural archive": From Mun (Mursi) lip-plates, to body painting and back again', *Paideuma*, 58, 245–59.

Fayers-Kerr, K. N., 2019. 'Becoming a community of substance: The Mun, the mud and the therapeutic art of body painting', in *Body Matters: Exploring the Materiality of the Human Body*, ed. L. Attala and L. Steel. Cardiff: University of Wales Press, pp. 109–33.

Gan, E., Tsing, A., Swanson, H., and Bubandt, N., 2017. 'Introduction: Haunted landscapes of the Anthropocene', in *Arts of Living on a Damaged Planet: Ghosts and Monsters of the Anthropocene*, ed. A. Tsing, H. Swanson, E. Gan and N. Bubandt. Minneapolis MN and London: University of Minnesota Press, pp. G1–G14.

Geggel, L., 2018. 'Ochre: The world's first red paint', *LiveScience*, November 2018. *www.livescience.com/64138-ochre.html* (accessed 3 May 2022).

Gell, A., 1998. *Art and Agency: An Anthropological Theory*. Oxford: Clarendon Press.

Govier, E., 2017. 'Creative practices: How Communities were "made" at Çatalhöyük', (unpublished PhD thesis, University of Wales Trinity Saint David).

Govier, E., 2019. 'Bodies that co-create: The residues and intimacies of vital materials', in *Body Matters: Exploring the Materiality of the Human Body*, ed. L. Attala and L. Steel. Cardiff: University of Wales Press, pp. 19–37.

Govier, E., and Steel, L., 2021. 'Beyond the "thingification" of worlds: Archaeology and the New Materialisms', *Journal of Material Culture*, 26(3), 298–317. *https://doi.org/10.1177/13591835211025559*.

Haraway, D., 2008. *When Species Meet*. Minneapolis MN and London: University of Minnesota Press.

Harris, O. J. T., 2014. 'Revealing our vibrant past: Science, materiality and the Neolithic', in *Early Farmers: The View from Archaeology and Science*, ed. A. Whittle and P. Bickle. Oxford: Oxford University Press/British Academy, pp. 327–45.

Heidegger, M., 1971. *Poetry, Language, Thought*, trans A. Hofstadter. New York NY: Harper and Row.

Henshilwood, C., and d'Errico, F., 2011. 'Middle Stone Age engravings and their significance to the debate on the emergence of symbolic material culture', in *Homo symbolicus: The Dawn of Language, Imagination and Spirituality*, ed. C. Henshilwood and F. d'Errico. Amsterdam: Benjamins, pp. 75–96.

Henshilwood, C., d'Errico, F., Yates, R., Jacobs, Z., Tribolo, C., Duller, G. A. T, Mercier, N., Sealy, J. C., Valadas, H., Watts, I., and Wintle, A. G., 2002. 'Emergence of modern human behavior: Middle Stone Age engravings from South Africa', *Science*, 295, 1278–80. *https://doi.org/10.1126/science.1067575*.

Henshilwood, C., d'Errico, F., Vanhaeren, M., van Niekerk, K., and Jacobs, Z., 2004. 'Middle Stone Age shell beads from South Africa', *Science*, 304, 404.

Henshilwood, C. S., d'Errico, F., and Watts, I., 2009. 'Engraved ochres from the Middle Stone Age levels at Blombos Cave, South Africa', *Journal of Human Evolution*, 57, 27–47.

Henshilwood, C. S., d'Errico, F., van Nierkerk, K. L., Coquinot, Y., Jacobsstein, Z., Lauritzen, E., and Menu, M., 2011. 'A 100,000-year-old ochre-processing workshop at Blombos Cave, South Africa', *Science*, 334, 219–22. *www.science.org/doi/10.1126/science.1211535*.

Henshilwood, C. S., d'Errico, F., van Niekerk, K., Dayet, L., Queffelec, A., and Pollarolo, L., 2018. 'An abstract drawing from the 73,000-year-old levels at Blombos Cave, South Africa', *Nature*, 562, 115–18.

Hovers, E., Ilani, S., Bar-Yosef, O., and Vendermeersch, B., 2003. 'An early case of colour symbolism: Ochre use by modern humans in Qafzeh Cave', *Current Anthropology*, 44(4), 491–522.

Ingold, T., 1993. 'The temporality of the landscape', *World Archaeology*, 25(2), 152–74.

Ingold, T., 2007. 'Materials against materiality', *Archaeological Dialogues*, 14, 1–16.

Ingold, T., 2010. 'Bringing things to life: Creative entanglements in a world of materials', Working paper 15, *Realities: ESRC National Centre for Research Methods. https://eprints.ncrm.ac.uk/id/eprint/1306/1/0510_creative_entanglements.pdf* (accessed 1 December 2023).

Ingold, T., 2012. 'Towards and ecology of materials', *Annual Review of Anthropology*, 41, 427–42.

Ingold, T., 2013. *Making: Anthropology, Archaeology, Art and Architecture*. Abingdon and New York NY: Routledge.

Jones, A. M., 2018. 'The archaeology of art: Practice, interaction and affect', in *The Archaeology of Art: Materials, Practices, Affects*, ed. A. M. Jones and A. Cochrane. Abingdon and New York NY: Routledge, pp. 19–30.

Knappett, C., 2006. 'Beyond skin: Layering and networking in art and archaeology', *Cambridge Archaeological Journal*, 16, 239–51.

Kopytoff, I., 1986. 'The cultural biography of things', in *The Social Life of Things: Commodities in Cultural Perspective*, ed. A. Appadurai. Cambridge: Cambridge University Press, pp. 64–91.

Lewis-Williams, D., 2008. *The Mind in the Cave: Consciousness and the Origins of Art*. London: Thames and Hudson (reprint).

Lewis-Williams, D., 2010. *Conceiving God: The Cognitive Origin and Evolution of Religion*. London: Thames and Hudson.

Lewis-Williams, J. D., and Dowson, T. A., 1990. 'Through the veil: San rock paintings and the rock face', *The South African Archaeological Bulletin*, 45, 5–16. *https://doi.org/10.2307/3887913*.

Lombard, M., 2007. 'The gripping nature of ochre: the association of ochre with Howieson's Poort adhesives and Later Stone Age mastics from South Africa', *Journal of Human Evolution*, 53, 406–19.

Macintyre, K., and Dobson, B., 2018. 'Ochre: An ancient health-giving cosmetic', *Anthropology from the Shed*. *https://www.anthropologyfromtheshed.com/ochre-an-ancient-health-giving-cosmetic* (accessed 1 December 2023).

Rifkin, R. F., 2011. 'Assessing the efficacy of red ochre as a prehistoric hide-tanning ingredient', *Journal of African Archaeology*, 9(2), 1–28.

Rifkin, R. F., 2012. 'Processing ochre in the Middle Stone Age: Testing the inference of prehistoric behaviours from actualistically derived experimental data', *Journal of Anthropological Archaeology*, 31, 174–95.

Rifkin, R. F., 2015. 'Ethnographic and experimental perspectives on the efficacy of ochre as a mosquito repellent', *South African Archaeological Bulletin*, 70 (201), 64–75.

Rifkin, R. F., Dayet, L., Queffelec, A., Summers, B., Lategan, M., and d'Errico, F., 2015. 'Evaluating the photoprotective effects of ochre on human skin by *in vivo* SPF assessment: Implications for human evolution, adaptation and dispersal', *PLOSOne*, 10(9). *https://doi.org/10.1371/journal.pone.0136090*.

Ronchitelli, A., Mugnaini, S., Arrighi, S., Atrei, A., Capecchi, G., Giamello, M., Longo, L., Marchettini, N., Viti, C., and Moron, A., 2015. 'When technology joins symbolic behaviour: The Gravettian burials at Grotta Paglicci (Rignano Garganico – Foggia – Southern Italy)', *Quaternary International*, 359–60, 423–41.

Roebroeks, W., Sier, M. J., Nielsen, T. K., de Loecker, D., Parés, J. M., Arps, C. E. S., and Mücher, H. J., 2012. 'Use of red ochre by early Neandertals', *PNAS*, 109(6), 1889–94. *https://doi.org/10.1073/pnas.1112261109*.

Rovelli, C., 2021. *Helgoland*. London: Allen Lane.

Sajó I. E., Kovács J., Fitzsimmons K. E., Jáger V., Lengyel G., Viola B., Talamo, S., and Hublin, J.-J., 2015. 'Core-shell processing of natural pigment: Upper Palaeolithic red ochre from Lovas, Hungary', *PLOS ONE* 10(7): e0131762. *https://doi.org/10.1371/journal.pone.0131762*.

Schotsmans, E., Busacca, G., Bennison-Chapman, L., Lingle, A., Milella, M., Tibbetts, B., Tsoraki, C., Vasić, M., and Veropoulidou, R., 2020. 'Pigment use at Neolithic Çatalhöyük', *Near Eastern Archaeology*, 83(3), 156–67.

Schotsmans, E., Busacca, G., Bennison-Chapman, L., Lingle, A., Milella, M., Tibbetts, B., Tsoraki, C., Vasić, M., and Veropoulidou, R., 2021. 'The colour of things. Pigments and colours in Neolithic Çatalhöyük', in *Communities at Work: The Making of Çatalhöyük*, ed. I. Hodder and C. Tsoraki. British Institute at Ankara Monograph 55, Çatalhöyük Research Project 15, London: Oxbow, pp. 263–88.

Sommer, M. (2007) *Bones and Ochre: The Curious Afterlife of the Red Lady of Paviland*. Cambridge MA and London: Harvard University Press.

Steel, L., 2020. 'Feats of clay: Considering the materiality of Late Bronze Age Cyprus', *Sustainability, Special Issue: Exploring Materiality in the Bronze Age*, 12. *http://doi.org/10.3390/su12176942* (accessed 1 December 2023).

Steffensen, V., 2019. 'Putting people back into the country', in *Decolonizing Research: Indigenous Storywork as Methodology*, ed. J. Archibald, J. B. J. Lee-Morgan and J. de Santolo. London: Bloomsbury Publishing, pp. 224–38.

Tarlach, G., 2018. 'What the ancient pigment ochre tells us about the human mind'. *www.discovermagazine.com/planet-earth/prehistoric-use-of-ochre-can-tell-us-about-the-evolution-of-humans* (accessed 15 April 2022).

Trinkaus, E., Buzhilova, A. P. Mednikova, M. B., and Dobrovolskaya, M. V., 2014. *The People of Sunghir: Burials, Bodies, and Behavior in the Earlier Upper Paleolithic*. Oxford: Oxford University Press.

Tsing, A., Swanson, H., Gan, E., and Bubandt, N. (eds), 2017. *Arts of Living on a Damaged Planet: Ghosts and Monsters of the Anthropocene*. Minneapolis MN and London: University of Minnesota Press.

Wenger, E. 2007. *Communities of Practice: Learning, Meaning, and Identity*. Cambridge: Cambridge University Press (reprint).

Wreschner, E. E., 1980. 'Red ochre and human evolution: A case for discussion', *Current Anthropology*, 21(5), 631–44.

Young, D., 2020. 'In the red: Substances and materials in the Australian Western Desert', *Journal of the Royal Anthropological Institute*, 26, 269–83.

3 HARD CORE, SOFT TOUCHES

A Story of Affect Between Caves, Rocks and Humans

Simone Sambento

And here come I,
a thing from a blue-green world,
an alien visiting alienation.
Thirsty for each black void
and sculpted crevice.
Limb and wind tested against disinterested
neutral stone.

At times these holes have hurt me;
but what's a tiff between lovers?
Each time is a consummation:
a union
with the cave.
(Extract from Jeffreys 2011)

Of Caves and Humans

Caves have long been looked at as testimonies to the history of humankind, witnesses to the evolution of our planet, biota and adaptation, climate change and the development of our species. It is therefore unsurprising that these same places that appear to us as time capsules of evolution are often seen as containers of facts and backgrounds to history. Ever curious, humans tend to interact with these as natural laboratory spaces in search of the answers that our emancipated, yet seemingly evolution-isolated species so eagerly seeks. The idea of an evolution-isolated species is important here. In the quest to understand our place in the world, humans have come to embrace the perspective of the evolutionary superiority of our species, a progressive distancing and isolation from all that is *other*, and the mastering of nature through the creative power of our minds. Animals, plants, rocks, mud and water are all, to varying degrees, perceived not just as distinct but also as separate from us. The rails are then laid down for the Cartesian dualism of mind versus material to run at full tilt, and the cave, which is formed of seemingly inert rock, is placed in the perspective of a passive foreign domain where knowledge is explored and harvested. This knowledge-harvesting allure of caves has steadily attracted a legion of disciplines as well as the curious – there are enough secrets tucked away in these ancient cathedrals to satiate the whole of the academic sciences. However, amid these paths of science and history also moves a different story of the human and the cave, one that bridges the ontological gap that separates the hard lithic world of rocks and the soft fleshy world of humans: a story of affect between caves and speleologists.

It was 2004 when, standing in front of a small muddy hole on a riverbank in the Scottish Highlands, I first entered a cave. As I squeezed myself and my oversized borrowed waterproofs and crooked helmet through the slimy gap, I remember my far larger friend squashing into the passage ahead of me shouting 'it's only dangerous when the waters rise'. We pressed on. The water, fortunately, did not rise, but my interest in caves did. Inside the cave, on coming upon an elevated chamber where we could sit almost upright, we found what, to my senses, were merely tiny sharp fragments cutting through my knees as I crawled along the passage. To the trained eyes of my friend though, a different story unfolded: we were sitting next to an accumulation of crushed shells that, according to him, could indicate a prehistoric feeding spot and suggested another ancient configuration of the cave. Validity of this interpretation aside, the idea that someone could reconstruct biological and geological history by interpreting those sharp fragments cutting through my trousers piqued my curiosity. What will forever be imprinted in my mind, however, is how fast my heart was pounding as I exerted all my energy squeezing and dragging my battered body along the cave's muddy constricted passages, each metre fought for, the fight between my human body and the cave body exhausting and exhilarating me in equal measure. Fast-forward six years and I was living deep in the midst of the caving community of the Basque Country and completely engrossed in the pursuit of cave exploration: speleology.

Emerging in the nineteenth century, the practice of modern speleology developed along the lines of a sporting-science that involved the exploration and systematic recording of caves and subterranean systems and attracted a wide range of disciplines and practices, including academic scientists and amateur practitioners. This overlapping of science, sport, scientists and amateurs has made speleology hard to define and, historically, different countries and speleological communities have carved their own paths, traditions and definitions of what the practice entails[1] (Cant 2006; Pérez 2012; Mattes 2015). However, in spite of geographical variations, speleologists' interactions with the subterranean world still largely converge in an empirical exploratory approach to the environment that they move in: searching, observing and recording, surveying, comparing data, and making informed predictions to explore further. Through this history, what often becomes forgotten though is that the interaction between caves and speleologists is first and foremost a physical process: exploring caves involves spending a considerable amount of time underground being cold, tired and covered in mud. It also involves many moments of awe and excitement for the speleologists, all the while sharing experiences and 'breaking bread' (Haraway 2008, 95) with their most intimate of companions: the caves. These relationships in fact become so strong that within caving communities they are commonly referred to as love affairs – occasionally reciprocated, often rocky – as illustrated in the opening poem.

This is a story about muddling traditional conceptions of the relationship between humans and the natural world around us. Predicated on new materialist debates, this chapter intends to challenge perceptions that have opposed the human and abiotic nature in a subject-object dualistic view of the world by looking at how the speleologist and the cave co-create each other in a process of constant becoming. It asks the questions: How are the seemingly distinct materialities of the speleologist and the cave creative actors in each other's existence? Who or what do they become through this encounter? Why does it matter? By illuminating these questions through theories and stories, this chapter thus attempts to shift the human from the pivotal centre from where all action springs and, more ambitiously, by lending a different gaze to what it is to be animate and inanimate, it hopes that the relational placing of humans and non-humans may bring forth a different becoming.

In the section 'Philosophies of the Mud', I start by drawing on Donna Haraway's (2008) concept of *becoming-with*, which challenges the separation between the human and non-human and emphasises the entanglements of co-existing in the world, and through this lens explore how speleologists and caves ontologically co-create and affect each other. To say that caves have the power to affect and shape the human entails questioning what it means to have agency. To address this, I turn to discussions that bring the non-human and the inanimate to the fore as actors that have the power to affect (Bennett 2010). I then broaden the discussion by contending that to understand this relationship of affect, the human must also be involved in the process of being a material entity (Derrida 1997a; 1997b).

'Stories of Affect' moves the narrative along to the subterranean world. Through a series of stories, it gives examples of how the ontological co-making of caves and speleologists takes place through the practices of exploration and surveying. It starts by using a cave song to illustrate the sensual connections between speleologists and caves and their material-discursive entanglements (Barad 2007). The discussion then moves to looking at how the cave and the human are co-created through movement during the acts of surveying and exploring. I then change the pace and tone of the narrative by introducing a diary extract that immerses the reader in the sensorial experience of cave exploration and illustrates the ontological making of caves and humans through their physical encounters. This section finishes with a mention of the vibrant and morphogenetic capabilities of rocks and caves and the role that they play in the making of the human-with-the-cave.

The chapter closes with an epilogue co-written with a fellow speleologist. Our final lines invite a thought: if we see our entanglements with the world as always relational, emergent and co-created, what type of worlds can we then choose to create and what type of humans can we choose to be?

Philosophies of the Mud

Co-creative actors

When I was first researching this topic my then university supervisor, Dr Luci Attala, suggested I read *When Species Meet* (2008) by a woman called Donna Haraway. Granted, I now know that both Haraway and her canine protagonists are a permanent fixture in anthropology, the social sciences and beyond, but back when I was studying as an undergraduate in a tiny rural Welsh village, this literary encounter was nothing short of a revelation. While I tried to make sense of my own and my caving companions' love affair with caves, here was this intelligent creative woman telling the world about her beloved canine companions, speaking of how through being deeply involved in each other's lives, dogs and humans co-created each other's existence as companion species – making kin with each other. To be frank, it all sounded a bit mad at the time, but so was our obsession with caves, so perhaps we were a good fit. Somehow, the concept of making kin ended up crystallising as a mental image of Haraway and her dogs galloping together in synchrony through agility obstacles, elegantly and with fabulous hair. In short, the antithesis of the relationship of my rocks and humans – I could not help thinking that such intellectual musings might not quite pan out for us. But, according to Haraway, there was no need to sashay elegantly through obstacles together, nor indeed was it necessary for our companions to align with us at all. What in fact mattered was what we *become-with* each other and, for this end, only one ingredient was truly necessary: being muddled in each other's lives and stories.

My caves and humans are of the mud, of the earth, encounters of the senses where their muddy entanglements are perhaps a lot stickier than one would like from their ideal companion species. Theirs is not a relationship of paced synchrony and warm companionship, nor is their touch always gentle and their regard high. My caves and humans do not always flow through each other's bodies in a choreographed dance. At best, they are a mix of admirably placed steps, hard blows and clumsy reaches. That is not to say that my human and rock creatures cannot interact; because they can and do. They do, however, pose different challenges. If through her agile argument about humans and canines, Haraway was able to bring the world-forming human and the poor-in-world dog (Heidegger 1995) out of their pre-established hierarchies and give them a more equal place in the democracy of relationships, much work still lies ahead for Heidegger's worldless rocks to come forth and make a statement. Put simply, the relationship between speleologists and rocky caves has the complication that one of the partners in this relationship not only does not speak, but also has no seemingly communicating existence that can have access to other beings (Heidegger 1995). How then is it possible that the 'inexpressive, unyielding, immobile' (Cohen 2010, 56) world of minerals and rocks can have any agency in affecting us?

In a fantastic conversation in the book *Stones According to Egill Saebjörnsson* (Bennett 2012), where Icelandic artist and musician Egill Saebjörnsson infuses rocks and minerals with life and explores human relationships with the inanimate, Jane Bennett discusses with the author the idea of worms and minerals as possible co-actants with the force of art. What she articulates is that if we stop seeing art as a representation of the world and instead see it as an active force (see also Alberti, Boyd, this volume), then all the things involved in its co-creative power no longer need to be looked at through the sticky classification of agency that is usually attributed to animate beings. Instead, things emerge as co-actants of that force. Why should the power to affect the world be measured against human agency? Seeking anthropomorphic characteristics in everything is missing the point, when all things, human and non-human alike, are *de facto* constant participants in the world (Latour 2004). So, when Bennett wrote her book *Vibrant Matter* (2010), she did something bold. Not only did she bring materials vibrating their way to life as co-actants, she allowed them a life that is independent from the human, that is latent and potential in spite of what encounter it forms: a vitality. Describing how independently of humans a pile of rubbish constantly becomes something else – something slimy, toxic, spreading – she convincingly makes a case for taking materials seriously as things that can influence and affect us through their potentially hazardous activity. That caves exist in spite of humans is a fact – they were here millions of years before us, are still continuously evolving, and will likely be here long after we are gone – but the very fact that we have a concomitant presence in the world means that we affect each other. So, although things can and do lead lives independently of the human, their independent existence and that of their assemblages has a 'liveliness intermeshed with human agency' (Bennett 2011, n.p.). In these assemblages, there are no no-consequence interconnections – be it at close or distant range – we are always affecting and being affected by the world, becoming with it through ongoing encounters. What is possible, however, is that the closer we become to things the more muddled we become with them, the more we break bread, the more they matter.

When attempting an argument about the lively and creative relationships between humans and the inanimate, it is the seemingly inert nature of the latter that always appears to constitute the challenge. My concern, however, rests more with the pre-conception of how the human arrives at these encounters. The blessing of working with the inanimate is that, since for so long we have relegated it to the domain of the silent and lifeless, it is not difficult to infuse it with whatever subjectivity we may wish – we can be a little creative when thinking about it. Humans, however, arrive at these encounters thinking they are fully formed, their existence assured, and little relativism can be conjured about them without being confronted with the sound of 'I can speak for myself!' But how can we start questioning what being human means in these relationships if we see ourselves as fully formed entities?

Philosophers, such as Jacques Derrida in his work 'And Say the Animal Responded?' (1997a), have contemplated that the greatest problem of projecting the questions of agency onto the other, is that the human is unlikely to see that it is their own place in the world that is due questioning. More fundamentally, according to Derrida, the Cartesian view – which only permits the animal's semiotic power to react and never to respond – is only possible to unpack if the focus that we have placed on the animal and the other is instead turned onto oneself to probe within the human. He takes his argument further and contends that it is only the fact that the human has the ability to conceptualise the idea of a subject in the first place that creates any difference between them and the other, therefore suggesting that the answer lies in how the human has constituted himself in relation to the other, and not how the other manifests itself in the world. This taking of consciousness takes physical form as Derrida (1997b) one day finds himself standing stark naked under his cat's gaze and scrutiny and, within the presence of the other, asks, 'Who am I?' Haraway, however, sees Derrida's cat story as a missed opportunity for the philosopher to learn 'how to look back' (Haraway 2008, 20) at the other and to be more curious and ask more, know more: Who is looking back? What do I touch when I touch the cave? Who are we creating together?

Stories of Affect

Hard core, soft touches

> If you ever get the horn, down below,
> Then your foreskin will get torn, down below,
> As you squeeze along those crawls,
> You will wear away your balls,
> And your screams will fill the halls, down below,
>
> If you ever want to screw, down below,
> Try between sumps 3 and 2, down below,
> Mike and Moira did it first,
> And his crutch piece nearly burst,
> But the mudbank came off worst, down below.
>
> (Extract from Traditional, attributed to Alfie Collins; Biddle 1976)

The world of caves and speleologists is, above all, physical. I find it surprising how often visceral encounters and involvements are absent from studies that seek first and foremost to look at the involvement of the human and non-human in a physical world of touching and sensing. Granted, this is a particularly crass song, but not unusual by any measure in its depictions of these human and cave relationships. Perhaps unsurprisingly then, during the course of my research I often found myself in the presence of these excited muddlings of the bodies of the cave and the speleologist where, despite the cave not necessarily becoming the bedding of sexual performance, it is being lived through a physical encounter that invokes intense physical and mental sensations. Stalagmites that thrust as penises, flowstone that resemble shapely breasts, constrictions and smotherings that assault our private parts. These visualisations and associations are in fact so common that parts of caves go on to be named after these conjurations, often following comical (and painful) episodes of the bodies of the speleologists and the caves being jammed and groped in a forceful fight that poses an assault on the senses: The Virgin's Delight (Swildon's Hole), Clitoris Crawl (Priddy Green Sink), The Sphincter (Uamh an Claonaite) and Coitus Corner (Quaking Pot), to name but a few. In the last two lines of the poetic passage of 'Down Below' (Biddle 1976) the fight between the crutch piece and the mudbank is illustrative of the ongoing opposing forces that the speleologist and the cave constantly exert on each other, where in this case the speleologist comes out feeling victorious knowing that, in spite of his suffering, the cave has also paid its toll. What is more, these encounters between the speleologist and the cave become repetitive as over and over again they experience interaction with each other in these erogenous zones, replicating and reinforcing the materiality of their physical becoming-together. It is not surprising then that due to the time speleologists spend with the cave and the suggestive sensuous embraces they offer, the relationship that emerges from spending time together is a visceral one and sometimes compared to having a love affair.

In a slightly surrealist book called *The Writings of Stones*, Roger Caillois (1985) digresses about the suggestive power that stones, their shapes and their lines have on humans. For him, these inanimate things bear an aesthetic and suggestive power that animates not only the imagination of the human, but the rock itself. For Caillois – and in line with Bennett's idea of art as a force (2010) – the fascination that humans have with lithic entities emerges from the fact that stones are vital forces that breathe and live and, through the course of their existence, form connections with everything around them; they are constantly throwing around spirals of suggestive co-creation that 'attracts onto itself that exact imagination which reveals the object more than inventing it' (Caillois 1973, in Warner 2008). Previous work (Cant 2003; Pérez 2012) undertaken with speleologists suggests that intimate and sensuous relations are constantly being formed between them and caves. For Cant, these encounters often find expression through creative mediums, possibly as a way to circumvent what she calls an expectation of 'tough masculinities' (Cant 2003, 68) that are embedded in caving pursuits and that can only vent the softer strokes that the cave bears on the human through a medium exterior to the cave environment and community: art. Also likely is that, due to the intense experiencing of the cave, expression becomes both paramount and complex, where not even borrowed words are able to capture effectively the vitality of matter (Bennett 2010) and its entanglements with the human. So much so that, alongside scientific records of cave exploration, it is not uncommon to find vast amounts of grey literature among clubs and caving communities where the visceral or sensuous encounters between caves and speleologists pour out in the form of creative drawings, comics, songs, prose and poetry, such as the verses in the opening of this chapter.

The material encounters of caves-speleologists and the discourses they seem to produce are not separate phenomena though. The affective entanglements between the materiality of the cave and the artistic musings they produce in fact bear notes of Barad's (2007) understanding of the world as existing through its material-discursive practices (see Alberti, this volume). In her view, there is no separation between things as matter and things as discourses – they are ontologically and epistemologically co-constituted. Under this lens, sensuous songs, cave toponymics, drawings and other discursive practices can in fact be seen as part of the co-creative configuration of things that form the ontologies of speleologists and the caves.

Movement and emerging the cave

During the course of my research, one of the most difficult things for human participants to express was what a cave is. Yet, once prodded, the answer seemed to be almost consensual: space. Spending a lot of time underground, speleologists somewhat resemble Ingold's (2011) mole, where the reality of its world is not that of objects and shapes, but tunnels, chambers and space. Consequentially, it is space that often constitutes challenge and fear for speleologists who, according to their size and moulding capability, are constantly assessing themselves against it (Pérez 2013): if the gap is too large for them to bridge, they will fall into the chasm, if the squeeze is too tight, they will be constricted. In her work about surveying and mapping, María Alejandra Pérez (2013) explores how speleologists, by pushing and moving their bodies along caves, form the space and contours of what then becomes the cave drawn on a paper. Surveying is one of the key activities of speleology: making use of a series of devices that measure distance, azimuth and inclination, a map is produced to represent the intricate passages of subterranean systems. A practitioner of speleology herself, to support her study Pérez sets out with a team to explain how this practice takes place. Drawing on Ingold's anthropology of lines (2007; 2011) she argues that as she moves along her exploratory path she is 'pushing passages' (Pérez 2013, 294), carving with her body the space that will define the cave and later be registered and contoured onto the map that becomes the cave, which is constantly being re-defined as the exploration progresses. The perspective that speleologists have of the cave as spaces and what the caves become through the act of surveying is thus embedded in the process of the cave becoming-with the intrusion of their bodies, the space it forms as it is occupied.

Although the example illustrates perfectly how the body of the speleologist creates what effectively becomes known as the cave, taking a solely human-centred perspective on how the cave is formed presents limitations and neglects the fact that the cave retains a vitality and existence that does not have to depend on the human (Bennett 2010; Haraway 2008). One could argue that the way the cave is formed for the human is not just a matter of perspective but also a matter of necessity: the spaces where the human body fits are the only ones that matter for them in terms of exploration because they are the ones that allow passage. That said, for the hydrologist for example, the maps drawn by speleologists – which are based on the lines formed through the movement of their bodies – might be irrelevant as they do not show all the wandering paths of what interests them: water (Florea and Vacher 2011). Long before the human set foot in the cave, other vital agencies were at play there, predominantly water. Although caves are formed through a series of complex ongoing processes, it is mainly water mixed with carbon dioxide that, through dissolution, forms many of the voids that make a limestone cave. It was water then, not the human, which carved most of the labyrinths where the human now pushes passages. The hydrogeologist could thus argue that he would much rather have water be the one drawing the map for them! Whereas a human-centred perspective would see the caves, and subsequently the survey maps, as being formed by the human body, a co-creative perspective would cast a wider gaze asking how the cave and the speleologist are forming each other. By shifting the focus even slightly from the human to other actors, not only would we start noticing the effects of the non-human world of water and air, we would also notice that in the act of moving through the cave the human is not actually pushing passages, it is chasing them: what appears on survey maps is therefore not the human carving a way through the cave, it is the human moving with it.

Into the belly of the beast: moving with the cave

After generously granting us a pleasant entrance and getting our hearts pounding, the cave started becoming elusive. Worst of all, she was breathing heavily into our faces, showing us her depth, but not disclosing the way through. Rivers' obsession was so compelling, and she so furtive, that we all became absorbed by it. I had never seen anyone spend so much time looking at a map – he was enthralled. We went back every weekend, sometimes for two days in a row, for months and months, spending the whole of our waking day inside her. She had become so difficult that Rivers scoured the grounds outside looking for clues of her doings, his hand acquiring a life of its own constantly measuring angles, searching for hints of the contours of her body along the landscape. Inside, the initial gallery was a sloping mass of debris from the roof collapse in which the entrance had opened. Flowstone had been growing its way for a long time and now laid itself as a petrified undulating cascade leading to the chaos of collapsed boulders amassed at the bottom end of the chamber. The place must be old, all the water had found its way to lower levels and long abandoned those passages of dripping calcite where everything felt still. It was through a small gap between these boulders that we found a way to go deeper: 'we need ropes!' The vertical crevices were awkward, not allowing us to place good rigging, banging and bruising ourselves onto her. The further in we moved, the more she squeezed us and changed her character. Soon past the first main vertical cracks, we were in a world of slime. She was not her peaceful calcite-clad and serene old self anymore, she was younger here, smaller passages but infants in the timescale of her life. Forcing us to a crawl, we dragged our mud-caked bodies and tackle bags through her insides, each movement seeing us more plastered with her thick viscosity. With the weight of her dampness and cold slowing us down, our bodies lost their vitality. She, on the other hand, seemed livelier than ever. Water dripped down along her turning vertical cracks into slippery crumbles of brittle wall. Jammed in the vertical abyss, a constellation of boulders dotted the landscape above and below us. The cave that I thought I knew was now spatially impossible for my senses to fully apprehend. What looked like ground was not ground, it was a temporary deposit of rock, soil, mud and things I did not understand and, as soon as I gave a few safe steps, she again opened herself beneath me. Space did not feel linear; it was a chaos of shapes with gravity turned upside down as we moved at impossible angles – a vertigo. A subtle breeze blew from a tight vertical section raising hopes that the cave may continue that way. At least now we were jammed between two walls, just like the precariously balanced rocks. Things grew in there though, things were growing inside me, my chest filling with humidity, spores and particles and slowly constricting. I did not know where my breath finished and hers began. Rivers was a man possessed and looked like he had the fever 'It's the air, the air does this to us', he said. Never had I been more sure that air does do things – her breathing was driving us all mad. Emerging from the immense chaos of her shapes, air was coming and going from all directions, clashing with itself, pushing its own passages and masses as we frenetically tried following it in search of her continuation. Seen from the outside it would have looked like Ingold's moles had gone mad: instead of giving form to the path we were moving in, we were literally moving not through the cave, but with it. We had entered a world in which we were witnessing its forming, and we were part of it. (Sambento 2013)

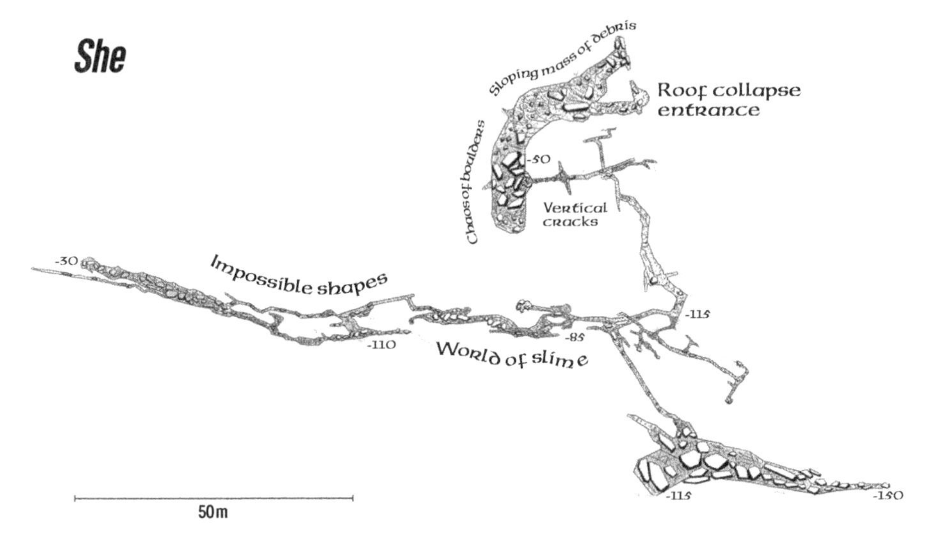

Figure 3.1 Survey map of 'She'.

Vibrant matter and haptic becomings

> What Deleuze and Guattari set their sights on is something else: a vibratory effluescence that persists before and after any arrangement in space: the peculiar motility of an intensity.
>
> (Bennett 2010, 57)

Deleuze and Guattari's (1980) project is to decentralise events as happening from the view of a subject. Instead, they offer a perspective that sees all things in a process of constant becoming, with no beginning or end point in sight. They argue that everything exists in a process of constant flux, never inert: the motility of an intensity. The cave and the human are moving, flowing, only in different time frames, making this flux almost undetectable to the human senses (Leveson 2006; Bennett 2010). The drifting of continents, the slow depositing of matter that assembles and is compressed, turned, folded, heated and shaped is invisible to the human eye. Yet the earth is alive. Defying hylomorphic models that see the inanimate material world as being formed only against its contact with living organisms (Ingold 2008; Bennett 2010), this rocky world has a life of its own. In a discussion about the life of materials, Bennett (2010) explores how metal vibrates through atoms quivering in its 'intercrystaline spaces' (Smith 1988, 134, cited in Bennett 2010, 59). Indeed, to see space as endemic only to the interstices between the surface of the rock and the body of speleologist is a conditioning of scale. Our senses are able to tell us about the life that runs through the cave corridors where we fit, where our vision enters, that our bodies feel. It might let us understand that wind and water were there carving the cave well before us, or that a mole, a bat or a worm all have contact zones in this interdependent dance that is the cave. But at the small interstices, the vitality of the soil, the rock, the air and the human evade us. Our naked senses cannot comprehend when Bennett's vibrant metal opens invisible lines of cracks, forces emergent from a series of causalities that are both cause and consequence of a time scale we cannot perceive. But these worlds are not always silent; they speak to those who have learned to interact with them. The blacksmith, for example, learns the materials' vibration, how to attune himself with it and be involved in a co-creative process (DeLanda 1999). These encounters are so visceral that DeLanda defines the way the blacksmith interacts with the metal not as an action of giving shape to matter but of interacting with it as living materials that are 'pregnant with morphogenetic capabilities and his role is teasing a form out of them' (DeLanda 1999, 11).

Teasing form out of things is not a prerogative solely of the human though. Of a photograph taken during exploration (see Figure 3.2), a colleague pointed out that it appeared as if the cave was giving birth to the speleologist, a perceptive comment indeed since as speleologists have an impact on the cave, so the cave very literally squeezes a form out of them. The assemblages of what becomes rock, against the assemblages of what becomes flesh and structure in the human, creates specific motions and points of contact where the cave and the human interact, their creative materialities becoming enacted according to what forces they meet (Bennett 2010). The speleologist's body becomes humanly crippled with aches, pains, distortions and movements, but at the same time also more adapted to the cave. To be able to interact with the body of the cave, the human learns how to move and approach it in specific ways. A case in point is when speleologists need to climb muddy cracks and slots that cause slipping under the surface friction of their bodies. They have learned that, to negotiate these surfaces, they must lean their backs against the slot and, moving

Figure 3.2 Cave giving birth to speleologist.

in opposition, push themselves up with every inch of their bodies trying for as much contact as possible between the human and the cave. So embedded does this become in the human that one day when I was climbing an outdoor sea crag with a climber-speleologist, he mentioned that he could tell I was a speleologist from the way I gave my back to a rocky slot trying to push my way up – in an outdoor rock environment, the human body and the rock usually flow better over each other's surface by facing it and placing weight in specific contact points. While climbing, sliding and tearing through mud and rock our bodies are assaulted and wrapped in the elements of the cave, partly regaining the electrical connection with the earth and encountering a balance through it, becoming-worldly, re-tying knots with the world (Haraway 2008). As speleologists exit the cave, she carries on with the human imprint in her endless story, the human does not define her, does not give her life, it becomes part of her. The human emerges wrapped in mud: Who do I touch when I touch the cave? Confronted with the mud, it feels scrutinised under the stark acknowledgement of being wrapped in her and, as it looks back, it sees itself becoming-with-her as a material entity in a world of affects.

Epilogue: Wrapping Affects

When considering what final thoughts I would like to leave the reader with, it occurred to me that often the purpose of telling a story is to let others see the world through different eyes. I therefore asked a fellow speleologist if he would like to read this little tale and, in his own words, share his conclusions. In true co-creative style, the following closing lines are an assemblage of this reader's interpretation of the discussion here presented, and my own final words.

> Any explanation of our Cartesian-driven perceptions inevitably muddy the central issues discussed here. An opportunity of freeing oneself from an essentially centralist view of what is understood to be an inanimate environment is exemplified by the speleologists' relationship with caves and rocks that not only changes and shapes them physically, but is inexorably bound up in a sensual encounter that denies the human actor from occupying centre stage. The basic premise has examined how everything, animate

> and other (inanimate) equally co-exist and evolve. The infinitely tiny movement of atoms in the seemingly solid, the creative forces of elements that proceed unseen, unheard, must lead to the conclusion that everything, animate and inanimate, has an equal presence in the world. Perhaps a more universal appreciation of this could have a positive effect on the current parlous state of the planet. Speleologists often light-heartedly propose a reason for caving as a 'back to the womb' impulse – perhaps we all need to emulate this example intellectually and be re-born into a different conceptual world where everything is recognised as being constantly in co-creative flux and in relationships of affect.

The cave will carry on existing without the human, as will the human existing without the cave, both vibrating along and forming events with the things that cross their path. But to say that they carry on existing regardless, does not exclude the premise that they carry on affecting. Any one point of contact holds, for a brief moment, all the potential of what it will become: the relationships we choose to forge with the world truly matter and are carried forward. This is above all a political project. To acknowledge that we are made with the world

Figure 3.3 We had entered a world in which we were witnessing its forming, and we were part of it.

is to take responsibility for the interactions and relationships we have with it, where the question *cui bono* – to whose benefit (Haraway 2008) – of one, is entangled in the *cui bono* of the other. To be involved is to be worldly.

Acknowledgements

A heartfelt thank you to Dr Luci Attala and Professor Louise Steel for inviting me to contribute to this volume. I am indebted to the club ADES Espeleologia Elkartea of Gernika for introducing me to the world of caves and caving communities, for their friendship, and for speaking candidly of personal experiences and allowing me to use their surveys and photographic material. This chapter comes with a stunning contribution by artist and illustrator Nuno Quaresma, who made an illustration especially for it – I am very grateful for his incredible skill in materialising my vision of the story. Special thanks to Alan 'Goon' Jeffreys, founder of the Grampian Speleological Group, for his Epilogue contributions and editorial makeover. To Professor Jane Calvert for comments on the initial draft. To the peer-reviewers for their insightful comments. To my colleague Dr Sophie Stone for lending her brain to some of our discussions. To David Brook for proofreading. And, last but not least, to all the caves and subterranean worlds that have been my companions.

Note

1. In the British tradition, the word 'speleology' has fallen into disuse as the scientific pursuit of cave knowledge (commonly referred to as 'cave and karst science' and mostly done by academic or professional scientists) and became separate from pursuits with the purpose of exploration or sport (known as 'caving' and done by amateurs). In many European countries, however, speleology is the most commonly used terminology, and science, exploration and sporting pursuits in caves are often intertwined. In the context of my research in the Basque Country, specifically, speleology is mostly used to refer to amateur expert practitioners who engage in cave exploration, which is how it will be used throughout this chapter.

References

Barad, K., 2007. *Meeting the Universe Halfway: Quantum Physics and the Entanglement of Matter and Meaning*. Durham NC and London: Duke University Press.

Bennett, J., 2010. *Vibrant Matter: A Political Ecology of Things*. Durham NC: Duke University Press.

Bennett, J., 2011. *Vibrant Matter, Zero Landscape: An Interview with Jane Bennett, in Philosophy in a Time of Error.* Interviewed by Klaus K. Loenhart. *www.eurozine.com/vibrant-matter-zero-landscape/* (accessed 23 September 2021).

Bennett, J., 2012. *Stones: Ten Questions to Jane Bennett, in Stones According to Egill Sæbjörnsson*. Interviewed by Egill Sæbjörnsson. Revolver Publishing/Künstlerhaus Bremen, pp. 27–36. Extract available from: *https://rocksstonesdust.com/essays/10_Questions.pdf* (accessed 23 September 2021).

Biddle, R., 1976. 'The caving songs of Mendip', *Grampian Speleological Group Bulletin*, 1–2.

Caillois, R., 1985. *The Writing of the Stones*. Charlottesville VA: University of Virginia Press.

Cant, S., 2003. 'The tug of danger with the magnetism of mystery: descents into the comprehensive, poetic-sensuous appeal of caves', *Tourist Studies*, 3(1), 67–81.

Cant, S., 2006. 'British speleologies: geographies of science, personality and practice, 1935–1953', *Journal of Historical Geography*, 32, 775–95.

Cohen, J. J., 2010. 'Stories of stone', *Postmedieval: A Journal of Medieval Cultural Studies* 1, 56–63.

DeLanda, M., 1999. *Deleuze and the Open-ended Becoming of the World. http://dephasage.ocular-witness.com/pdf/delanda_mettalurgy.pdf* (accessed 23 September 2021).

Deleuze, G., and Guattari, F., 1980. *A Thousand Plateaus: Capitalism and Schizophrenia*. London: Athlone Press.

Derrida, J., 1997a. 'The animal that therefore I am (more to follow)', in *The Animal that Therefore I Am*, ed. M.-L. Mallet, 2008, trans. D. Willis. New York NY: Fordham University Press, pp. 1–51.

Derrida, J., 1997b. 'And say the animal responded?', in *The Animal that Therefore I Am*, ed. M.-L. Mallet, 2008, trans. D. Willis. New York NY: Fordham University Press, pp. 52–118.

Florea, L., and Vacher, H., 2011. 'Communication and "forestructures" at the geological intersection of caves and subsurface water flow: Hermeneutics and parochialism', *Earth Sciences History*, 30(1), 85–105.

Haraway, D., 2008. *When Species Meet*. Minneapolis MN: University of Minnesota Press.

Heidegger, M., 1995. *The Fundamental Concepts of Metaphysics: World, Finitude, Solitude*. Bloomington IN: Indiana University Press.

Ingold, T., 2007. *Lines: A Brief History*. New York NY: Routledge.

Ingold, T., 2008. *Bringing Things to Life: Creative Entanglements in a World of Materials*. *http://eprints.ncrm.ac.uk/1306/1/0510_creative_entanglements.pdf* (accessed 23 September 2021).

Ingold, T., 2011. *Being Alive: Essays on Movement, Knowledge and Description*. London: Routledge.

Jeffreys, A. L., 2011. *De Profundis: A Personal Miscellany of 50 Years Impressions in Verse*. Self-published.

Latour, B., 2004. *Politics of Nature: How to Bring the Sciences into Democracy*. London: Harvard University Press.

Leveson, D., 2006. 'Extract of "the innocence of rock"', in *Bedrock: Writers on the Wonders of Geology*, ed. L. E. Savoy, E. M. Moores and J. E. Moores. San Antonio TX: Trinity University Press, pp. 13–15.

Mattes, J., 2015. 'Disciplinary identities and crossing boundaries: The academization of speleology in the first half of the twentieth century', *Earth Sciences History*, 34(2), 275–95.

Pérez, M. A., 2012. 'Exploration, Science and Society in Venezuela's Cave Landscape' (unpublished PhD thesis, University of Michigan).

Pérez, M. A., 2013. 'Lines underground: Exploring and mapping Venezuela's cave environment', *Cartographica: The International Journal for Geographic Information and Geovisualization*, 48(4), 293–308.

Sambento, S., 2013. Unpublished researcher's diaries.

Warner, M., 2008. 'The writing of stones, Roger Caillois's imaginary logic', *Cabinet Magazine*, 29, n.p. *www.cabinetmagazine.org/issues/29/warner.php* (accessed 23 September 2021).

4 PLASTERED

People-Plaster Relationships in the Neolithic Near East

Joanne Clarke and Alexander Wasse

> We must abandon something that seemed most natural to us: the simple idea of a world made of things.
>
> (Rovelli 2021, 164)

Introduction

In 1925, a young German physicist spent the summer on a small barren island, Heligoland, in the North Sea, to give himself respite from severe asthma. While on the island he formulated the theory of quantum physics, a mathematical structure by which he explains the properties of electrons. Prior to Heisenberg's discovery, it was assumed that electrons were particles that orbited around the nucleus of an atom in precise orbits before suddenly making miraculous, unexplained leaps into another orbit – quantum leaps (Rovelli 2021, 10). During his stay on Heligoland, Heisenberg imagined a way to mathematically describe these incongruous leaps of electrons from one orbit to another; instead of individual entities moving in defined pathways, electrons, he theorised, behaved as matrices, only existing relative to other matrices. As a matrix, the position of an electron becomes a probability factor, that is, the probability of it being in any one position is a relationship to other electrons being at any one position at any given time. In simple terms, electrons cannot be directly observed because they exist only in relationship to other electrons and then only as a probability of their position.

The idea that electrons exist only in relationship to other electrons forms the point of departure for this short exploration of the significance of plaster in the Neolithic Near East. In his recent book *Helgoland*, Rovelli explains to the lay person how the laws of quantum physics underpin 'the nature of experience' (Rovelli 2021, 3). He says that 'the solidity of the world seems to melt into air ... Entities are nothing other than ephemeral nodes [in a web of relationships]' (Rovelli 2021, 164). Rovelli is, of course, not the first to offer up this explanation of existence (see Barad 2007), but his articulation is made more powerful for the simplicity of its delivery. Yet, even in the second century CE, the Buddhist philosopher Nāgārjuna (Westerhoff 2009; 2010) wrote on the emptiness of 'substance', where his principal treatise was that nothing has its nature intrinsically and independently (Westerhoff 2010). Recently, physicist and new materialist Karen Barad has written that things should be imagined as relationships rather than as 'distinct entities' (Barad 2003, 813) and that 'quantum physics forces us to confront ... the nature of nature and meaning making' (Barad 2007, 24). This has profound consequences for how we envision humanity and humanity's place in the world, because if nothing has substance intrinsically or independently then, as Barad says (2007, 153) '[b]odies are not objects with inherent boundaries and properties; they are material-discursive phenomena'; we only exist as relationships of matter (see Alberti, this volume).

That there is no such thing as things but only relationships of matter, where everything is only substantive in as much as it is in relationship with everything else, has also been expressed in the context of social anthropology and material culture studies. Tim Ingold talks of meshworks where:

> a meshwork consists not of interconnected points but interwoven lines. Every line is a relation but the relation is not *between* one thing and another ... [r]ather the relation is [the] line *along* which materials flow, mix and mutate. Persons and things, then, are formed in [a] meshwork as knots or bundles of such relations. (Ingold 2007, 35)

This idea of a meshwork is very similar to Rovelli's concept of ephemeral nodes in a web of relationships.

Like Nāgārjuna, Rovelli, Barad and Ingold, in this chapter we abandon the notion of a 'world of things' to better understand how plaster shaped secular and spiritual life in the Neolithic Near East. We argue that people and plaster were enmeshed (to use a term derived from Ingold) to the extent that they were co-dependent and co-producing; the way in which one existed was because of the way the other existed. During the Levantine Middle Pre-Pottery Neolithic B (MPPNB), a period of some 700 years from 8,300 calibrated years (cal.) BCE to 7,200 cal. BCE (Finlayson and Makarewicz 2020, 58), the co-dependency and co-production of people and plaster allows us to view in some small way what Rovelli means when he asks us to give up the notion that the world is full of things in preference for a world full of relationships.

Plaster

The term 'plaster' is used here to describe a broad range of material, the base component of which is ordinarily varying percentages of calcium carbonate ($CaCO_3$). As only a small percentage of Neolithic plasters have been analysed and confirmed as lime-based (Goren et al. 1991), the term plaster also often describes mud and gypsum plasters, which are sometimes used interchangeably with lime plasters at MPPNB sites (Croucher 2012, 95). Different compositions of plasters, with more or less $CaCO_3$, have different properties of storage and use. Some plasters are altered by heating – lime and gypsum plasters, for example (Kingery et al. 1988, 221) – while other 'plasters' can be created simply by mixing chalk, crushed limestone or mud with water and other bonding materials such as clay or ash to create a hard, unfired surface. It is likely that the distinction between the use of fired and non-fired plaster was predicated to a certain extent on the knowledge of how to fire stone at temperatures above 800°C. Given that fired plaster is the first pyrotechnology to emerge in the ancient Near East, and given that the process had the potential to be quite explosive, it is unsurprising that the skill required to make good quality lime products appears to have been restricted to some parts of the region.

One of us has previously argued (Clarke 2012, 180) that in the Pre-Pottery Neolithic Levant (see Figure 4.1) plaster enhanced daily life through its widespread application and use across a range of secular and religious media. By the MPPNB plaster was used expertly, and different production methods were thoroughly understood. Availability of raw material was important but more so was an understanding of the base ingredients needed to produce the requisite finished product

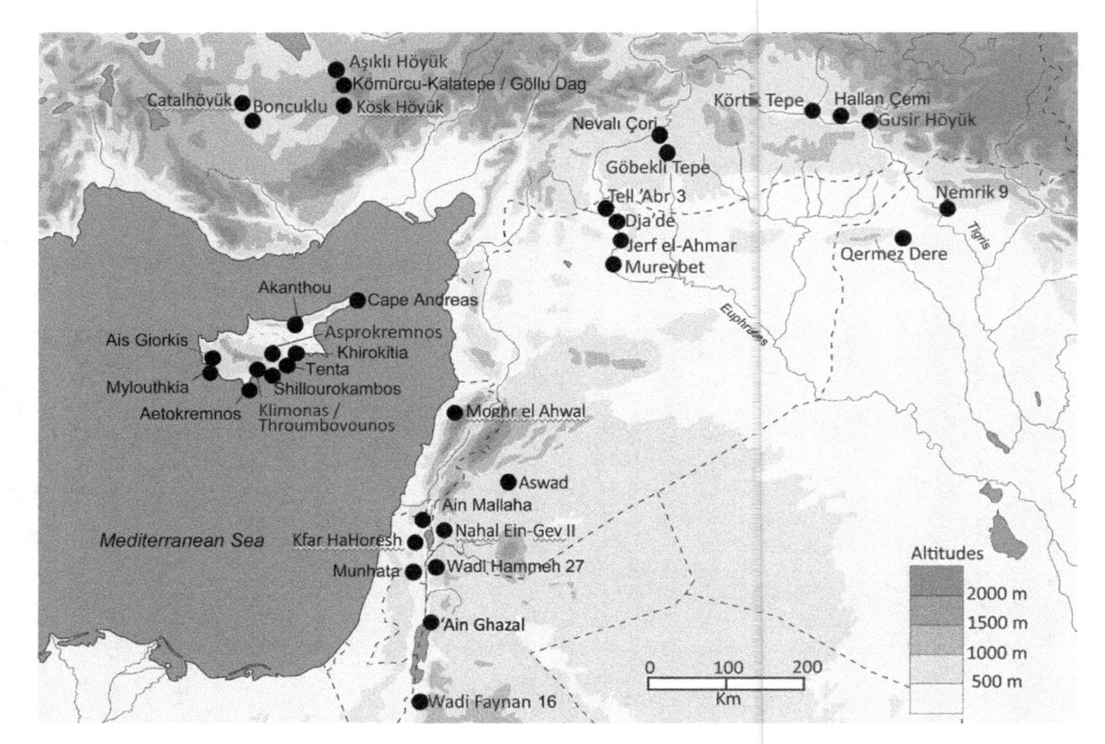

Figure 4.1 Map of Neolithic sites in the Near East.

for the requisite use. This had to be learned as different kinds of plaster produce different finished products. Also important was the way in which different properties of plasters, such as whiteness, hardness, plasticity and (in the case of pure lime plaster) antisepsis (Clarke 2012, 178), were conceived and applied.

The two principal fired plasters found in the MPPNB were pure lime plaster and hydraulic lime plaster. Differences between the production and application of the two were well understood by this period. The former has a very high concentration of $CaCO_3$, can be stored under water as putty for extended periods, is malleable on application and remains relatively soft even after drying. The latter is made from clay-bearing limestone and quickly sets hard on reaction with water in the air and thus would have been used expediently (Holmes and Wingate 1997, 12). Neolithic communities also knew how to source the appropriate material for making these different kinds of fired plaster. Fundamental differences in material properties not only contributed to their different applications, but possibly their different cultural significance, associations and relationships with other materials. Hydraulic lime was frequently used for flooring because of its expediency and its hardness when dry, but pure lime plaster was used for floor platforms at Çatalhöyük, a settlement in central Anatolia dated late in the Neolithisation of the Near East and some 500 years later than the MPPNB. This may have been in order to easily access the human remains buried beneath and also perhaps for its antiseptic qualities. Mud plasters were used for flooring in regions where raw materials or technological knowledge were lacking. At 'Ain Ghazal, a site with easy access to limestone, Rollefson has said that there appears to have been a hierarchy in the use of fired lime in plasters, with floor plaster having the least lime content, then statuary, and finally plaster used for modelling skulls with the highest amount of lime (Rollefson, pers. comm.). At Çatalhöyük, there is ample evidence that plaster was used differentially and discriminately, with the whitest, purest, lime plasters reserved for platforms and hydraulic (dirty) plaster used for cooking areas (Hodder 2006, 60).

Plaster: Discovery and Use

Communities that had ready access to limestone, and where firing temperatures of upwards of 800°C could be achieved, were more likely to make fired lime plasters (Fornhammar 2016). Therefore, it is probably not coincidence that use of fired lime plaster in the Near East emerged first in the Jordan Rift Valley at sites like 'Ain Mallaha and Nahal Ein-Gev II where air temperatures and atmospheric pressure are higher (Fornhammar 2016, 137).

Archaeological evidence for the use of lime plaster before the MPPNB is patchy. The first confirmed example comes from Sinai during the Levantine Middle Epipalaeolithic (*c.*16,000–13,000 cal. BCE) at Lagama North VIII, where it was used as an adhesive for hafting tools (Kingery et al. 1988, 220; Friesem et al. 2019; 2020). During the Early Natufian (*c.*12,300–10,800 cal. BCE), examples of the use of lime plaster for architectural features include benches and walls at 'Ain Mallaha (Kingery et al. 1988, 239; Valla et al. 2017, 295), while a small plaster-lined stone bin at Moghr el Ahwal in Lebanon (Garrard 2013, 50) is evidence that the knowledge of how to make fired lime products had spread beyond the Jordan Valley. Lime plaster was also reported in burial contexts at 'Ain Mallaha (Valla et al. 2007), but its unequivocal association with mortuary practice comes from the Late Natufian site of Nahal Ein-Gev II where, in a cemetery, eight individuals were found covered by a 40cm-thick layer of white lime plaster (Friesem et al. 2019).

During the Pre-Pottery Neolithic A (PPNA), the use of fired lime plasters appears to decline (Friesem et al. 2019, 21). This might be an artifice of the archaeological record, or it might indicate a change in peoples' preference for raw materials. Whatever the case, the significance of 'plaster' and its relationship with human remains seems to have only increased. At Wadi Faynan 16, mud plaster was used to model the floor of a large communal building (O75). Finlayson et al. (2013, 46) report that the floor was moulded as a single surface with a cup-hole mortar built into it on either side of a central axis. The floor had been divided into sectors by plaster divisions running in a herring bone style and had been re-plastered on numerous occasions (Finlayson et al. 2013, 47). Also at Wadi Faynan 16, Mithen et al. (2015, 107) describe the placement of a skull in the floor makeup of a building:

> The adult skull faced north and had been severely damaged by an animal burrow. The burial fill contained white flecks, possibly gypsum, and the skull had traces of a white residue on its top and the left-hand side, possibly a gypsum-based paste. A series of linear black marks were present on the back of the skull. These might be stains from a basket on which the skull had been resting or deliberately applied pigment. It is possible, therefore, that this skull had been decorated with both a plaster-like substance and a black pigment, seeming to act as a precursor for the presence of such decoration in the PPNB.

Here, for the first time we observe the deliberate commingling of human skeletal material, specifically a skull, with plaster and pigment. Although the characteristic plastered skulls of the MPPNB were some hundreds of years in the future, the incorporation of a human cranium with plaster and other floor elements to create a 'web of relationships' is an early precursor to the fully developed plasterings of the MPPNB. That PPNA Wadi Faynan also has evidence of skull manipulation and marking of the location of skulls in burials with the probable intention of later removal (Mithen et al. 2015) reinforces an early Neolithic beginning for the relationship between plaster and skulls.

Thus, by the PPNA, plaster and human skeletal material had come into intimate relationship beyond simply one of pragmatism (sealing burials for antiseptic purposes), a relationship that for the first time appears to have been intentional through the incorporation of a human skull into the mud plaster matrix of a floor. In addition, apparently deliberate plastering and pigmentation of the skull in the floor is one of the earliest examples of commingling human remains with pigment, a practice that was to become very common in the MPPNB.

If one were to contextualise these relationships within a new materialist way of conceiving the world, we would think of the skull and the floor as being conjoined and in dynamic relationship. For Ingold (2007), the floor and skull create a meshwork where neither has meaning nor substance without the interconnecting webs of significance that flow between them. For Bennett (2010, 23) the skull and floor exist in a relationship of vibrant materiality where one is only made vital through interaction with the other. For Rovelli (2021), the relationship between skull and floor allows for the existence of each.

In actuality, removing the skull from the floor makeup would have left a void, undermining the integrity of the floor. The skull, meanwhile, would have returned to being simply human skeletal material, its meaning and significance lost. Barad (2007, 141) would describe this relationship as intra-action; a dynamic 'topological reconfiguring/entanglement/relationality/re-articulation of the world'.

Notwithstanding the significance of the association of plaster with skeletal material at Wadi Faynan 16, it is not until late in the long transition from hunting and foraging to farming and herding, that is to say during the MPPNB, that plaster becomes ubiquitous across broad swathes of the region that now comprises Syria, Lebanon, Israel, the Palestinian Territories and Jordan. Plaster was used in the creation and maintenance of everything from walls and floors, basins, bins and hearths, to internal features such as platforms, piers and buttresses, for a number of enigmatic creations such as the small plaster balls found at Abu Hureyra (Kingery et al. 1988, 227), and for statuary and figurines, for lining burials, for sprinkling on the body of the deceased and bundling post-cranial material (Mithen et al. 2015), and crucially for plastering skulls. Plaster had become the material of choice for 'making the world' but more than this, through the modelling of human skulls, it also became entangled in the materiality of life and death. Arguably a kind of transformation had taken place where plaster was no longer simply a useful material, but a material expression of a way of life linking the living with the dead, the sacred with the everyday, and the past with the present – and by the MPPNB all contextualised within the domestic space. The materiality of plaster had acquired agency, while the properties of the material 'plaster' were now intrinsic to 'becoming-with' (Haraway 2008).

Later, during the seventh millennium BCE – more than 500 years after its apogee in the Levant – plaster emerges as an important material in Anatolia where people at some sites used it to model architectural elements and installations, decorative features on walls and floors, and in ritual and mortuary contexts, including plastered skulls at Çatalhöyük (Erdogu and Ulubey 2011) and Köşk Höyük (Özbek 2009). Why there is such a large gap between the disappearance of plastered skulls in the Levant and their appearance in Anatolia remains a mystery, but its coincidence with the adoption of agriculture in both regions is noteworthy due to the 'more intense house-based ritual and symbolic practices [and] increasingly structured use of domestic space' (Baird et al. 2018, E3085), an observation that will be returned to later.

Plastering Life and Death

There has been considerable speculation as to why MPPNB society, and seemingly not at any other time – at least in the southern Levant – plastered skulls (Kuijt 2002; 2008; Kuijt et al. 2009; Benz 2010). Although here is not the place to examine this topic in detail, plastered skulls perhaps represent, better than any other use, the extent to which the significance of plaster resided not in what was made from it but how people were in dynamic relationship with it as a material. How complex this relationship was can be glimpsed through the lens of human/plaster interdependency and the plastering of skulls.

To date, more than 100 plastered skulls have been found at sites in the Levant and all are dated to a time span of around 900 years between ~8300 and ~7200 cal. BCE (Finlayson and Makarewicz 2020, 58). There are a great deal fewer plastered skulls than headless individuals and there are also a great deal fewer headless individuals than human skeletal remains, thus, the number of human burials reflects only a fraction of the MPPNB population. What this suggests is that only certain individuals were chosen to have their skulls modelled in plaster, but all ages and all sexes were represented (Croucher 2012, 97). Like the 'floor-skull' at Wadi Faynan 16, plastering was often coincident with colouring, mostly in ochre but occasionally in cinnabar (Goren et al. 2001, 685). Skull plastering has thus been interpreted as re-fleshing, perhaps even revitalising certain deceased individuals (Casella and Croucher 2014, 100). This theory seems plausible, at least in the case of some skulls, given the wide range of colours and variations in the application of pigments. Moreover, there are examples of the addition of calcite to plaster and burnishing of the plaster surface to create a lustre (Goren et al. 2001, 681). Nevertheless, some plastered skulls were modelled to appear asleep, or even possibly dead; for example, those found at Aswad (Stordeur and Khawam 2007; Stordeur 2015). It is therefore not certain that re-fleshing or revitalising also meant 'bringing back to life'.

Irrespective of the way in which faces were modelled, the process of plastering skulls involved people in a complex performance of life and death, one that was embodied, enactive, embedded and extended (Gibbs Jr. 2019, 33). By way of illustration, after decomposition the grave of an individual identified for secondary skull treatment was opened and the skull removed. At this point people began to interact with the skull. What this interaction involved is not altogether clear but there is ample evidence for routine handling (Croucher 2012, 94). Some skulls were never plastered, while others were plastered and then 'unplastered' (Croucher 2012, 108). Painting was a process that some skulls received, but not all, and in some examples, painting was applied directly onto the skull without the addition of plaster. There is also evidence for the incorporation of hair or head dresses (Croucher 2012, 95). At some point – and for reasons that are beyond our understanding – plastered skulls were removed from circulation and carefully curated in caches under floors or in association with burials, or both (Croucher 2018, 110). What is not fully understood or even written about is that skull plastering was part of a greater performance and that the outcome was not to create a plastered skull but rather to be in a protracted dynamic relationship with the burial, with the body, with the skull, with the plaster and with the pigment. The point of the performance was not a finished entity – a plastered skull – the point was the intra-activity (cf. Barad 2003; 2007) of living and non-living matter co-produced and co-constituted through performance (Steel 2019); a process of materials and meaning 'becoming' together.

Time was also an important factor in these MPPNB performances of becoming. At 'Ain Ghazal one structure incorporated the remains of twelve individuals beneath its floors, not only suggesting the house was in use over a significant period, but that the house literally became incorporated with the individuals beneath the floors (Rollefson 2000, 169). Even if there were gaps between the interment of individual members, the placement of each would presumably have been known and remembered by the generations that inhabited the house, suggesting that memory and memorialisation were situated in mortuary practice and contextualised and practiced within domestic space. Hodder and Pels (2010) have a term for houses that contained significant numbers of burials: 'history houses'. They argue that at Çatalhöyük certain buildings accumulated more transcendent knowledge and symbolic capital than others and were in use and remodelled over many hundreds of years (Hodder and Pels 2010, 164). Over time more people were buried in history houses than would have lived in them. As such, they became houses more for the dead than for the living. As at 'Ain Ghazal, houses at Çatalhöyük with large numbers of burials were also more elaborate. Plastered bucrania, platforms, mouldings on walls and plastered skulls were found to be much more prevalent in the history houses than in other structures. Also like 'Ain Ghazal, memory and memorialisation appear to have been elaborated through plastering. There is evidence that pits were dug down from later houses to retrieve plastered installations from the walls and floors of earlier houses, suggesting that houses and house installations were 'passed down' through generations of inhabitants (Hodder and Pels 2010, 182). In sum, human remains, mortuary ritual, memorialisation and plaster were contextualised within the intra-action of matter, meaning, and in the case of the Neolithic Near East, time (cf. Barad 2003; 2007).

At Kfar HaHoresh, time, memory and mortuary ritual were expressed through the materiality of plaster. This is exemplified by the so-called Bos Pit, which contained at its base the partly articulated skeletons of at least eight aurochses, apparently part of a feasting ritual (Goring-Morris and Horwitz 2007, 906). The pit was then filled with earth and a small unworked limestone slab was placed on top surrounded by angular stones that were piled over and around the slab and the mouth of the pit. On top of the slab was the burial of a young adult male, the body scattered with lime plaster mixed with crushed chalk and then sealed with a lime-plaster capping. At a later date a small hole was cut through the lime-capping to remove the skull and a second lime-plaster surface was then laid to seal the hole. In this example time, materials and praxis intra-act; people and plaster combine in elaborate rituals involving life, death and plaster, layered as events performed over time, creating and structuring memory. Social memory is articulated through plaster, structured to a great extent by the affordances of the materials plaster is made of that are ascribed meaning through the practices and conceptions of spiritual life and memorialisation.

Plaster and plastering, therefore, not only regulated the workaday activities of MPPNB society, such as repairing houses (plastering walls and floors), storage (bins and *vaisselles blanches*) and food preparation (hearths), but also regulated spiritual life through its employment in mortuary rituals that played out over time (Goring-Morris and Horwitz 2007; Clarke 2012, 183). Memory and memorialisation were part of those rituals and plaster was a material through which memorialisation was realised. The reappearance of plastered skulls in the seventh and sixth millennia BCE in Anatolia at Çatalhöyük and Köşk Höyük, with no apparent connection to their MPPNB Levantine antecedents, might be explained through an emerging awareness of ancestry (Kuijt et al. 2009), this being a likely outcome of the adoption of the principles of delayed return (explained below) as well as being necessary for the performance of social memory.

In this context it is useful to refer to Maurice Halbwachs' theory of social memory (Halbwachs 2020). First, the past is used by members of a group to serve their objectives, whether that be legitimating a particular socio-political reality, laying claim to territory or forging an identity. Importantly, social memory does not constitute a literal or accurate reconstruction of the past but, rather, a reconstruction using material from the present in context-specific theatres of memory. Second, social memory is a process, toggling between past and present. It is always changing and operates in two temporal directions: the present shapes views of the past, and the past shapes interpretations of the present. Third, social memory is a narrative. To be comprehensible it must be structured within a familiar story with a beginning, middle and end. Social memory does not have to be tethered to a physical site but can be performed in any number of contexts and in any number of iterations that create subtly different renderings of a way of being in the world. Performance, however, requires a medium (Ingold 2007) or matrix (Rovelli 2021), or indeed a mnemonic device that enables rituals to be remembered. In parts of the Neolithic Near East that role was ascribed to plaster. Plastering a skull or plastering a building was an act of renewal and in these acts of renewal layers of memory and meaning were embedded.

Plastering a Changing World View

It is unlikely to be coincidence that the widespread use of plaster in the MPPNB happened in near lock step with the transition to agriculture. Plaster-making transforms inert stone into a versatile material that can be used for a variety of purposes. The symbolic significance of this transformation cannot have been lost on people whose way of 'being in the world' was transitioning for the first time to one where expending energy and time enabled an imagined outcome – cultivation – to come to fruition. Agriculture is not simply an economic choice, it is a way of life and a way of imagining the world (Watkin 2023). With the transition to agriculture a fundamental ontological shift took place whereby people moved from living in the environment to living beyond it. In the process, the way in which people engaged with their material world also changed, as new technologies were required to support this new way of life. Prior to the emergence of agriculture people were shaped by their material world, including everything living and non-living in it, but with agriculture came a requirement for greater extraction and manipulation of material resources. Manipulation of materials was not simply an economic necessity, material resources become saturated with meaning and symbolism, what Barad (2007, 153) calls 'material-discursive phenomena'. The notion that agriculture represents far more than an economic adaptation is deeply embedded in the anthropological literature:

> The dichotomies of good and evil, right and wrong express this farming project: control comes with separating manipulable resources from the rest of the environment and working with determination and consistency against all that might undermine this endeavour. (Brody 2001, 307)

In a series of writings, Ingold (1980; 1986; 2002; Ingold and Kurttila 2000) articulated a vision of change in human-animal-material relations across the hunter-herder transition that cuts to the heart of this ontological change. This can be summarised as a transition from principles of 'trust' to principles of 'domination' (Ingold and Kurttila 2000; Ingold 2002). It has been asserted that hunter-gatherers, 'instead of attempting to control nature ... concentrate on controlling their relationship with it' (Ridington 1982, 471). As such, they may be considered as dwelling within nature rather than transcending it, a notion that frequently accords with their own world views insofar as these are known (Descola 2013). If this premise is accepted, it follows that pre-agricultural modes of life were predicated on the expectation ('trust') that nature would yield the materials required to sustain life regardless of human intervention, as 'one cannot appropriate that within which one's being is wholly contained' (Ingold 1980, 135). Thus, for agriculture to be practised at all, humans needed to transcend nature, moving at least partially beyond its realm in order to control it ('domination').

Of particular interest is the fact that the *principles* of 'trust' and 'domination' are seen as inseparable from the *activities* of sharing, on the one hand (Ingold 2011, 69), and owning, on the other. For example, Ingold (2011, 76) have described how the shift from hunting to pastoralism among northern Eurasian reindeer herders was accompanied by a shift from egalitarian social relations to those of dominance and subordination. This fundamental integration of *principle* and *activity* enables us to explore how the former (i.e., the principles of 'trust' and 'domination') may have played out during Levantine Neolithisation through archaeological examination of the material correlates of the latter.

Leaving aside the contentious issue of when nuclear families became the basic domestic unit in Levantine prehistory (Byrd 2000; 2005; Banning 2003; Banning and Chazan 2006), curvilinear houses have long been associated with varying combinations of mobility, communal living and egalitarianism, more often than not features of hunter-gatherer societies. In contrast, rectilinear houses are typically described as offering greater opportunity for segmentation of space, expansion and subdivision, all factors of importance to sedentary farmers tied to increasingly bounded plots of cultivable land (Byrd 2005). The replacement of curvilinear by rectilinear houses during the PPNB has therefore been linked to the transition from hunting and gathering to agriculture. Although additional factors, such as marriage, control of storage and the socialisation of production, consumption and risk management, have more recently been emphasised (Byrd 1994; 2005; Flannery 2002), it remains true that mode of life remains at the heart of this strand of the debate (e.g., Goring-Morris and Belfer-Cohen 2008; 2013).

Privileging the symbolic over the economic, Cauvin (2000, 132) has interpreted the same empirical observation, *viz.* the PPNB shift from circular to rectilinear house plans, as representing a transition from 'that which transcends man and remains beyond his reach' to the 'manifest, the concrete, that which has been realised'. Noting that the rectilinear form is rare in nature and that the transition was typically accompanied by a shift from semi-subterranean to above-ground living. Cauvin (2000, 132) proposed that this reflected the emergence of a mental attitude, presumably at community level, that imposed 'an entirely new, preconceived form on a basic need for shelter'.

The transition from living within nature to living beyond nature was in no way straightforward or a linear evolutionary process, but at one end was a way of life where agriculture had not yet been imagined, and at the other end was a way of life where agriculture has become fundamental to human existence. In between is a multitude of behaviours involving more or less of one or the other ways of life, all remaining mutable and fluid for some 4,000 years until the beginning of urbanism in the fourth millennium BCE. The transition from hunting, gathering and foraging to farming and herding in the ancient Near East may have taken thousands of years, but the process was original; that is, hunter-gatherers had no concept of food-producing ways of life until they adopted or otherwise came into contact with them (see Finlayson and Makarewicz 2020 on why modern hunter-gatherers make poor analogues for the earliest developments in food production). The process was not simply social and economic, it was also cognitive and involved profound shifts in the way in which people conceived their world. This conceptual shift was also irreversible; once people understood the extent to which their environment might be manipulated for communal or personal benefit, the fruit of the forbidden tree had been tasted and could not be put back on the branch. Hunting still contributed significantly to the proportion of meat in the diet of early farmers and herders, but the way in which people hunted necessarily changed, frequently becoming a matter of choice rather than of absolute necessity. This conceptual transition towards 'domination' is no better illustrated than in the painted hunting scenes from Çatalhöyük, in which painted images on white plastered walls show animals being effectively 'baited' as tails and tongues are pulled (see Figure 4.2). Another example of human 'domination' over the natural world might be sought in the so-called 'desert-kite' hunting traps of northern Saudi Arabia and the Jordanian *badia*. Hundreds of kites were constructed, open to the east and closed to the west, extending across the steppic rangelands in vast chains. As gazelle migrated west to east they would have been directed down the long v-shaped 'funnels' of the kites into a corral trap often located out of sight over the brow of a

Figure 4.2 Wall painting showing teasing and baiting of stag from Çatalhöyük.

hill or in a dip in the landscape. As such, kites effectively 'weaponised' the landscape, allowing for hundreds of animals to be captured, in all likelihood far more than were needed for subsistence alone (Bar-Yosef 2016, 117; Martin et al. 2016, 216). The use of kites has been argued to have begun in the PPNB as an intensifying, quasi-commodified hunting strategy practised by mobile herders as a means of maximising the 'take' from otherwise marginal site catchments (Wasse 2019, 273–4). Hunting by the PPNB, therefore, can no longer be considered on its own, prelapsarian terms, but must be looked at from the perspective of the extent to which it was similar to, or different from, herding.

Becoming Plaster

It has been argued in multiple writings that the shift from hunting and gathering to farming and herding entangled people and things in increasing degrees of dependency (Hodder 2012; 2014). Hodder (2014, 33) says that '[s]ince a dependence on made things became an evolutionary pathway, there has been one long movement, initially slow, but speeding up exponentially as the strands of human-thing entanglement lengthened and intensified'. Hodder may be talking about things rather than matter or materials but he agrees that the intra-action of matter – humans and non-humans, living and inert – has been one of ever-increasing enmeshment:

> Once humans had invested in things, they had become trapped in maintaining that investment and the benefits that it produced … There is a long-term trend towards greater human-thing entanglement that is a product of the fact that human 'being' depends on things, and of the fact that things depend on other things and on humans. (Hodder 2014, 32)

We argue that in the MPPNB plaster played a unique role in the co-dependency and co-production of matter and materials and that it was the special properties of plaster that afforded it this unique role.

Plaster would have been made in open pits, using limestone quarried from nearby cliffs and outcrops. Firing pits would have offered little protection from the intense heat of burning limestone, or the potential danger of slaking quicklime, but it will have allowed for an intimate, close-up experience of what would have been a remarkable transformative process. Chunks of limestone (the most common base material) are burned to produce quicklime (for a fuller discussion of the lime-burning process see Fornhammar 2016, 136), which is then combined with water to produce slaked lime. During the slaking process the emergent plaster appears to come to life depending on how much water is added. Slaking animates the material in a potentially explosive chemical reaction. It expands and breaks up the fired stones from the inside, at which point the stone falls apart into a sludge (Fornhammar 2016, 137). It is at this point, at the end of the transformation of inert stone into 'living' plaster, that in the MPPNB bone and other materials were often added to make it stronger and improve its properties of application and use (Fornhammar 2016, fig. 4).

The chemical reaction that happens when quicklime is slaked cannot have gone unobserved by Neolithic plaster pyrotechnicians, although what significance they placed on it is uncertain. Although considerably earlier than the MPPNB, the fact that at the Natufian site of Nahal Ein-Gev II plaster was not only incorporated into burials but was actually made on top of the burials themselves, suggests its significance in mortuary practice was already beginning to emerge 1,000 years earlier. It was not necessary for slaking to take place on the top of burials – although carrying quicklime any distance would have been hazardous – this must have been a choice made for reasons that are beyond our understanding. During the process other material became incorporated into the plaster acting as unintentional *pozzolans*.[1] Friesem et al. (2019) are frustratingly silent on the exact nature of this material, particularly on whether bone fragments that they report were found in the mix were human (from the burials) or animal (from some other source). Nevertheless, plaster at Nahal Ein-Gev II appears to have been made by hot mixing. In the conventional method pozzolans are mixed with lime that has been previously slaked and then cooled before incorporation of other material, in the hot mixing method quicklime is mixed with pozzolans and then slaked with water. This generates great heat and, in the case of Nahal Ein-Gev II, was sufficiently hot to burn the bones from the sediment that had been unintentionally incorporated into the plaster. Irrespective of whether the incorporated bone was human or animal, hot mixing quicklime on top of a burial and observing the chemical reaction that took place was undoubtedly a powerful experience, if not an actual metaphor for 'coming alive'.

If making plaster was conceived of as 'bringing to life that which was not alive' (stone) in an act of material transformation, then undertaking this procedure on top of human remains could, by association, have metaphorically animated the human remains as well. Thus plaster, we argue, was the material expression of a transformation metaphor of 'coming alive'. Plaster embodied the fusion of what was once living (people) with what was never living (stone) and through a process of chemical transformation, animated both in the creation of a new material. In this context, it is not surprising that plaster was used so ubiquitously. The most obvious act of 'coming alive' was to plaster human skulls, but plaster was used for so much more than simply plastering human skulls, arguably plaster made vibrant everything that was made from it or decorated with it. As Jane Bennett (2010) suggests, matter is vibrant and for MPPNB society, no matter was more vibrant than plaster.

We have argued that during the Neolithic in the Near East, lime plaster had significance and meaning far beyond its material properties of whiteness, purity, plasticity and antisepsis (Clarke 2012, 177). Plaster did not simply represent the ancestors, or even revitalise them; in the act of making plaster, of plastering skulls, of plastering walls and floors, of plastering basins and benches and small balls of animal bone, plaster was incorporated into every aspect of daily life and made vibrant everything that came in contact with it. Plaster and people became enmeshed. More than this, the act of plastering wove a metaphorical thread of revitalising everything that was plastered. Although some plasters were not fired, their association with and similarity to fired plasters may have afforded them a degree of specialness. However, it is probably not chance that it was pure lime plaster that was mostly used for plastering skulls, for creating the statues found at 'Ain Ghazal and for the platforms that covered burial plots in the houses at Çatalhöyük.

In sum, like Heisenberg's theory of quantum physics, where nothing is in and of itself, during the MPPNB people lived in relationship with plaster. Plaster brought to life and gave meaning, vibrancy and substance to the world. Just as the electrons of Heisenberg's mathematical theorem exist only in relationship to other electrons, so too in the Neolithic Near East plaster provided a matrix in which disparate material culture elements were enmeshed and in relationship to everything else. It might be argued that had there been no plaster, MPPNB society would have been entirely different; it would have been as if it never existed at all.

Acknowledgements

Very many thanks to Karina Croucher for her informal review.

Note

1. Pozzolans are additives that enable non-hydraulic lime plasters to set more rapidly and today typically include ash and brick dust (Gibbons 2019). Non-hydraulic lime plasters do not naturally contain minerals that enable them to harden as do the marl-based (hydraulic) plasters.

References

Baird, D., Fairbairn, A., Jenkins, E., Martin, L., Middleton, C., Pearson, J., Asouti, E., Edwards, Y., Kabukcu, C., Mustafaoğlu, G., Russell, N., Bar-Yosef, O., Jacobsen, G., Wu, X., Baker, A., and Elliott, S., 2018. 'Agricultural origins on the Anatolian plateau', *Proceedings of the National Academy of Sciences*, 115(14), E3077–86.

Banning, E. B., 2003. 'Housing Neolithic farmers', *Near Eastern Archaeology*, 66(1–2), 4–21.

Banning, E. B., and Chazan, M., 2006. 'Structuring interactions, structuring ideas: Domestication of space in the prehistoric Near East', in *Domesticating Space: Construction, Community and Cosmology in the Late Prehistoric Near East*, ed. E. B. Banning and M. Chazan. Berlin: Ex Oriente, pp. 5–14.

Bar-Yosef, O., 2016. 'Changes in 'demand and supply' for mass killings of gazelles during the Holocene', in *Bones and Identity: Zooarchaeological Approaches to Reconstructing Social and Cultural Landscapes in Southwest Asia*, ed. N. Marom, R. Yeshuran, L. Weissbrod and G. Bar-Oz. Oxford: Oxbow Books, pp. 113–24.

Barad, K., 2003. 'Posthumanist performativity: Toward an understanding of how matter comes to matter', *Signs: Journal of Women in Culture and Society*, 28(3), 801–31.

Barad, K., 2007. *Meeting the Universe Halfway: Quantum Physics and the Entanglement of Matter and Meaning*. Durham NC: Duke University Press.

Bennett, J., 2010. *Vibrant Matter: A Political Ecology of Things*. Durham NC and London: Duke University Press.

Benz, M., 2010. 'Beyond death – the construction of social identities at the transition from foraging to farming', in *The Principle of Sharing: Segregation and Construction of Social Identities at the Transition from Foraging to Farming*, ed. M. Benz. Studies in Early Near Eastern Production, Subsistence, and Environment 14. Berlin: Ex Oriente, pp. 249–76.

Brody, H., 2001. *The Other Side of Eden: Hunter-Gatherers, Farming and the Shaping of the World*. London: Faber and Faber.

Byrd, B. F., 1994. 'Public and private, domestic and corporate: the emergence of the southwest Asian village', *American Antiquity*, 59(4), 639–66.

Byrd, B. F., 2000. 'Households in transition: Neolithic social organization within Southwest Asia', in *Life in Neolithic Farming Communities: Social Organization, Identity, and Differentiation*, ed. I. Kuijt. New York NY: Kluwer Academic/Plenum Press, pp. 63–98.

Byrd, B. F., 2005. 'Reassessing the emergence of village life in the Near East', *Journal of Archaeological Research*, 13(3), 231–90.

Casella, E. C., and Croucher, K., 2014. 'Decay, temporality and the politics of conservation: An archaeological approach to material studies', in *Objects and Materials: A Routledge Companion*, ed. P. Harvey, E. C. Casella, G. Evans, H. Knox, C. McLean, E. B. Silva, N. Thoburn and K. Woodward. London: Routledge, pp. 92–103.

Cauvin, J., 2000. *The Birth of the Gods and the Origins of Agriculture*. Cambridge: Cambridge University Press.

Clarke, J., 2012. 'Decorating the Neolithic: An evaluation of the use of plaster in the enhancement of daily life in the Middle Pre-pottery Neolithic B of the Southern Levant', *Cambridge Archaeological Journal*, 22(2), 177–86.

Croucher, K., 2012. *Death and Dying in the Neolithic Near East*. Oxford: Oxford University Press.

Croucher, K., 2018. 'Keeping the dead close: Grief and bereavement in the treatment of skulls from the Neolithic Middle East', *Mortality*, 23(2), 103–20.

Descola, P., 2013. *Beyond Nature and Culture*. Chicago IL: University of Chicago Press.

Erdogu, B., and Ulubey, A., 2011. 'Colour symbolism in the Prehistoric architecture of Central Anatolia and Raman spectroscopic investigation of red ochre in Chalcolithic Çatalhöyük', *Oxford Journal of Archaeology*, 30(1), 1–11.

Finlayson, B., Mithen, S., al-Najjar, M., Smith, S., and Jenkins, E., 2013. 'The origins, development and practice of economic and social strategies in the Middle East from earliest times to the modern day. Excavations at Wadi Faynan 16, a Pre-Pottery Neolithic A site in southern Jordan', *Bulletin for the Council for British Research in the Levant*, 5(1), 46–8.

Finlayson, B., and Makarewicz, C. A., 2020. 'Beyond the Jordan: Multiformities of the Pre-Pottery Neolithic', *Documenta Praehistorica*, 47, 54–75.

Flannery, K. V., 2002. 'The origins of the village revisited: from nuclear to extended households', *American Antiquity*, 67(3), 417–33.

Fornhammar, U., 2016. 'Identifying the geographic area with best conditions for discovering lime burning: Could the lime industry have been born in the Dead Sea region?', *Journal of Archaeological Science: Reports*, 8, 135–41. *https://doi.org/10.1016/j.jasrep.2016.05.059*.

Friesem, D. E., Abadi, I., Shaham, D., and Grosman, L., 2019. 'Lime plaster cover of the dead 12,000 years ago: new evidence for the origins of lime plaster technology', *Evolutionary Human Sciences*, 1. *https://doi.org/10.1017/ehs.2019.9* (accessed 1 December 2023).

Friesem, D. E., Anton, M., Waiman-Barak, P., Shahack-Gross, R., and Nadel, D., 2020. 'Variability and complexity in calcite-based plaster production: A case study from a Pre-Pottery Neolithic B infant burial at Tel Ro'im West and its implications to mortuary practices in the Southern Levant', *Journal of Archaeological Science*, 113, 105048.

Garrard, A., 2013. 'The Qadisha Valley Prehistory Project, Northern Levant', *Bulletin for the Council for British Research in the Levant*, 5(1), 48–50.

Gibbons, P., 2019. 'Pozzolans for lime mortars', Cathedral Communications Ltd. *www.buildingconservation.com/articles/pozzo/lime-pozzolans.htm* (accessed 22 March 2022).

Gibbs Jr, R. W., 2019. 'Metaphor as dynamical-ecological performance', *Metaphor and Symbol*, 34(1), 33–44.

Goren, Y., Goldberg, P., Stahl, P. W., and Brinker, U. H., 1991. 'Petrographic thin sections and the development of Neolithic plaster production in northern Israel', *Journal of Field Archaeology*, 18(1), 131–40.

Goren, Y., Goring-Morris, N. A., and Segal, I., 2001. 'The technology of skull modelling in the Pre-pottery Neolithic B (PPNB): Regional variability, the relation of technology and iconography and their archaeological implications', *Journal of Archaeological Science*, 28, 671–90.

Goring-Morris, A. N., and Belfer-Cohen, A., 2008. 'A roof over one's head: Developments in Near Eastern residential architecture across the Epipalaeolithic-Neolithic transition', in *The Neolithic Demographic Transition and its Consequences*, ed. J. P. Bocquet-Appel and O. Bar-Yosef. Dordrecht: Springer, pp. 239–86.

Goring-Morris, A. N., and Belfer-Cohen, A., 2013. 'Houses and households: a Near Eastern perspective', in *Tracking the Neolithic House in Europe*, ed. D. Hofmann and J. Smyth. New York NY: Springer, pp. 19–44.

Goring-Morris, N., and Horwitz, L. K., 2007. 'Funerals and feasts during the Pre-Pottery Neolithic B of the Near East', *Antiquity*, 81, 902–19.

Halbwachs, M., 2020. *On Collective Memory*. Chicago IL and London: University of Chicago Press (reprint).

Haraway, D., 2008. *When Species Meet*. Minneapolis MN and London: University of Minnesota Press.

Hodder, I., 2006. *Çatalhöyük: The Leopard's Tale. Revealing the Mysteries of Turkey's Ancient 'Town'*. London: Thames and Hudson.

Hodder, I., 2012. *Entangled: An Archeology of the Relationships Between Humans and Things*. Chichester: Wiley-Blackwell.

Hodder, I., 2014. 'The entanglements of humans and things: A long-term view', *New Literary History*, 45(1), 19–36.

Hodder, I., and Meskell, L., 2011. 'A "curious and sometimes a trifle macabre artistry": Some aspects of symbolism in Neolithic Turkey', *Current Anthropology*, 52(2), 235–63.

Hodder, I., and Pels, P., 2010. 'History houses: A new interpretation of architectural elaboration at Çatalhöyük', in *Religion in the Emergence of Civilization: Çatalhöyük as a Case Study*, ed. I. Hodder. Cambridge: Cambridge University Press, pp. 163–86.

Holmes, S., and Wingate, M., 1997. *Building with Lime: A Practical Introduction*. Rugby: Practical Action Publishing.

Ingold, T., 1980. *Hunters, Pastoralists and Ranchers: Reindeer Economies and Their Transformations*. Cambridge: Cambridge University Press.

Ingold, T., 1986. 'Reindeer economies: And the origins of pastoralism', *Anthropology Today*, 2(4), 5–10.

Ingold, T., 2002. 'From trust to domination: an alternative history of human-animal relations', in *Animals and Human Society*, ed. A. Manning and J. Serpell. London: Routledge, pp. 13–34.

Ingold, T. 2007. 'Writing texts, reading materials. A response to my critics', *Archaeological Dialogues*, 14(1): 31–8.

Ingold, T., 2011. 'From trust to domination: An alternative history of human-animal relations', in *The Perception of the Environment. Essays on Livelihood, Dwelling and Skill*. Abingdon: Routledge, pp. 61–76.

Ingold, T., and Kurttila, T., 2000. 'Perceiving the environment in Finnish Lapland', *Body and Society*, 6(3–4), 183–96.

Kingery, D. W., Vandiver, P. B., and Prickett, M., 1988. 'The beginnings of pyrotechnology, part II: production and use of lime and gypsum plaster in the Pre-Pottery Neolithic Near East', *Journal of Field Archaeology*, 15(2), 219–43.

Kuijt, I., 2002. 'Keeping the peace: Ritual, skull caching, and community integration in the Levantine Neolithic', in *Life in Neolithic Farming Communities: Social Organization, Identity, and Differentiation*, ed. I. Kujit. New York NY, Boston MA, Dordrecht, London and Moscow: Kluwer Academic Publishers, pp. 137–64.

Kuijt, I., 2008. 'The regeneration of life: Neolithic structures of symbolic remembering and forgetting', *Current Anthropology*, 49(2), 171–97.

Kuijt, I., Özdoğan, M., and Pearson, M.P., 2009. 'Neolithic skull removal: Enemies, ancestors, and memory [with Comments]', *Paléorient*, 35(1), 117–27.

Martin, L., Edwards, Y., Roe, J., and Garrard, A. N., 2016. 'Faunal turnover in the Azraq basin, eastern Jordan 28,000 to 9000 cal yr BP, signalling climate change and human impact', *Quaternary Research*, 86, 200–19.

Mithen, S., Finlayson, B., Maricevic, D., Smith, S., Jenkins, E., and Najjar, M., 2015. 'Death and architecture: The Pre-Pottery Neolithic A burials at WF16, Wadi Faynan, Southern Jordan', in *Death Rituals, Social Order and the Archaeology of Immortality in the Ancient World: 'Death Shall Have No Dominion'*, ed. C. Renfrew, M. Boyd and I. Morley. Cambridge: Cambridge University Press, pp. 82–110.

Özbek, M., 2009. 'Remodeled human skulls in Köşk Höyük (Neolithic age, Anatolia): A new appraisal in view of recent discoveries', *Journal of Archaeological Science*, 36(2), 379–86.

Ridington, R., 1982. 'Technology, world view, and adaptive strategy in a northern hunting society', *Canadian Review of Sociology/Revue canadienne de sociologie*, 19(4), 469–81.

Rollefson, G. O., 2000. 'Ritual and social structure at Neolithic 'Ain Ghazal', in *Life in Neolithic Farming Communities. Social Organization, Identity, and Differentiation*, ed. Ian Kuijt. New York NY: Springer, pp. 165–90.

Rovelli, C., 2021. *Helgoland*. London: Allen Lane.

Stordeur, D., and Khawam, R., 2007. 'Les crânes surmodelés de Tell Aswad (PPNB, Syrie). Premier regard sur l'ensemble, premières réflexions', *Syria: Archéologie, art et histoire*, 84, 5–32.

Steel, L., 2019. 'Embodied encounters with the ancestors', in *Body Matters: Exploring the Materiality of the Human Body*, ed. L. Attala and L. Steel. Cardiff: University of Wales Press, pp. 89–108.

Stordeur, D., 2015. 'Neolithic plastered skulls from Tell Aswad (Syria): A funerary tradition in the Near East', in *The Chinchorro Culture: A Comparative Perspective: The Archaeology of the Earliest Human Mummification*, ed. N. Sanz, B. T. Arriaza and V. G. Standen. Arica: Unesco Publishing. pp. 177–96.

Valla, F., Khalaily, H., Valladas, H., Kaltnecker, E., Bocquentin, F., Teresa, C., Mayer, D. B. Y., Le Dosseur, G., Regev, L., Chu, V., and Weiner, S., 2007. 'Les fouilles de Ain Mallaha (Eynan) de 2003 à 2005: Quatrième rapport préliminaire', *Journal of the Israel Prehistoric Society*, 37, 135–379.

Valla, F., Khalaily, H., Samuelian, N., Bocquentin, F., Bridault, A., and Rabinovich, R., 2017. 'Eynan (Ain Mallaha)', in *Quaternary of the Levant: Environments, Climate Change and Humans*, ed. Y. Enzel and O. Bar-Yosef. Cambridge: Cambridge University Press, pp. 295–302.

Wasse, A., 2019. 'A joy of wild asses, a pasture of flocks: hunting and herding in the greater Syrian desert during the PPNB and Late Neolithic', in *Decades in Deserts: Essays on Near Eastern Archaeology in Honor of Sumio Fujii*, ed. S. Nakamura, T. Adachi and M. Abe. Tokyo: Rokuichi Shobou, pp. 269–85.

Watkin, T., 2023. *Becoming Neolithic: The Pivot of Human History*. London and New York NY: Routledge.

Westerhoff, J. C., 2009. *Nagarjuna's Madhyamaka: A Philosophical Introduction*. Oxford: Oxford University Press.

Westerhoff, J. C., 2010. 'Nāgārjuna', *Stanford: Stanford Encyclopedia of Philosophy*. *https://plato.stanford.edu/entries/nagarjuna* (accessed 21 July 2021).

5 A MELDING OF MODELS

A New Materialist Approach to the Earthy Constituents in the 'Ceremonial' Hoard from Kissonerga *Mosphilia*

Natalie Boyd

Introduction

This chapter considers the earthy components of a mixed material group of objects that formed a singular temporal and spatial deposit from the Middle Chalcolithic site of Kissonerga *Mosphilia* in south-western Cyprus, applying theoretical approaches from the new materialisms. It aims to contribute to the understanding of this unique artefact assortment by exploring how the earthy elements of this depositional group emerged within an entangled network, interacting with each other as well as with other things, the environment and people, and thus how their meaning and understanding has changed through treatment and time. The application of post-humanistic theories, in particular the new materialities, will help us engage with these pieces in a more immersive way, placing humans on an equal footing with other actors in the material world. In particular, assemblage theory offers a potent tool for asking questions about what we do not or 'cannot' know. It provides a different way to approach the taphonomic process and relationality of archaeological sites and artefacts not as fixed in time but as holding many relations with multiple elements down the ages (see, e.g., Govier and Steel 2021, 309–11) (including, but not limited to, people) and not forgetting today's archaeologists.

The New Materialisms, Materiality, Agency, Vibrancy and Assemblage

The new materialisms form part of a move away from viewing humans as privileged and 'other' by comparison to non-human beings and the material world (Barad 2003; Bennett 2010; Coole and Frost 2010; Attala and Steel 2019; Steel 2018; 2020; Cifarelli 2021; Govier and Steel 2021). Humans are repositioned in the material world, as part of the ever flowing and reconfiguring matter of which everything is formed. The relationships and entanglements (Boivin 2010; Ingold 2013; Govier and Steel 2021) between people, animals and objects (see, e.g., Averett 2020) can therefore be explored as interactions between equals, each having the capacity to have an impact on the others, each contributing to the creation and formation of the world around them. In addition to their physical properties, the new materialisms assert that everything, not just humans, has agency, as everything is formed from matter, and matter itself has agency, by dint of the fact that it has the ability to do things, build things and affect things (Gell 1998; Latour 2005; Steel 2020). Applying the new materialisms to the Kissonerga material allows us to explore this without our modern, western social constructs, outside of the hylomorphic model that has become more and more ingrained since it was proffered by Aristotle (Ingold 2010; 2013) and that limits our ability to engage with and interpret things from a culture outside of our canon in terms of geography, time and social customs. Both Bennett (2010) and Ingold (2010) question the perspective that material, the world and objects are inert and waiting for humans to interact with or act upon them. In the case of the Kissonerga group, the figurines, the house model and all the elements of this group, have relationships with each other, regardless of whether humans are involved. The new materialisms therefore allow us to explore the complex and multivalent meshwork of this assemblage without prioritising ourselves, removing some of the self-imposed barriers to understanding that are created when we stand humans at odds with everything else (Harris 2014a; Latour 1993).

As well as the properties of entities as individuals, the new materialisms also allow for the exploration of groups of things as assemblages and how this impacts on their dynamics (Witmore 2007; 2014; Webmoor and Witmore 2008; Bennett 2010; Ingold 2013; Harris 2014a; 2014b; 2017; Marshall and Alberti 2014; Fowler and Harris 2015; Olsen and Witmore 2015; DeLanda 2016; Conneller 2017; Crellin 2017; Fowler 2017; Hamilakis and Jones 2017; Jones 2017; Lucas 2017; Steel 2018; Govier and Steel 2021). In this way, the relationships between the elements of the complex assemblages of homogenous, heterogenous, human and non-human elements that make up the world can be explored. In this chapter, an assemblage-based approach is favoured to explore the carefully selected, thematic, ceremonial deposit from Kissonerga *Mosphilia*. This represents a unique and purposeful grouping of objects – ceramic (see Figures 5.3), stone and shell – in time and space, and considering them as an assemblage allows for a different perspective on this temporal snapshot. The components of this collection of tools, figurines and models were deliberately selected and deposited together as a single group; even so, we need not assume that they had necessarily been constant companions. Moreover, we should consider the various materials and substances used to create the individual components of the hoards (clay, pigments), as well as the people who worked 'in partnership' with these substances (see Jones 2018, 22), responding to their capacities (Bennett 2010; Rovelli 2021, 67–8, 78; see also Steel, this volume) to create the objects. Here, I contend that considering the groups, subgroups, possible uses and other relationships of these earthy entities allows us to explore their social lives (cf. Kopytoff 1986), how they were variously in relationship and thus their meaning to each other as well as to the people of Kissonerga *Mosphilia*. This might also allow us to explore changes within cultural practices resulting in these items being decommissioned and removed from circulation. This ancient social world and our knowledge of it is nothing more than 'the result of interactions that generate meaningful information' (Rovelli 2021, 148).

Bennett (2010, 23) describes assemblages as 'ad hoc groupings of diverse elements, of vibrant materials of all sorts. Assemblages are living, throbbing confederations'. This differs slightly from the more traditionally accepted understanding of the word assemblage in archaeology, which describes a collection of typologically related objects, or a group of objects that have been deposited in the same archaeological feature or at the same site (Lucas 2011; Crellin 2017; Govier and Steel 2021, 306). Assemblages in this sense are temporary, fleeting arrangements. Crellin (2017, 113) uses the example of a bus. At any one time there are a different number of passengers, each different from the others, a driver, the luggage, the bus and everything that makes it, extending out to include the road, the environment, the bus company, and so forth. No two moments on the bus are the same, let alone two journeys, and, although there are traces left in the archaeological record (e.g., the bus, tickets, CCTV, litter), we cannot truly recreate and fix that moment in time. Assemblages can be made of a single item, or can be as vast as the universe, which therefore gives us 'a unique way of approaching the problem of linking the micro and macro-levels of social reality' (DeLanda 2006, 17). Assemblages are active, the components that make them take on properties as a result of their place within the assemblage (Conneller 2017). However, a reconfiguration of these objects, either within this or part of another assemblage, creates different relationships, properties and meanings (DeLanda 2006; Crellin 2017), although not all properties will be altered and those that do change will not necessarily change at the same rate (Fowler and Harris 2015). While tears are lost in rain, paper will rapidly disintegrate, metal will slowly rust, and glass will be unchanged, therefore, while the elements of an assemblage are changing, the rate of change can vary as widely as the size and complexity of an assemblage. These differing qualities are what Bennett (2010) posits as the vibrancy of objects, each object having its own vitality, which can be enhanced or muted by its proximity and relationship with other objects within an assemblage. The variations in vibrancy can help us to identify and map change in assemblages, social practices and places.

The 'Ceremonial' Hoard from Kissonerga *Mosphilia*

The Chalcolithic site of Kissonerga *Mosphilia* lies in the south-west of the island of Cyprus (see Figure 5.1) and was excavated by the Lemba Archaeological Project in the 1980s (Peltenburg 1991a). It is one of the largest prehistoric sites in Cyprus (Peltenburg 1990), although only a limited area near the centre of the site was available for excavation. The site revealed evidence of five periods of occupation, from the late Neolithic, through the Chalcolithic to the Early Bronze Age (Peltenburg 1990). The settlement was densely populated, with typically circular buildings ranging in size up to around 15 metres in diameter, and often clustered together (Peltenburg 1991a). Most of the buildings in the settlement seem to have been domestic houses (Peltenburg 1990). The houses of Chalcolithic Cyprus had a very distinctive layout, whose origins are illusive, but it does appear to be a Cypriot design rather than externally influenced. The circular plan

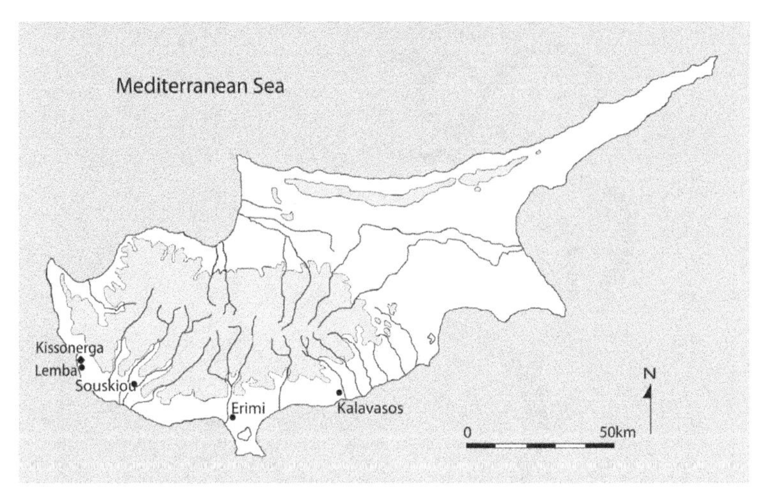

Figure 5.1 Map of Cyprus, showing location of Kissonerga *Mosphilia*.

was in use for around 1,000 years with regional and chronological variations in the internal layout (Bolger and Peltenburg 1991). The houses were of circular plan, with doors that were hinged on a pivot, usually facing south, a central hearth, radial ridges that divided the internal space into three, decorated floors and walls and a platform that was usually opposite the entry. In 1987, while excavating a Middle Chalcolithic open extra mural area of the site, deemed to be ceremonial due to the number of atypical and seemingly ritual activities evidenced here, two pits containing unusual and purposeful deposits of objects were discovered (see Figure 5.2) (Peltenburg and Thomas 1991). One of these pits, labelled Unit 1015, was discovered containing a collection of fifty-seven objects made of pottery, stone, bone and shell within an ashy soil fill (Peltenburg 1990; Goring 1991; Peltenburg and Thomas 1991). The deposited items included a building model, filled and surrounded by stone and ceramic figurines and a birthing stool model, stone tools, 'people-shaped' pebbles, a complete triton shell and a drilled pig tooth, and was topped by ceramic bowls, both broken and complete (see Figure 5.3) (Goring 1991; Bolger 1992; 1996; Beausang 2000). Due to its non-domestic nature, its non-funerary context and its careful deposition, the group has been referred to as ritual or ceremonial. The form and decoration of the stone and pottery figurines within the collection have led to its identification as a

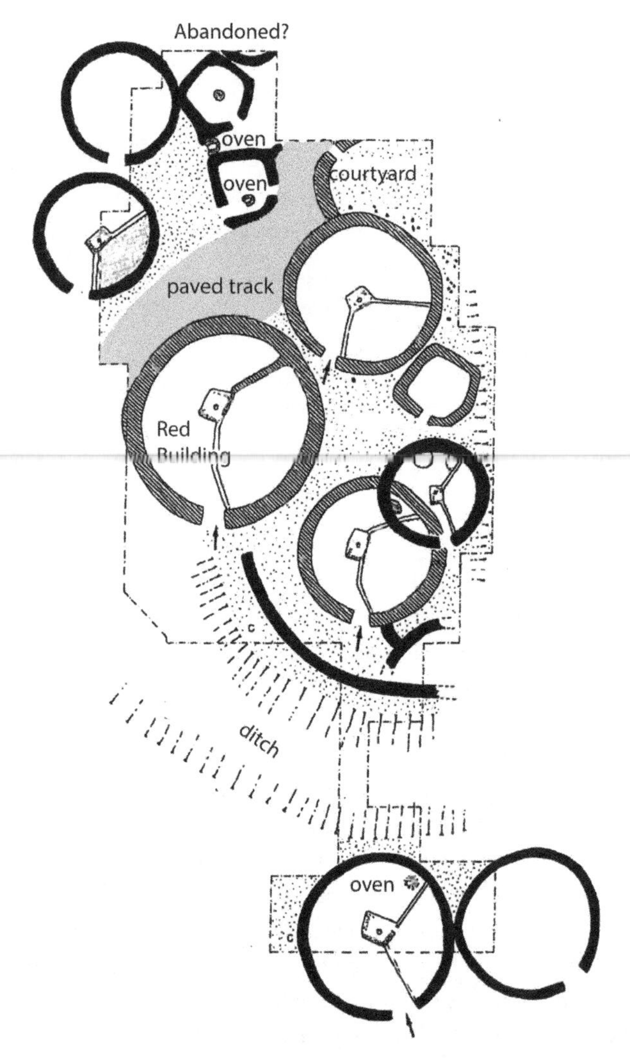

Figure 5.2 Plan of the 'ceremonial area' at Kissonerga *Mosphilia*.

childbirth collection, whether for teaching or use during parturition. The building model has a number of features that so closely match excavated buildings that the excavators note it can be narrowed to a type with 'restricted chronological duration' and it may be 'a western regional variant' (Bolger and Peltenburg 1991, 17). In particular, the features that correlate include the circular plan, the entrance, the door and pivot, the protuberances above the entry, the hearth, the radial ridges, the platform and the decorated floors and walls.

The earthy components of this grouping (see Figures 5.3) comprise the building model and the coating used to conceal its decorations, a series of ceramic figurines, with decoration, who appear to represent various stages of pregnancy and childbirth, a grotesque vessel, a model birthing stool, decorated ceramic bowls, and the fill of the pit. At least one of the stone tools has surface traces of ochre (see also Steel, this volume). The application of assemblage theory to this grouping of items will allow for the consideration of not only how they relate to each other and how they work together, but also how they came to be together and what they might tell us about societal change and when it happened. The new materialisms will allow us to gain an insight into how the inhabitants of Chalcolithic Kissonerga *Mosphilia* interacted with the materials of their world, how they saw themselves and their environment, and how they recreated these with their hands, manipulating earthy matter to replicate themselves, those around them, those who were other or from the outside, and the buildings they inhabited (see also Alberti, this volume).

The Ceramic Elements of the Hoard

There is evidence of humans working with clay and firing it since the Palaeolithic, indicating the length of the relationship that we have had with this transformative substance (Vandier et al. 1989; Steel and Attala, this volume). Not only is clay a very malleable and mouldable material, but it is known to have spiritual meaning to a number of societies (Boivin and Owic 2013). As Steel (2020, 12) states:

> making pottery is an essentially haptic process, in which the potter works with clay and responds to its physical properties. During this process, the boundaries between the matter of the potter's hands and the substance s/he manipulates are blurred, permeable and fluid.

The potter and the clay become equals in a creative relationship (Malafouris 2013), where the clay determines whether the ideas of the potter can be realised, and compromises can be made on both sides; for example, the potter simplifying their design or adding a temper to manipulate the clay. The clay is then fired, a risky and difficult process, which requires another understanding relationship between the person creating the fire, the fire, and the vessel(s) being fired, but one that, when successful, transforms the soft, slippery, malleable clay into a hard, durable material that holds the shape that it has been given. Even at this stage, there was a chance the slipping and decoration could fail or the artist could make a mistake, which would cause the object to be different from that which was originally intended, for better or worse. These material interactions between the people who procured, shaped and fired the materials, as well as the resulting objects, are part of the ongoing matter flows comprising the relational assemblage of the ceremonial deposit (see Harris 2014b, 334).

The proficiency of the potters who created the ceramic elements of the ceremonial deposition is especially clearly evidenced in the building model (see Figure 5.3a). This model is the 'earliest unambiguous model of a structure from Cyprus' (Peltenburg 2001, 123) and is a realistic representation of the standard building plan for the houses of the settlement (Peltenburg, 2001). The model is based on Red-on-White Lattice Ware (RWL) bowls from this period, with a flat base supporting thick walls and a rounded rim. The bowl has a rectangular aperture that represented the doorway, with a broken loop and a depression on the interior that once supported the functioning modelled door (Peltenburg 2001). The interior was decorated, with the base painted red, the white walls decorated with red geometric designs, which differ from the designs found on other ceramics from the period and may

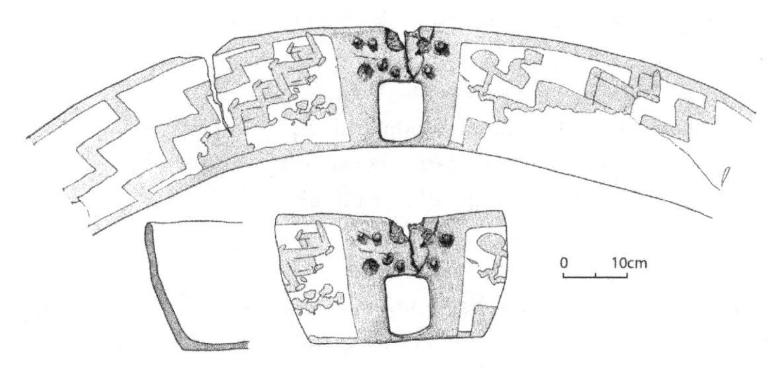

Figure 5.3a Building model from Kissonerga *Mosphilia*.

be more closely related to wall paintings or decoration, painted plaster having been recovered during excavations (Bolger 1996). Raised ridges in the base, accurately represented the divisions revealed in the excavations of the buildings of Kissonerga-*Mosphilia*, and the modelled square hearth in the centre has similar parallels. Peltenburg (2001, 126) notes that aside from one area of the exterior of the model that showed signs of coming into contact with heat, the model showed little signs of wear, indicating that it was either relatively new, had been treated with care, or both. Nine knob-like protrusions on the exterior of the model above the door have been snapped off, along with one to the right of the doorway on the interior, and a layer of white plaster had been used to obscure areas of the model before deposition, so the object is not pristine (Bolger and Peltenburg 1991, 15–16).

The person(s) who crafted this model must have not only been very skilled at producing RWL bowls, but must also have had intimate knowledge of the layout, dimensions and significance of the features of the houses of Chalcolithic Cyprus. The knowledge and experience of a building, an assemblage, that this craftsman was very familiar with is reflected in the creation of a miniature version, a smaller, mirroring or mimetic assemblage (Taussig 1993) of the original (see also Alberti, this volume).

As all the pottery from this site is handmade, there is a more simple, two-way relationship between the potter and the clay that they are working with (see Malafouris 2013; Steel 2020). Bolger (1991) notes that this can add difficulties in identifying types and can hinder the identification of production methods. However, it would appear that the vessels from Unit 1015, and from the ceremonial area of the site in which the pit was located, are all RW Group C, which is a buff-coloured clay with micaceous filler, and would have been either slab or coil-built, with red banding and lattice patterns. Five of these bowls were recovered from Unit 1015, all from Period 3 (*c*.3000 BCE), but are noted as not forming a stylistically homogenous group (Bolger 1991, 32). The building model forms the most unusual of the bowls. The other bowls can be separated by their designs, with the uppermost bowl (KM1444) being quite typical of the patterning found on other bowls across the site, with carefully planned and executed parallel bands and lattice designs. The two below (KM1445 and KM1495) are fragmentary and upside down, so would have created a cover for the objects below in the pit. The patterning on these is unusual in that the decoration is irregular and asymmetrical, the paint thick, and some of the design aspects being without parallel on the site. Bolger suggests that these two may have been painted by the same artist due to the similarity in the treatment of the paint and the designs on the two vessels. It is not clear whether the artist was inexperienced or whether there was an intention behind the difference in the decoration of these two bowls. However, the relationship between the artist, the brush, the paint and the bowls created two vessels that became 'other' or in some way deemed suitable to provide shelter for the objects in the pit below.

The final vessel within this pit is an anthropomorphic vessel (see Figure 5.3b; KM1449), categorised as probably male (Bolger 1991), although there are no obvious sexual indicators, found lying on its back along the rim of the building model. It had been deliberately broken prior to deposition and may have included the removal of any indicators of gender. The vessel has what Bolger describes as an 'intense facial expression' (1991, 32), but the contents it may have once held have left no trace. While there are other anthropomorphic figures from Chalcolithic Cyprus, none share the features or style of this one.

Within and around the building model at the base of the pit were eight pottery figurines, representing various stages of pregnancy and childbirth (see Figure 5.3) (Goring 1991). The date for the creation of each figure is unknown, most likely all were made within the Middle Chalcolithic, but not necessarily at the same time, coming together as a group at some point before their deposition. The figurines, while representing a very female experience, have a definite phallic appearance, with long necks and upturned faces, and outstretched arms. Breasts, buttocks hips and thighs seem to have been important for the makers to include and the red decoration serves to highlight these areas. One of the models includes paintwork showing a baby emerging from between the figurine's legs; this figure is also wearing a necklace that seems to include a pendant similar to the figurines (Goring 1991). Birthing stools were included with some of the figurines, and one as a standalone object. All these figurines had been deliberately broken before deposition. As it is impossible to say whether these were produced as a group or were an agglomeration of practice and time, it is equally impossible to determine whether these were commissioned or made by a single person or artist. The wear patterns of

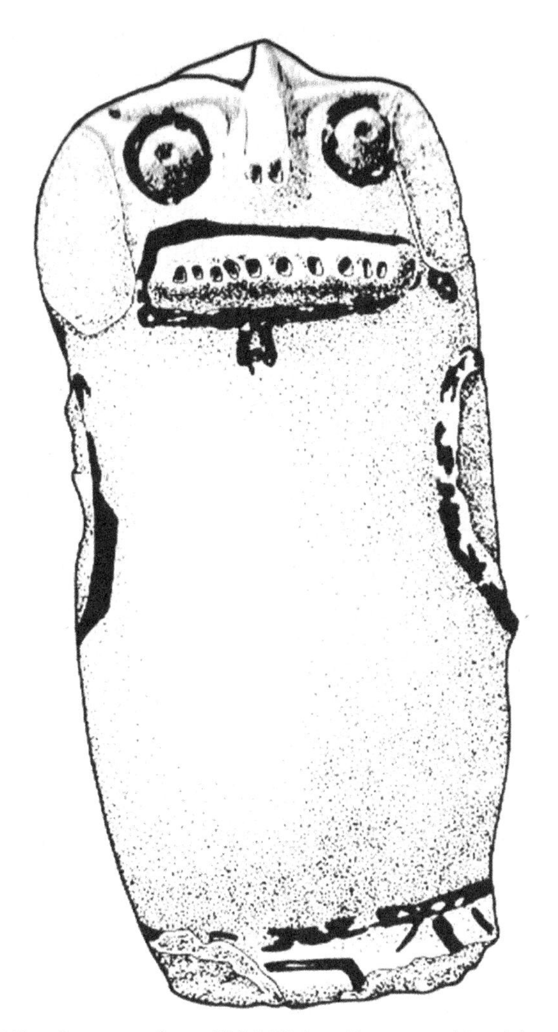

Figure 5.3b Grotesque figure KM14499 from Kissonerga *Mosphilia*.

these figures suggest they were held around their waists, between the outstretched arms and the rounded hips, an area where they were largely undecorated, and the wear suggests they were well-handled. They were not made for the pit but had lived a life beforehand (see Kopytoff 1986). It has been suggested that these figurines may have been teaching aids to indicate to an expectant mother what she would encounter in the weeks ahead, or as part of a birthing ritual (Goring

1991). An engagement with these figurines must have seen the handler imagining or reliving the pregnancy and parturition processes, the process of engagement would have seen the handler identifying with and *becoming*-with the earthy figurines in that moment (Haraway 2008; Malafouris 2008; Attala and Steel 2019; Averett 2020), a material-semiotic intra-action where the handler and the figures cannot easily be distinguished from one another, no longer person and representation, instead these are mutually constituting bodies in a non-causal world, rather than things to be observed, represented or reflected (Barad 2007). This would enable the person handling the object to gain a different perspective and an increased awareness of the experiences that lay ahead of them, and in some way would link and connect them with all of the women who had previously held that object and lived that pregnancy experience, a type of assemblage in themselves, without having to be present in the same place or time, an osmotic exchange of knowledge, custom and experience. In this way, the materials are not just an extension of the body (Walsh 2019), but are also a bridge between people of the community, past, present and future.

It is possible that the figurines were used in conjunction with the building model, providing a form of puppet show, but one that would see further blurring of boundaries, with the person(s) controlling the figures within the building model becoming those figures, creating a scene in which people are acting and engaging with a building through models.

The Deposition

At some stage in the Middle Chalcolithic, this group of objects came together as part of a planned and purposeful deposition. A pit was dug in the open, ceremonial area of the site (Peltenburg and Thomas 1991). Elements of the building model were broken off, and a plaster was applied, concealing the decoration. The bowl was laid in the base of the pit, surrounded and filled by the figurines and other objects (see Figure 5.4), many of which had also been fragmented, scratched and damaged. One of the figurines (KM1475) was selected to be lain on its side completely blocking the south-facing door of the house model (Goring 1991). This act gave the figurine agency (cf. Gell 1998), whether it had any before or not, as its task now, apparently, is to guard the door and restrict access to the building model. This figurine differs slightly from the others in that the arms are pressed into the shoulders and breasts (Goring 1991) rather than being outstretched, which may have been a factor in its being chosen for this task. The anthropomorphic vessel was laid on top of the rim of the building model, separated from the rest of the figurines and highlighting its 'otherness', then the two fragmentary bowls were laid upside down to cover the figurines, before the final, complete bowl was sat on top, correctly orientated. In an unknown location, something was burned,

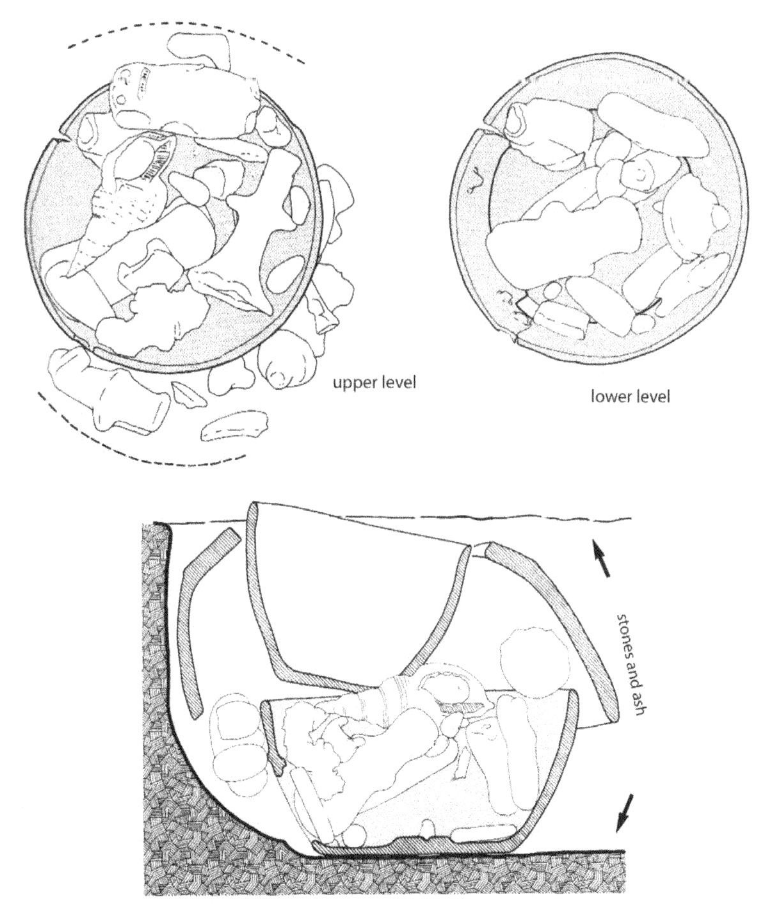

Figure 5.4 Cross-section and plan of objects packed into the building model.

possibly in a pit that had remains of a feast within it, as fragmentary animal bones were included. Once cool, this ash was mixed with soil, again from an unknown location, and used to fill the pit, sealing the group below. It is not clear where this ashy, earthy fill came from, but it was another purposeful choice for inclusion in this assemblage. The contents of the fire may have been related or unrelated to the materials or processes of pregnancy and childbirth.

The purposeful collection, destruction and deposition of these objects in this way has marked them as special, and their treatment as part of a ceremony or ritual (Peltenburg 1991b, 88–94). They form a vibrant and quite powerful grouping, laden with meaning and narrative.

Later Interactions

The open, ceremonial area of the site fell out of use, or activities were relocated, and the area was slowly infilled with other structures (Peltenburg and Thomas 1991). A very unusual rectangular building (B1000) was constructed here, but it was later dug away and its function has been lost. A circular building of the more common Chalcolithic Cypriot type was constructed (B994), its walls partially overlying Unit 1015, and the rim of the uppermost bowl possibly protruding through the floor. Aside from a small amount of damage to the rim, the deposit does not seem to have suffered any disturbance or damage. The builders must have been aware of its presence, if not of its contents and meaning. However, they gently incorporated it into the building, allowing it to be a part of this new assemblage, and carefully lived with and around it until the building fell out of use.

Other buildings fell out of use, and the area may have been used as a dump (Peltenburg, 2001). After an apparent break, new activity took place in this part of the site, in Period 4, mostly seeming to relate to graves and large pits. Unit 1015 seems to have avoided any disturbance in this repurposing of this area of the site.

Following this, the ceremonial hoard laid undisturbed until its discovery in the late 1980s. Its meaning and life then changed again, becoming part of an archaeological dig and a study collection, displayed as individual objects within a museum display. Our relationship with these objects is now a visual one (Sonik 2021), where originally it would once have been tactile; our engagement is removed, limited. Without the understanding of the meaning of the objects, and with their separation, their agency and vibrancy are dulled. Their life essence is altered further by their representation as words and static, often black-and-white images in publications, removing all interaction with them; though, conversely, their influence increases through the ability of publications to introduce these things to new audiences, their images reformed in print and pixel, their matter transferring and transforming, although never replicating the entire experience of the originals. Instead, they act as catalysts in new experiences and engagements, provoking thought, discussion and imagination, creating links between matter across time and space. As noted by Averett (2022, 171), assemblages are unstable and ever evolving, disrupting temporal and physical boundaries and understandings, challenging the linear concept of time.

The Hoard as Assemblage

The ceremonial hoard from Kissonerga *Mosphilia* is a grouping of things that appear to have a common theme in that they relate to pregnancy and childbirth. However, while these things were deposited at the same time, it would appear that they were produced and came into use at various times over a period of many years. Each one was formed from a different collection of materials, a different creation time, likely different potters, artists and hands procured the necessary materials, crafted the tools, collected the fuel, lit the furnace, and so forth (Harris 2014a; Steel 2020). Different minds had the ideas and realised the images. These creators were supported by a wider network of relations, providing the food they ate, the clothes they wore, the beds they slept in. All these relationships, these matter flows, mingling and influencing and leading to the production of these objects.

However, the objects themselves are not an end point, they are waymarkers on another journey (Ingold 2010). It is not known how they were used, whether together or apart, with people or not, and there are an untold number of further unknown relationships – were they washed, anointed with oils, wrapped or stored when not in use, whether one owner or many? The size and tactile nature, along with the wear patterns, tells of unnumbered people, women, mothers who engaged, held and caressed these objects. The visual engagement with the decorations, likely an exchange of information between the painter, the model and the handler, some elements of which bind us to them in recognition across time; for example, the image of the baby emerging from the mother, a message that transcends time and culture. Traces of ochre on a stone tool indicate another, more fleeting relationship network of mixed materials and people: the stone grinding the earthy ochre (see Steel, this volume) before it is mixed and used, whether for decoration, body paint or painkiller. Flints possibly for slicing the umbilical cord, separating mother and baby, halting the flow of nutrients and fluids between the two, while confirming that creation of a new life, two from one. The needles for stopping that immediate matter flow from the mother. The ashy fill of the pit perhaps the remnants of the burning of the unclean sheets and clothing used during parturition. The relationships, the networks, the flows and exchanges too innumerable to list.

The one certainty that they give us is that sometime around 3000 BCE there was a change. These items were no longer to be used and were to be removed from society. Defaced, damaged, broken, covered, these hands unknown, possibly the same as those who created and used, possibly new. Despite this clear marker within the flows of the matter and relationships of these things, this bringing together of objects to form a cohesive, vibrant and emotive assemblage, the relationships and changes continue, albeit at a changed rate. The hoard becomes encased within the earth from which its components were made and sourced, it becomes the 'underneath' for the building constructed above it. Exposed during excavation, it builds new relationships with the open earth, the sky, the modern world and the excavators (see Harris 2014b, 334; Govier and Steel 2021, 309–11). The elements of the group are separated, counted, classified, studied, organised, stored, displayed, viewed, sketched, photographed, described. At each point the elements of the hoard move into and out of assemblages with each other, with other objects, with those studying them, recording them, the equipment used, the paper and screens they are described on, even this chapter, the book it forms a part of and the shelves it will sit on. The flows and exchanges continue, forming new relationships, new assemblages, each highlighting different qualities and features. Through time the techniques for engagement change, from a manual environment to a digital representation, from a cheirotic experience to an exhibit shielded behind glass; from an exclusive grouping in a sealed pit to a public, doorless space as part of an island's history on show (Averett 2022, 173). Part of constantly shifting intra-actions, knowledges, customs and relationships in an eternal matter flow.

Conclusion

This chapter explores a new materialisms approach to the earthy constituents of the non-mortuary hoard from Kissonerga *Mosphilia*, which aims to demonstrate how the engagement with and between these objects can allow us a different insight into the meaning, power and interactions they may have had. From the selection of the materials to the production of the objects and then their consumption, numerous hands had numerous engagements, forming numerous relationships and assemblages of varying vibrancy. These engagements would have formed blurred boundaries at several stages of the creation and life of the objects, imbuing them with memories and experiences and demonstrating that human agency cannot be privileged over the rest of the material world. While we may not be able to untangle the original intent or purpose of the earthy elements of this deposit, we can have a better understanding of the relationships between people, materials and their worlds, and the fluid and porous nature of matter.

References

Attala, L., and Steel, L. (eds), 2019. *Body Matters: Exploring the Materiality of the Human Body*. Cardiff: University of Wales Press.

Averett, E. W., 2020. 'Blurred boundaries: Zoomorphic masking rituals and the human-animal relationship in ancient Cyprus', *World Archaeology*, 52, 724–45. *https://doi.org/10.1080/00438243.2021.1900903*.

Averett, E. W., 2022. 'Beyond representation: Cypriot sanctuaries as vibrant assemblages', *Ancient Art Revisited: Global Perspectives from Archaeology and Art History*, ed. C. Watts and C. Knappett. Abingdon and New York NY: Routledge, pp. 170–98.

Barad, K., 2003. 'Posthumanist performativity: Toward an understanding of how matter comes to matter', *Signs: Journal of*

Women in Culture and Society, 28(3), 801–31. *https://doi.org/10.1086/345321.*

Barad, K., 2007. *Meeting the Universe Halfway: Quantum Physics and the Entanglement of Matter and Meaning.* Durham NC and London: Duke University Press.

Beausang, E., 2000. 'Childbirth in prehistory: An introduction', *European Journal of Archaeology*, 3, 69–87. *https://doi.org/10.1179/eja.2000.3.1.69.*

Bennett, J., 2010. *Vibrant Matter: A Political Ecology of Things.* Durham NC and London: Duke University Press.

Boivin, N., 2010. *Material Cultures, Material Minds: The Impact of Things on Human Thought, Society, and Evolution.* Cambridge: Cambridge University Press.

Boivin, N., and Owic, M. A. (eds), 2013. *Soils, Stones and Symbols Cultural Perceptions of the Mineral World.* London: Routledge.

Bolger, D. L., 1991. 'Other ceramics', in *Lemba Archaeological Project* II.2. *A Ceremonial Area at Kissonerga*, ed. E. Peltenburg. SIMA LXX.3. Göteborg: Åströms Verlag, pp. 28–37.

Bolger, D. L., 1992. 'The archaeology of fertility and birth: A ritual deposit from Chalcolithic Cyprus', *Journal of Anthropological Research*, 48, 145–64.

Bolger, D., 1996. 'Figurines, fertility, and the emergence of complex society in prehistoric Cyprus', *Current Anthropology*, 37(2), 365–73.

Bolger, D., and Peltenburg, E., 1991. 'The building model', in *Lemba Archaeological Project* II.2. *A Ceremonial Area at Kissonerga*, ed. E. Peltenburg. SIMA LXX.3. Göteborg: Åströms Förlag, pp. 12–27.

Cifarelli, M., 2021. 'Dress, sensory assemblages, and identity in the early first millennium bce at Hasanlu, Iran', in *The Routledge Handbook of the Senses in the Ancient Near East*, ed. K. Neumann and A. Thomason. London: Routledge, pp. 141–66.

Conneller, C., 2017. 'Commentary: Materializing assemblages', *Cambridge Archaeological Journal*, 27(1), 183–5. *https://doi.org/10.1017/S0959774316000652.*

Coole, D. H., and Frost, S. (eds), 2010. *New Materialisms: Ontology, Agency, and Politics.* Durham NC and London: Duke University Press.

Crellin, R. J., 2017. 'Changing assemblages: Vibrant matter in burial assemblages', *Cambridge Archaeological Journal*, 27(1), 111–25. *https://doi.org/10.1017/S0959774316000664.*

DeLanda, M., 2006. *A New Philosophy of Society: Assemblage Theory and Social Complexity*. London and New York NY: Continuum.

DeLanda, M., 2016. *Assemblage Theory, Speculative Realism*. Edinburgh: Edinburgh University Press.

Fowler, C., 2017. 'Relational typologies, assemblage theory and Early Bronze Age burials', *Cambridge Archaeological Journal*, 27(1), 95–109. *https://doi.org/10.1017/S0959774316000615*.

Fowler, C., and Harris O. T. J., 2015. 'Enduring relations: Exploring a paradox of new materialism', *Journal of Material Culture*, 20(2), 127–48. *https://doi.org/10.1177/1359183515577176*.

Gell, A., 1998. *Art and Agency: An Anthropological Theory*. Oxford: Clarendon Press.

Goring, E., 1991. 'Pottery figurines: The development of a coroplastic art in Chalcolithic Cyprus', *Bulletin of the American Schools of Oriental Research*, 282–3, 153–61. *https://doi.org/10.2307/1357268*.

Govier, E., and Steel, L., 2021. 'Beyond the "thingification" of worlds: Archaeology and the New Materialisms', *Journal of Material Culture*, 26(3), 298–317. *https://doi.org/10.1177/13591835211025559*.

Hamilakis, Y., and Jones, A. M., 2017. 'Archaeology and assemblage', *Cambridge Archaeological Journal*, 27(1), 77–84. *https://doi.org/10.1017/S0959774316000688*.

Haraway, D., 2008. *When Species Meet*. Minneapolis MN and London: University of Minnesota Press.

Harris, O. J. T., 2014a. '(Re-)assembling communities', *Journal of Archaeological Method and Theory*, 21, 76–97. *https://doi.org/10.1007/s10816-012-9138-3*.

Harris O. J. T., 2014b. 'Revealing our vibrant past: Science, materiality and the Neolithic', in *Early Farmers: The View from Archaeology and Science*, ed. A. Whittle A. and P. Bickle. Oxford: Oxford University Press/British Academy, pp. 327–45.

Harris, O. J. T., 2017. 'Assemblages and scale in archaeology', *Cambridge Archaeological Journal*, 27(1), 127–39. *https://doi.org/10.1017/S0959774316000597*.

Ingold, T., 2010. 'Bringing things to life: Creative Entanglements in a world of materials', Working paper 15, *Realities: ESRC National Centre for Research Methods*. *https://eprints.ncrm.ac.uk/id/eprint/1306/1/0510_creative_entanglements.pdf* (accessed 2 December 2023).

Ingold, T., 2013. *Making: Anthropology, Archaeology, Art and Architecture*. Abingdon and New York NY: Routledge.

Jones, A. M., 2017. 'The art of assemblage: Styling neolithic art', *Cambridge Archaeological Journal*, 27(1), 85–94. *https://doi.org/10.1017/S0959774316000561*.

Jones, A. M., 2018. 'The archaeology of art: Practice, interaction and affect', in *The Archaeology of Art: Materials, Practices, Affects*, ed. A. M. Jones and A. Cochrane. Abingdon and New York NY: Routledge, pp. 19–30

Kopytoff, I., 1986. 'The cultural biography of things', in *The Social Life of Things: Commodities in Cultural Perspective*, ed. A. Appadurai. Cambridge: Cambridge University Press, pp. 64–91

Latour, B., 1993. *We Have Never Been Modern*. Cambridge MA: Harvard University Press.

Latour, B., 2005. *Reassembling the Social: An Introduction to Actor-Network-Theory*, Clarendon lectures in management studies. Oxford and New York NY: Oxford University Press.

Lucas, G., 2011. *Understanding the Archaeological Record*. Cambridge: Cambridge University Press. *https://doi.org/10.1017/CBO9780511845772*.

Lucas, G., 2017. 'Variations on a theme: Assemblage archaeology', *Cambridge Archaeological Journal*, 27(1), 187–90. *https://doi.org/10.1017/S0959774316000573*.

Malafouris, L., 2008. 'At the potter's wheel: An argument for material agency', in *Material Agency: Towards a Non-Anthropocentric Approach*, ed. C. Knappett and L. Malafouris. Boston MA: Springer, pp. 19–36. *https://doi.org/10.1007/978-0-387-74711-8_2*.

Malafouris, L., 2013. *How Things Shape the Mind: A Theory of Material Engagement*. Cambridge MA: MIT Press.

Marshall, Y., and Alberti, B., 2014. 'A matter of difference: Karen Barad, ontology and archaeological bodies', *Cambridge Archaeological Journal*, 24(1), 19–36. *https://doi.org/10.1017/S0959774314000067*.

Olsen, B., and Witmore, C., 2015. 'Archaeology, symmetry and the ontology of things. A response to critics', *Archaeological Dialogues*, 22(2), 187–97. *https://doi.org/10.1017/S1380203815000240*.

Peltenburg, E., 1990. 'Figures in a bowl: Evidence for Chalcolithic Religion from Kissonerga Mosphilia', *Archaeologia Cypria (Κυπριακή Αρχαιολογία)*, 2, 25–31.

Peltenburg, E., 1991a. 'Kissonerga-Mosphilia: A major Chalcolithic site in Cyprus', *Bulletin of the American Schools of Oriental Research*, 282–3, 17–35. *https://doi.org/10.2307/1357260* (accessed 2 December 2023).

Peltenburg, E., 1991b. 'Contextual implications of the "kissonerga ritual"', in *Lemba Archaeological Project* II.2. *A Ceremonial Area at Kissonerga*, ed. E. Peltenburg, Göteborg: Åströms Förlag, pp. 85–108.

Peltenburg, E., 2001. 'A ceremonial model: Contexts for a prehistoric building model from Kissonerga, Cyprus', in *'Maquettes architecturales' de l'antiquite: Regards croisés (Proche Orient, Égypte, Chypre, Bassin Égéen et Grèce, du néolithique à l'époque hellénistique)*, ed. B. Muller. Paris: de Boccard, pp. 123–41.

Peltenburg, E., and Thomas, G., 1991. 'The context and contents of the ceremonial area', in *Lemba Archaeological Project* II.2. *A Ceremonial Area at Kissonerga*, ed. E. Peltenburg. SIMA LXX.3. Göteborg: Åströms Förlag, pp. 1–11.

Rovelli, C., 2021. *Helgoland*. London: Allen Lane.

Sonik, K., 2021. 'The distant eye and the ekphrastic image: Thinking through aesthetics and art for the senses (Western/non-Western)', in *The Routledge Handbook of the Senses in the Ancient Near East*, ed. K. Neumann and A. Thomason. London: Routledge, pp. 530–57.

Steel, L., 2018. 'Watery entanglements in the Cypriot hinterland', *Land*, 7, 104. *https://doi.org/10.3390/land7030104* (accessed 2 December 2023).

Steel, L., 2020. 'Feats of clay: Considering the materiality of Late Bronze Age Cyprus', *Sustainability*, 12, 6942. *https://doi.org/10.3390/su12176942*.

Taussig, M., 1993. *Mimesis and Alterity: A Particular History of The Senses*. London and New York NY: Routledge.

Vandier, P. B., Soffer, O., Klima, B., and Svoboda, J., 1989. 'The origins of ceramic technology at Dolni Věstonice, Czechoslovakia', *Science*, 246, 1001–8.

Walsh, C., 2019. 'A cup for any occasion? The materiality of drinking experiences at Kerma, in *Body Matters: Exploring the Materiality of the Human Body*, ed. L. Attala and L. Steel. Cardiff: University of Wales Press, pp. 173–95.

Webmoor, T., and Witmore, C. L., 2008. 'Things are us! A commentary on human/things relations under the banner of a "social" archaeology', *Norwegian Archaeological Review*, 41(1), 53–70. *https://doi.org/10.1080/00293650701698423*.

Witmore, C. L., 2007. 'Symmetrical archaeology: Excerpts of a manifesto', *World Archaeology*, 39, 546–62. *https://doi.org/10.1080/00438240701679411*.

Witmore, C., 2014. 'Archaeology and the New Materialisms', *Journal of Contemporary Archaeology*, 1, 203–46. *https://doi.org/10.1558/jca.v1i2.16661*.

6 'CORBUSIAN PIGGERIES' AND 'TOYTOWN COTTAGES'

The Social Lives of Concrete and Brick in Twentieth-Century Liverpool

Alexander Scott

In November 1987, *Sunday Times* columnist Simon Jenkins highlighted a 'battle of styles' that was 'making the cultural history of the 1980s as exciting as any decade this century'. Jenkins effused that the reappearance of 'pediments and porticoes, pitched roofs and dormers, coloured stone and brick ... all over Britain are a sign that architecture is striving once again after art'. For Jenkins, this was a *material* as much as an aesthetic judgement: 'better, if we must [have] an Asda vernacular superstore with red bricks and slate roof than a concrete Arndale or Elephant and Castle shopping centre'. Jenkins was gratified by the unpopularity of concrete architecture signalled by Labour-controlled local authorities – most notably the far-left Liverpool City Council – deciding to replace multistorey concrete tower blocks with low-rise brick housing. 'Even the Liverpool Militants,' Jenkins concluded, 'have been forced to blow up their Corbusian "Piggeries" and construct toytown cottages instead' (Jenkins 1987, 33). This chapter explores a 'battle of materials' – between brick and concrete – that ran analogue to Jenkins' 'battle of styles'.

Ingold (2007; 2013) argues that material culture studies' tendency to focus on objects underestimates how their constitutive materials shape human lives. Materials possess distinct characteristics and physical capacities, but also affective, meaning-making propensities. This chapter thus adopts a new materialities perspective, rejecting the notion that matter is inert and instead focusing on how humans and things co-create each other (Attala and Steel 2019a; 2019b). Recognising people and matter as *materials-in-relationship*, the chapter focuses on interactions between concrete, brick and humans, surveying a range of archival sources to explicate the differing ways materials were used and conceptualised in the city of Liverpool and the United

Kingdom at large throughout the twentieth century. It documents how the city's built environment and political landscape were shaped by materials. It highlights the very different relationships that emerged between people, concrete and bricks in the later twentieth century and demonstrates how an ideological consensus formed in favour of brickwork and against concrete by the mid-1980s. In this sense, the chapter explores the agency of concrete and brick, and their component matters (cf. Ingold 2007), revealing them as actors in networks that link together humans and innumerable other materials and substances (Latour 2005).

Concrete, broadly speaking, was associated with advancement in the early twentieth century, and its promise to facilitate higher, faster and cheaper building chimed with wider political agendas and infrastructural needs. Perceived as a progressive alternative to brick architecture, concrete became a material of choice in the reconstruction of Liverpool's housing stock in the 1940s–1960s. However, many structural and societal problems were linked to concrete tower blocks, including those namechecked by Jenkins, the 'Piggeries' in Liverpool – formally known as Haigh, Crosbie and Canterbury Heights (Jenkins 1987, 33). With concrete eventually seen as symptomatic of social democracy's apparent ills, brick's popularity recovered during the 1970s and 1980s. According to Samuel (1996), this 'return to brick' complemented the policies of Margaret Thatcher's premiership. Brickwork's use in conservation projects was part of broader developments that placed newfound emphasis on tourist potential of industrial heritage (simultaneous to the diminution of Britain's manufacturing capacity). Likewise, preferences for brick in the housing market and urban regeneration projects reflected Thatcherism's 'gravitational shift from public-sector to private-sector [and] tenancy to owner-occupation' and the 'business recolonisation of the inner city' (Samuel 1996, 128).

Concrete and brick, the chapter thus shows, were implicated in numerous aesthetic, social and political causes throughout the twentieth century. This encapsulates what Latour (2004) terms 'matters of concern'; the ways that non-human actants perform, produce tensions and shape actions. Deviating from an anthropocentric conceptualisation of concrete and brick as utilitarian 'objects', the chapter emphasises the *agency* of materials to impact on physical, socio-economic and ideological landscapes. New materialities scholarship foregrounds substances' capacity to influence and work with humans, 'other-than human beings' and the environment at large (Attala and Steel 2019a; 2019b). By attending to brick and concrete's physical properties, the chapter interprets architectural structures as products of collaborations between people and other matters. Consequently, the chapter documents concrete and brick's various *social and material effects*: what they do and 'how they have meaning, how they are known and what social and cultural forms happen through and around them' (Drazin 2015b, 14). It additionally emphasises the *affects* – the types of emotions, moods and imaginings – that concrete and brick elicited in Liverpool.

Social and Material Histories of Brick and Concrete

As Ingold reminds us, '[t]o describe the properties of materials is to tell the stories of what happens to them as they flow, mix and mutate' (2007, 14). This is particularly relevant when considering the distinctive characteristics of brick and concrete. Neither are singularities; they are assemblages (cf. Bennett 2010, xvi–xvii, 20–6) of different matters with multiple varieties. First developed c.3500 BCE (see Steel and Attala, this volume), fired bricks – the type most regularly used today – combine silica (sand), alumina (clay) and lime with ammonia and iron oxide (Campbell and Pryce 2003); mudbricks use a different formula of loam, mud, sand and water and can be cut and left to air dry. Fired bricks are produced by heating clay at temperatures exceeding 900°C, strengthening molecular bonds to form a hard, strong substance. Because clay is liable to cracks and shrinkage, sand is added for bulk and durability. Sand's colour also presents aesthetic advantages, allowing brickmakers to vary appearance and texture (see Steel, this volume, on the affect of colour). Bricks are held in place using a binding material, such as mortar – a viscous substance combining cement (slaked lime), sand and water. Mortar hardens as it absorbs carbon dioxide, lending structural stability by filling gaps between bricks (Hynes 2019).

Similarly, concrete is an amalgam of sand, an aggregate (typically crushed rock or pebbles) and cement (often lime or calcium silicate-based) that binds and toughens through hydration. Unlike bricks, concrete is described as a complete building material that simply needs water to be added. In its viscous state, concrete is extremely pliable, and can be fitted into moulds of different shapes and sizes, which in turn permits multiple construction uses, including roads, pavements and bridges, as well as buildings. Concrete requires cement to be heated at 1,400°C – a resource-intensive process responsible for *c*.4–8 per cent of global CO_2 emissions (Forty 2019), which also uses substantial amounts of water. The underutilisation of concrete's recycling potential also generates mountains of landfill, prompting Watts (2019) to consider it 'the most destructive material on Earth'.

Concrete and brick both exert anatomical tolls. The physiological hazards include breathing noxious chemicals and dust, which contributes to numerous respiratory problems among manufacture and construction workers (see Govier 2019, for bodies becoming-with substances though inhalation). Musculoskeletal disorders are common among bricklayers and long hours spent walking on hard concrete surfaces, such as hospital floors, is associated with chronic heel pain. Such ailments speak to Stacy Alaimo's concept of 'trans-corporeality', and its emphasis on how 'substantial material interchanges' shape human bodies (Alaimo 2018, 435).

Liquid Stone, Dried Earth

Like brick, concrete has been used for millennia, with examples found in ancient Roman and Mayan architecture. However, with wood, plaster, stone and brick favoured around the world, concrete's usage was not widespread until the early twentieth century. This resurgence saw concrete reconceptualised as a material synonymous with innovation, the avant-garde and the future – even 'a kind of modernity in and of itself' (Gandy 2014, 173).

The materiality of concrete lends itself to such associations. Concrete's versatility allows for experiments in form (including concrete 'cloth', canoes and now printed houses) in ways that uniform bricks cannot. Moreover, in tandem with iron, reinforced concrete enabled the construction of skyscrapers and vast infrastructure projects such as dams. Concrete expanded architecture's technical and epistemological possibilities. Coupled with its ability to resist compression and weather forces, concrete's malleability was constitutive of a plethora of new architectural aesthetics, forms and structures (Huppatz 2019).

For Allen (2015), however, concrete's physical properties make it a 'divisive and contradictory material … [because it is] fixed yet fluid, solid yet brittle, composite yet uniform' (Allen 2015, 237). Concrete's initial amorphousness challenges normative notions of building, requiring penning and shuttering to prevent sprawl and spread before the material dries and hardens. The ubiquitous descriptor 'concrete jungle' employs 'metaphors of wildness and disorder' (Gandy 2014, 173) and suggests a threatening, untameable character. Concrete, therefore, is a way of thinking – a set of possibilities that, coupled with people, produces form.

The above illustrates concrete's negative reputation. Concrete is 'more associated with death than life', with the phrase 'concrete over' hinting at 'cutting people off from or obliterating nature' (Forty 2019, 9, 43). In contrast, there is a linguistic tendency to emphasise brick's organic qualities over the technological character of its production. For example, Hall (2015, 7) has written that bricks are 'just earth – the humblest thing imaginable', while Cruickshank (2015, 9) marvelled at the 'alchemy' by which brickmaking 'transform[s] … the elements of earth and water … into a material more durable than stone'. Brick is valued for its interactions with other elements. Dwellers of brick buildings express affection for the material's 'smell of earth when exposed to rain', likewise perceiving moss growth on bricks as reassuring evidence of 'a natural aging process' (Sofian et al. 2020, 7).

As the phrase 'brick-by-brick' exemplifies, building with bricks is a slow, incremental process reliant on intuition, patience and embodied knowledge. While bricks themselves are often standardised and factory-made (Moran 2004), bricklaying requires a caring, personal touch, which confers a sense of homeliness and domesticity (Nettleton et al 2020). This contrasts with the impersonal monolithic capacities of prefabricated concrete structures. For Unwin (2014, 161), the structural stability of brick walls constitutes a 'social geometry' that aligns bricks' material solidity with feelings of solidarity and permanence, hence its emergence as the preferred building material in Liverpool in the later twentieth century. Latour (2005, 74) uses an account of human-material interactivity on a building site – 'a shouted order to lay a brick, the chemical connection of cement with water, the force of a pulley unto a rope with a movement of the hand, the strike of a match to light a cigarette offered by a co-worker, etc.' – to explain actor-network theory's supposition that it is 'absurd ... to put material and social entities on two different shelves'.

One striking aspect of the agency or thing-power (Bennett 2010) of concrete and brick is their 'embodied emissions' (essentially the total energy requirements of making, transporting and maintaining building materials) – a significant contributor to anthropogenic climate change (Harrabin 2021). While less resource intensive than concrete, brick has a damaging ecological footprint, generating considerably more embodied emissions than bio-composites such as hempcrete (naturally grown hemp bonded with lime) and also contributing to landfill (Jankovic 2022).

The built environment is co-created by networks of people and materials. Materials accordingly determine the look, feel and identities of places. This is evidenced by the divergent status of concrete and brick within the national culture of the United Kingdom. Nationalism factors into the materials' respective reputations – certainly in a UK context. As Samuel (1996, 129) observed, brick is conceived as the 'most "English" of materials', distinguishable from the stone and granite buildings predominant in neighbouring Wales and Scotland. Accordingly, brick gives shape to national traits, being thought of as 'honest, down-to-earth, plain and unvarnished, not flashy like marble ... no[r] artificial like concrete' (Samuel 1996, 129). Contrariwise, concrete is historically associated with continental Europe: patented by Francois Hennebique in 1892, reinforced concrete was initially regarded as a distinctively French technological triumph (Newby 2001). In the early twentieth century, concrete became a cosmopolitan emblem of the 'machine age', feted by Italian Futurists and exponents of 'International Style'-architecture such as Le Corbusier and Bauhaus (Forty 2019, 101–42).

These contrasts should not be drawn too starkly, and any assumptions of concrete's 'newness' are misleading. As noted above, natural concretes were used by the Mayans and in some of the most famous buildings of Ancient Rome (the Pantheon and Colosseum). Nor was concrete uniquely 'modernist' – as evidenced by the brickwork buildings of Alvar Aalto and Willem Marinus Dudok. 'The return to brick' too was an international phenomenon: Sharon Zukin's (1989)

Loft Living: Culture and Capital in Urban Change showed how a trend that began in 1960s New York for converting industrial buildings into artists' studios 'transformed into bourgeois chic … wood floors, exposed red brick walls and cast-iron facades' (Zukin 1989, 2). By the same token, concrete's 'foreignness' from a British standpoint can be overstated. Following the appearance of the world's first skyscraper in Chicago in 1885, British cities harnessed concrete's potential for building upwards. Liverpool's Royal Liver Building, completed in 1911, prefigured an era when reinforced concrete structures were heralded as solutions for cities' residential and commercial needs. The exposed concrete surfaces of 1950s–1970s Brutalism were part of a 'native' architectural idiom that (while influenced by continental trends) addressed UK-specific concerns. Coined by Alison and Peter Smithson, 'the New Brutalism' denotes a style of architecture typically used for public institutions (such as universities, libraries, hospitals, town halls and social housing), which were material manifestations of the utilitarian and egalitarian ethos of 'welfare state modernism' (Ortolano 2019). Concrete's status as the end-product of an advanced technological process also complemented Harold Wilson's 1963 pledge to 'forge a new Britain in the white heat of the scientific revolution' (Powers 2007). More latterly, Britain's post-war 'Concretopia' has been critically rehabilitated – with several Brutalist landmarks now recognised as Listed Buildings by English Heritage (Grindrod 2013).

Even within one national context, then, concrete and brick's reputations have waxed and waned considerably. Despite connotations of certitude, solidity and security, perceptions of both materials – like their constituent substances – are malleable and subject to chronological and geographical variation. Overgeneralisation can obscure regional nuances, so the rest of the chapter concentrates on and examines the *local* resonances of concrete, brick and other materials in a Liverpudlian context. In the process, it embraces the methodological challenge of materialising concrete and brick's historic agency. Doing so relies on a degree of inference, because archival sources often contain little explicit commentary on materials' agentive qualities. As Latour (2005, 79) concedes, 'once built, the wall of bricks does not utter a word'; 'to make them talk', historians thus have 'to produce scripts of what [materials] are making others – humans or nonhumans – do'.

The Materiality of Liverpool's Pre-Second World War Architecture

The bedrock of south Lancashire comprises strata of Carboniferous rocks, including ample reserves of sandstone from the Permian-Triassic period (c.210–90 million years ago) (Broadhurst 2006). Sandstone has been used architecturally on Merseyside since the Neolithic period, as exemplified by the Calderstones – six monoliths found at a park in south Liverpool thought to have been a Bronze Age burial ground (Cowell 2006). Readily accessible and durable, sandstone remains a distinctive feature of Liverpool's cityscape: its Anglican Cathedral, for instance, is made from sandstone quarried at nearby Woolton (Broadhurst 2006).

By contrast, brick assumed prominence relatively late in Liverpool's architectural history. Brick became a 'status symbol' in the sixteenth century, being used in mansions such as Speke, Croxteth and Knowsley Halls (Pevsner et al. 2006, 36). Its application became more widespread during the Industrial Revolution, as improved means of transportation (canals, railways) reduced dependency on locally sourced materials. Brickwork was pervasive in Victorian-era terraced houses, tenements, factories, docks and warehouses. It also distinguished the University of Liverpool's Victoria Building, which remains a byword for the 'redbrick' universities founded in the late nineteenth century (Whyte 2015).

Concrete architecture supplemented brickwork during Liverpool's apex as an Edwardian 'city of empire' (de Figueiredo 2003). The interior of the Mersey Docks and Harbour Board Building used individual steel frames encased in concrete, while the neighbouring Royal Liver Building and Cunard Building were pioneering applications of reinforced concrete technology (whereby concrete is embedded inside a steel 'skeleton'). Even before this, concrete had been used in municipal housing. Impressed by its adaptation in dock walls and hydraulic systems, Liverpool's City Engineer, John Alexander Brodie, researched concrete's utility for 'economical and suitable dwellings for the poorer classes' (Brodie 1905, 3). Completed in 1905, Brodie's Eldon Street Labourers' Dwellings consisted of twelve residences across three storeys. Floors, ceiling and walls of each were precast from a concrete admixture of recycled clinker (Brodie 1905). Attesting to materials' unruly capacity to resist human expectations and intent, Eldon Street over-ran its budget. Concrete housing thus did not appear on a large scale until after the Second World War (Finnimore 1989).

Interwar Liverpool was characterised by a culture of architectural experimentation and an expanded network of actors (architects, builders, manufacturers) and actants (materials) co-creating the urban environment. The University of Liverpool's School of Architecture was renowned for its cosmopolitan curriculum, and many graduates spent periods studying overseas – including Herbert J. Rowse, whose India Buildings and Martins Bank in central Liverpool emulated high-rise offices observed in North America (Richmond 2001). Internationalism was also a feature of municipal housebuilding. Sir Lancelot Keay, Liverpool's City Architect and Director of Housing from 1925–48, based several multistorey estates on high-density schemes in continental Europe (Keay 1935a, 28–9).

Such stylistic innovations were the exception rather than the rule, though. Four-fifths of homes built by Liverpool City Council during Keay's tenure were one or two storeys in height and detached and semi-detached properties remained the norm in the public and private sectors alike (Bradbury 1967, 19; Pooley and Irish 1987). This tallied with a UK-wide fashion for historical allusions in domestic architecture. Interwar housing in Liverpool suburbs was typically made from brick and timber, and often adorned with 'Tudorbethan' or 'Neo-Georgian' flourishes that bespoke a 'nostalgia' that 'combine[d] the comforting spirit of Old England with modern living' (Sugg Ryan 2018, 159). Whether real or imagined, such associations with the past are indicative of brick's affective pull.

As such, while Liverpool provided fertile ground for architectural novelty in the decades prior to the Second World War, this did not amount to a wholesale adoption of the International Style – or concrete. Even enthusiasts for modernism erred towards other materials and technologies, as evidenced by the brickwork exteriors of Keay's St Andrew's Gardens (see Figure 6.1) and Rowse's art-deco design for Liverpool Philharmonic Hall. In 1935 Keay conceded that precast concrete had yet to be 'utilised to its uttermost' due to prevailing preferences for 'traditional forms of planning' (Keay 1935b, 628–9). Moreover, Keay's pre-war housing made a conspicuous virtue of craftsmanship and manual labour. Conceived as workers' quarters,

Figure 6.1 St Andrew's Gardens, Central Liverpool.

the now-demolished flats at Gerard Gardens were decorated with two reliefs, one depicting an architect and the other a hod-carrier transporting bricks.

Concrete in the Rebuilding of Liverpool, *c.*1945–65

The Second World War provided impetus for architectural change. While offering the inadvertent benefit of levelling some of the city's worst slums, the Liverpool Blitzes of 1940 and 1941 destroyed 10,000 houses and left 70,000 people homeless (Imperial War Museum n.d.). Nationwide 460,000 dwellings were destroyed, and 4 million homes damaged. Shortfalls in the construction industry exacerbated matters. With labour and materials directed towards wartime priorities, the number of construction workers halved work between 1939 and 1945, and brickmakers' output underwent precipitous decline. This provoked national debate about how to restore Britain's housing stock, with Churchill's wartime coalition commissioning research into how non-traditional building methods might address the 'housing question' (Tbsubaki 2000; Wall 2013).

Keay's housing department was involved in one such initiative in early 1945. The War Damage Commission (est. 1941) reimbursed

Liverpool City Council for trialling two methods of concrete construction at Norris Green. The Unit Construction Company was contracted to build houses using concrete mixed and cast on site, while Costain and Sons erected properties made from pre-cast, factory-built components. Concrete was seen to change the rhythms of the working day, and to yield economic benefits. Keay was particularly impressed by Unit's 'brickless house', which noticeably reduced labour hours and was therefore eminently suitable for the construction of homes (Post 1945, 3).

Keay's positivity about prefabrication suited the national political mood. The Housing (Temporary Accommodation) Act 1944 offered respite to homelessness by commissioning 125,000 temporary houses nationwide – including Liverpool's Belle Vale estate, where 1,300 factory-made aluminium bungalows were bolted onto brick bases (Bradbury 1967; Vale 2005). Prefabrication was deemed more than a stopgap, though. In *Rebuilding Britain: A Twenty-Year Plan* (1945), Ernest Simon, recommended a long-term reorganisation of the construction industry around factory production to 'leave as little as possible to be done on-site'. Simon deemed the volume of labour necessitated by brick housing 'wasteful' and incompatible with 'modern methods'. He predicted that 'steel, timber, concrete and so on' would soon supplant 'the brick house, so successful since the days of Babylon' (Simon 1945, 34–5, 52–5). Bricks, furthermore, were hard to come by in the war's immediate aftermath, with a lack of bricks and bricklayers reducing housebuilding programmes to 'a hand-to-mouth existence' (Echo 1950, 5).

With c.40,000 people waiting for homes, Ronald Bradbury – Liverpool's City Architect and Director of Housing from 1948 to 1970 – sought creative solutions. The post-war era saw 'a radical departure from tradition' with architects 'utilising new materials and new structural techniques' – including various forms of reinforced concrete (Bradbury 1956, 537). This differed 'fundamentally from the brick and timber method' and was seen as harbinger of a time when houses 'in the main will be built-up of factory-made prefabricated sections' (Bradbury 1956, 539). Bradbury foresaw more traditional materials having a role alongside futuristic technologies, discussing the likelihood of houses being 'moulded in plastic … steel or aluminium' and the prospect of using mudbricks in domestic architecture (Hertford 1956, 6).

Bradbury's leadership of projects such as the Kirkby overspill estate earned him a reputation 'as the man who did more to alter Liverpool's skyline than any other individual' (Echo 1963, 9). Trained at Columbia University and married to a US citizen, Bradbury – like Rowse and others before him – drew inspiration from American urbanism. His designs for Everton Heights, north Liverpool, were informed by a 1954 visit to inspect public housing in New York. Noting that American urbanites enjoyed better living standards than their British counterparts, Bradbury resolved that high densities were achievable 'without undue sacrifice of amenities' and that multistorey housing 'is not a bad thing, provided the architectural solution is intelligent and … carefully conceived' (Liverpool City Council (LCC) 1954, 53). A series of tower blocks were built, set back from main roads to limit vehicular access and affording 'fine views of the River Mersey and across to North Wales' (LCC 1958, 7). Bradbury's choice of material enhanced the desired aesthetic effect: tower blocks were clad in concrete as opposed to the 'rustic brick' that he felt made New York apartments 'monotonous and tiresome' (Echo 1955, 15). The *Liverpool Echo* fulsomely endorsed Bradbury's design, commending the 'incomparable panorama' that had replaced 'countless mean cottages of uniform drab brick separated by narrow ditches of streets' (Echo 1957, 6). Everton Heights, the *Echo* said, proved 'it makes more sense to build skywards within the bounds of a city than to go on engulfing acres of farmland in a tide of brick' (Echo 1959b, 8). It is striking that, when expressing concerns about brick housing's capacity to overwhelm Liverpool's greenbelt, the Echo deployed organic metaphors ('ditches', 'tide') not wholly dissimilar to the 'concrete jungle' trope that later became commonplace.

Everton Heights reflected the political culture of Liverpool in the mid-to-late 1950s. Its two ten-storey centrepieces of Everton Heights were named 'The Braddocks' in honour of the husband-and-wife team that dominated the local Labour Party 'machine' in the post-war era: John 'Jack' Braddock and Elizabeth 'Bessie' Braddock. Winning control of the city council for the first time in 1955, Labour politicians were staunch advocates of high-rise housing. The council refocused attention on inner-city projects, undertaking 'a burst of multistorey building using any available land: point blocks and slab blocks, suburban sites and slum clearance sites' (Glendinning and Muthesius 1993, 254–5).

Labour's financial investment was matched by political bombast. Defending one scheme at Menlove Avenue in 1959, Alderman Joseph Morgan vowed to 'build multistorey flats whether residents like it or not' (Echo 1959b, 8). Bessie Braddock similarly branded critics of tower blocks at Sefton Park (see Figure 6.2) a 'snobocracy' (Echo 1959a, 7).

With the Conservative Governments of the 1950s and 1960s incentivising high-rise architecture nationally (Scott 2020), tower blocks enjoyed bipartisan support. After regaining control of Liverpool City Council in 1961, the Conservatives commissioned a delegation to visit Paris and observe 'new and advanced *prefabricated* techniques for housing ... pioneered in the use of reinforced concrete' (Echo 1962a, 3, my emphasis), highlighting the distinctive capacities of the material that enabled rapid post-war reconstruction. The travelling party visited factories where precast concrete components were produced and studied housing estates built using concrete systems. Suitably impressed, the delegation left France 'convinced that ... the production of precast concrete dwellings on the factory conditions ... could greatly increase housing output and considerably reduce the time taken in the construction of individual housing' (LCC 1962). Council leader Maxwell Entwistle told the *Echo* that 'the whole thing

Figure 6.2 Flats at Croxteth Drive, Sefton Park.

is … quite revolutionary … and represents the first big break with traditional building methods for years' (Echo 1962b, 9). In subsequent years, concrete manufacturers became significant players in Liverpool's municipal life, moving into the network of relationships that altered the city's skyline. The city council entered a contact with the Camus company – a specialist in the prefabricated housing that formed a 'concrete cordon' around post-war Paris (Urban 2012, 37–58). Partnering with the local Unit Construction company, a Unit Camus factory opened at Kirkby in 1964. By the end of 1965, seventy-nine multistorey blocks containing 5,864 flats were built (Bradbury 1967, 46). Perhaps fittingly, one of the new properties, a twenty-storey block at Harding Street, Toxteth, was named Entwistle Heights to recognise the former council leader's 'services to the city' (Bradbury 1967, 43).

Liverpool's 'Concrete Jungle', c.1965–79

Municipal housebuilding whetted a wider appetite for concrete architecture. In July 1967, the industry journal *Concrete* (1967) ran a feature on 'Concrete Redevelopment in Liverpool' that discussed concrete's role in various construction projects, including St John's Beacon, a new shopping precinct and the recently consecrated Liverpool Metropolitan Cathedral. Concrete's presence in the Metropolitan Cathedral design (see Figure 6.3) held spiritual significance, evoking 'an architecture concerned with modernising progress' at a time when the Catholic Church was undergoing major liturgical reform (Proctor 2014, 116). Concrete structures were a prominent feature of the architect Graeme Shankland's Liverpool City Centre Plan (1964). Although only partially realised, Shankland's plan led to the construction of several high-rise offices, new civic spaces and a series of inner-city motorways and overhead walkways. Given a remit of fostering 'mobility, leisure and prosperity', Shankland (1964, 117) wanted to make the city centre 'a place worth coming to … for great civic occasions, personal recreation, fun and adventure'.

Shankland's vison failed to materialise. By the 1970s, Liverpool's port and manufacturing industries entered inexorable decline, contributing to a process of depopulation that continued into the twenty-first century. Partly because of this, the Shankland plan became widely reviled: Jenkins likened Shankland to 'Bomber Harris' (Saumarez

Figure 6.3 Liverpool Metropolitan Cathedral.

Smith 2019, 89), while Samuel (1996, 67) dubbed him 'the butcher of Liverpool' whose 'fetish for building brand new' encapsulated 'the planning disasters of the 1960s'. In 1976, the *Echo* published a plaintive by Richard Whittington-Egan (1976, 6) – author of several books on Liverpool history – which claimed that Shankland 'had turned the city of my dreams into a concrete nightmare'. Labelling the new city centre 'a Swiss-clean, clinically dull, impersonal, undistinguished Metropolisville', Whittington-Egan (1976, 6) accused Liverpool's 'City Fathers' of neglecting their role as 'guardians *ad litem* to their bricks and mortal charges'. He dismissed Shankland's overhead walkways as 'concrete rat mazes' and St John's Beacon as 'a concrete mushroom' only fit for 'providing a magnificent panorama of the havoc they [town planners] have wrought' (1976, 6). Turning attention to outer districts, Whittington-Egan (1976, 6) spoke to residents 'marooned, high and dry, in tower-blocks'. They told him that 'Life was much better the way things were … There's no street life now. We all seem to be separate. The flats are lonely.'

These comments were indicative of a sweeping turn of public opinion against concrete architecture in response to its materiality. The 1968 collapse of Ronan Point in London focused national attention on safety concerns and multistorey housebuilding curtailed considerably thereafter. In September 1970, Liverpool City Council abandoned high-rise flats in favour of new two-storey houses – a move Bradbury reasoned would restore 'community feeling', since 'it was often said that you could travel right up a skyscraper block and not meet a soul' (Echo 1970, 3). The changing mood was expressed by the folksong 'Back Buchanan Street'. Written by Harry and Gordon Dison, the song's refrain 'don't want to go to Kirkby' captured many displaced Liverpudlians' disillusionment with their experiences of living in concrete tower blocks:

> We'll miss a lot of little things,
> Like putting' out the cat,
> For there's no back door
> On the 14th floor
> Of a Unit Camus flat.
>
> (Echo 1967, 8)

Liverpool's flirtation with industrialised housing terminated when the Unit Camus factory at Kirkby shut in 1972.

This policy shift, and resulting new material environment, was expedited by a resurgence of the Liberal Party. Between 1974 and 1983, the Liberals formed a series of coalitions with the Conservatives on Liverpool City Council, implementing a wholesale reversal of housing strategy. Demurring against newbuild schemes, the Liberals advocated conservation of existing properties and opposed large-scale municipal ownership. Pre-dating the Thatcher government's 'Right to Buy' policy, the Liberal-Conservative coalition sold off some council properties and issued a moratorium on municipal housebuilding. A 'build for sale' scheme was also instituted – effectively a subsidy for private sector house building on municipally owned land. In addition, the Liberals encouraged the founding of independent housing co-operatives, which transferred ownership of council houses to residents' groups. Liverpool co-ops attracted national attention and were heralded as exemplars of 'community architecture' – a planning ethos in which residents rather than professionals led the design process (Thompson 2020).

The Liberals claimed that voters were tired of 'the Labour and Tory machines' and their 'concrete jungles of multistorey flats unsuitable for young families' (Carr 1967, 8). The 'concrete jungle' metaphor was routinely applied to Liverpool's Netherley estate. Located beside farmland at the extremities of the city boundaries, Netherley was notorious for its remoteness. A 1974 sociological study described the estate as 'a system of pedestrian motorways leading nowhere', noting that many tenants found living in '"cellars in the sky" ... worse than solitary confinement' (Spence 1974, n.p.). The author, Phoebe Spence (1974, n.p.), added: 'The claustrophobic nature of flats increases the feeling of isolation. Reinforced concrete can transmit sounds loud and clear, so sleeping is difficult.' The causal relationship between concrete's acoustic properties and insomnia gives a very clear example of materials' trans-corporeal impact on humans.

The psychophysiological effects of living, indeed becoming-with concrete were discussed in a 1977 *Spare Rib* cover story on Netherley headlined, 'It's Colditz or the Concrete Jungle'. This reported that poor drainage caused 'high incidence of diarrhoea and dysentery' and 'that mental illness figures [were] high especially among housewives and mothers' (Flowers 1977, 10). These findings were consistent with research elsewhere in the United Kingdom, which demonstrated that working-class women (especially young mothers) were disproportionately prone to the physical and social isolation engendered by high-rise housing (Abrams et al. 2019). More broadly, the gendered experience of Netherley's residents is symptomatic of the marginalisation of women by the male-dominated professions of architecture and town planning, which have in effect rendered cities as 'patriarchy written in stone, brick, glass and concrete' (Darke 1996, 88). At the same time, the *Spare Rib* report affirmed women's ability to 'claim space' in man-made urban environments (Kern 2020). The magazine foregrounded acts of resistance by female residents, profiling Maria O'Reilly of Netherley Flat Dwellers Action Group – who staged a series of protests against the City Council, including roadblocks, occupations and depositing rubbish and vermin at Liverpool Town Hall (Flowers 1977). In July 1979, the Flat Dwellers had a case upheld by the local government ombudsman, which ruled that the 'indifferent workmanship and failure to meet design specifications' were an 'injustice' to residents (Ellis and Neild 1979, 7). The Council agreed a relocation scheme, and the tower blocks were demolished in September 1981. Photographed at the demolition site, Councillor Derek Hatton told the *Echo*: 'It's a great victory for the Labour Party and the flatdwellers. It shows the disaster of cheap building and putting things up without thinking about what people really want' (Echo 1981, 3).

The 'Return to Brick' in Domestic Architecture, c.1979–2000

Hatton was the public face of Militant, a far-left 'tendency' that dominated the Liverpool Labour Party in the mid-1980s. When Labour won outright control of the Town Hall in 1983, it initiated an ambitious programme of municipal spending – a deliberate contravention of the Conservatives' commitment to reducing local authority expenditure. Costed at £130 million, the programme aimed to replace poorly maintained properties with newbuilds that would rehouse around 40,000 residents (Taaffe and Mulhearn 1988). Rejecting 'the disastrous mistakes of post-war municipal building' (LCC c.1987, n.p.), the Militant-influenced council forsook the Liberals' 'build for sale' policy and cut funding to housing co-ops. It also targeted high-rises built by previous Labour and Conservatives administrations, which saw 'thousands of people living substandard walk-up and maisonettes' (LCC c.1987, n.p.). The Piggeries and The Braddocks were bulldozed, with the council pointedly insisting that its 'Homes for the People' were 'houses and bungalows ... with traditional through streets' and 'no pedestrian/vehicular separation' (LCC 1985, 8). Entwistle Heights was also demolished, as were several of Keay's 1930s tenements. The council described its approach as 'old fashioned', rejecting modernist experiments with collective living (Hetherington 1984, 4). Reporting on the construction of 'neat, redbrick semis with walls round their gardens', *The Guardian* summarise the changes as 'not so much a revolution as a return to former values' (Andrews 1985, 17).

The council's critique of post-war urbanism shared common ground with Thatcher – otherwise a staunch ideological adversary. In 1981, Thatcher recalled opening Netherley Comprehensive School and encountering 'a big new housing estate ... built by architects of course, but not the sort of houses that they would like to live in' (BBC Radio 2

1981). Returning to theme in 1986, Thatcher asserted that 'they [architects and planners] took long streets of houses where people knew one another ... turned them up into blocks of flats and expected people still to have the same relationship' (Granada Television 1986).

Liverpool underwent a widescale 'return to brick' during the Thatcher era. A 1979 *Echo* feature described ten 'build-for-sale' houses in West Derby as 'very traditional, simple ... and built in dark red brick' – a taste for 'natural materials echoed in the timber framed windows' and the inclusion of 'stone setts instead of concrete kerbs' (*Echo* 1979, 1). Brickwork too was commonplace in co-operative housing. A 1982 feature by *Architects' Journal* observed that the red brick used throughout the Weller Street co-operative (see Figure 6.4) lent it a 'simple, almost utilitarian' feel (Wates 1982, 57). This uniformity conformed with the 'egalitarianism' of the co-op's left-wing leadership – but it was also the result of ordinary members' design preferences (McDonald 1986, 112). One resident recalled that although neighbours were theoretically 'in favour of using different colour bricks', ultimately 'everyone wanted red in their own courts' (Wates 1982, 57; see also Steel this volume on the affective pull of colour). These choices were motivated by a combination of bricks' affect – their aesthetic and symbolic connotations – and their haptic characteristics. Brickwork was said to lend 'a graininess or a feel for detail' (Anderson 1984, 50)

Figure 6.4 Copperfield Close, part of Weller Street Housing Co-operative.

that departed from the 'inhuman', grey facades of council-built properties: a member of Hesketh Street co-op took pride that their new homes looked 'very expensive – totally different from a "corpy estate"' (Anderson 1984, 51). Co-operative housing thus mirrored trends in the private market during the 1970s and 1980s, with volume housebuilders especially using brickwork to bestow a 'patina of rusticity' on otherwise formulaic designs (Samuel 1996, 121). This provides a clear example of architectural designs shifting in response to the specific material properties of brick (see Ingold 2007).

Brickwork's renewed popularity was aided by shrewd marketing. In 1976, an industry lobby group named the Brick Development Association (BDA) took out a full-page advert in *The Sunday Times Magazine* celebrating brick as 'a national asset'. Brick, the BDA claimed, was 'an indigenous material' with a '"homegrown" character 'insulated from world economics' (BDA 1976, 77). Furthermore, brick's thermal properties were deemed particularly advantageous in the context of the era's international energy crises: other BDA adverts stressed that reverting to brick architecture could 'check residents' ever-rising fuel costs' and 'reduce import bills' (BDA 1977, 39). In 1980, the BDA (1980, 16) adopted the slogan 'Brick Keeps Britain Beautiful' and an advert playing up a belief that bricks' materiality was in harmony with the elements:

> Some houses ... have a layer of beautiful British brick on the outside, while inside lurk ... materials from abroad [that] haven't stood the test of time in our damp, drizzly climate. Before you buy that new house, check it's brick right through ... Only then can you be sure you've got the best Britain can offer. And not some risky foreign alternative.

Implicitly, concrete was one such 'foreign' material. BDA publicity emphasised brick's capacity to 'humanise otherwise soulless structures' (BDA 1973, i) and to correct flaws associated with concrete architecture. Recalling Netherley Flat Dwellers' noise complaints, the BDA campaigned to replace 'walls made from breeze block and plasterboard' with 'solid, brick-built partitions' that provided better sound insulation – a matter of some urgency since residents of modern homes 'can hear the neighbours have a session ... [with] all the groans, squeals and laughter' (Mirror 1975, 7). Brick's capacity to mute noisy neighbours established it as a material peculiarly well adapted to socially conservative 'family values'. An advert for the 'family-size brick' from 1978 alleged that, unlike 'flashier materials', brick 'has a lovely rustic quality that everyone recognises ... ask a child to draw a house and he'll [*sic*] draw one made of brick' (BDA 1978a, 6). Another advert announced that brick confounded 'uniformity, ugliness ... institutionalism ... banality, boredom, [and] ready-made ideas' (even though the accompanying photograph showed 'a machine-made pressed Calcium Silicate Brick') (BDA 1978b, 111).

Brick and Heritage-Led Urban Regeneration in 1980s Liverpool

BDA marketing harmonised with Thatcherism's 'family-centred individualism' (Lawrence and Sutcliffe-Braithwaite 2012, 134). Brickmaking for its part was a rare manufacturing success story during the 1980s. In 1985, the *Financial Times* reported that Conservative urban regeneration policies – such as the creation of Urban Development Corporations and Enterprise Zones – had been 'a boon' to the brick industry, which had increased its 'market share as part of the revolt against the drab concrete structures which symbolised Britain's post-war rebuilding' (David 1985, vii). London Docklands Development Corporation, for example, used redbrick landscaping at Canary Wharf to inject 'English tradition' into an environment otherwise associated with global capital (Edwards 1992, 159).

Liverpool fitted this wider picture. The Merseyside Development Corporation (MDC, est. 1981) oversaw a series of regeneration schemes that were said to have 'revive[d] confidence in [Liverpool's] future', testifying that 'people ... having tested the modernist concrete "machines for working and living in" ... again welcome brick as reviving the traditional English vernacular style' (Brick Bulletin 1988a, 3–5). To prove the point, the BDA's magazine *Brick Bulletin* devoted several pages to Liverpool's Albert Dock – the refurbishment of which 'demonstrate[d] powerfully the versatility of brickwork as a structural medium' (Brick Bulletin 1988b, 17–18). First opened in 1846, Albert Dock had seen declining use for the better part of a century prior to closing in 1972. It thereafter fell into disrepair before being renovated by the MDC. By 1984, the dock's condition had improved sufficiently to host its first public events, with Tate Liverpool art gallery opening four years later.

Brick's role in the Albert Dock redevelopment attracted considerable commentary within the nascent field of heritage studies. Samuel (1996) mentioned the dock in his critique of Britain's heritage industry, while Reas (1993) photographed it to demonstrate how 'the heritage process … unifies the past into a single romantic and idealised version'. Walsh (1996, 143–4) similarly regarded Albert Dock as a 'de-historicised … playground' that serviced 'ersatz tourism'. Williams (2004, 114–7) compared its combination of art spaces and des-res apartments to processes of inner-city gentrification analysed by Zukin (1989) and highlighted how the redevelopment accentuated warehouses' 'picturesque' qualities. This analysis was apposite to Tate Liverpool, designed by James Stirling. A native Liverpudlian, Stirling (1960, 89) recognised 'the quality of vernacular brick buildings such as the Liverpool warehouses and … the great virtuosity English 19th-century brick architecture in general'. Stirling consequently ensured that Tate Liverpool retained the dock's original brickwork and layout.

Ironically, however, Stirling also designed one of post-war Britain's most ill-starred concrete housing schemes – the Southgate Estate at Runcorn, just south of Liverpool. Southgate was made up of an assortment of concrete flats and maisonettes supposed to house 6,000 people. The quirky designs of Stirling's buildings quickly became objects of derision: residents likened their circular windows to washing machines, and its combination of colourful plastic cladding and rectilinear forms earned Southgate the nickname 'Legoland' (Weston and Bona 2021). A BBC documentary *Where We Live Now* (BBC 1979) concurred, dismissing Southgate as 'a romanticised version of the Machine Age' and 'a colossal ego trip by the architect'. Although visually distinct from concrete towers such as The Piggeries, Southgate was beset by social and material problems familiar to inner-city estates. Populated mainly by low-income families, the estate's flats proved hard to let and experienced recurrent heating, insulation and maintenance issues. Summarising its apparent failure, Architects' Journal (1989, 5) labelled Southgate 'Britain's Pruitt-Igoe' – a reference to a notorious housing project in St Louis, Missouri, the 1972 demolition of which Jencks (1984, 9) memorably pronounced 'the death of modern architecture'. Southgate was duly demolished in 1990 and replaced with 'a pleasant, landscaped estate of brick houses, bungalows and flats with gardens' (Young 1993, 14).

Nevertheless, equating Southgate's demise with the triumph of traditional brick architecture versus concrete modernism oversimplifies matters. Stirling's writings offered less a *rejection* of twentieth-century architecture than an exploration of the influence that historical materials, forms and styles had *on* modernism: '"The Functional Tradition" and Expression' cited both 'anonymously designed buildings in England of a regional type, such as farmhouses, barns, warehouses, mills, etc.' and the 'uniformity' of Victorian terraces as precursors to the 'uncompromising appearance' favoured by Le Corbusier (Stirling 1960, 89, 91). Historical allusions of this type were, in fact, discernible in Stirling's Runcorn houses. Plastic and concrete trappings notwithstanding, Stirling considered the Georgian terraces of Bath as a reference-point for Southgate's courtyard layout and high density. The 'washing-machine' windows were supposed to be reminiscent of steamship portholes – a nod to Merseyside's maritime heritage that Stirling repeated when designing apertures for Tate Liverpool (Hennebury 2014).

Conclusion

Stirling's oeuvre further complicates efforts to demarcate 'battlelines' between concrete and brick. Crinson (2006) uses Stirling and Gowan's 1961 housing estate in Preston to show that historic brickwork techniques remained popular among some avant-garde architects even while the concrete structures of welfare-state modernism predominated. If this problematises interpretations that attribute the advent of the heritage industry to Thatcherism, Stirling's penchant for historicism and corresponding admiration for Le Corbusier also suggests that the 'return to brick' did not eventuate a wholesale turn away from modernism. Ultimately, Stirling thought the decision to use concrete, brick or any other building material was one made 'entirely at a practical level and … never emotionally' (Crinson 2006, 225).

This chapter has shown that, contrary to Stirling's indifference, whether to use concrete or brick frequently *was* a choice that freighted social, political and cultural – even emotional – significance in twentieth-century Liverpool. Exploration of the material characteristics of concrete and brick reveal that both were implicated in a tangle of architectural and socio-political meanings and choices after the Second World War. Building materials have been shown to co-create places, sometimes with unexpected results. Where concrete tower blocks once evoked modernity and progress, by the 1970s and 1980s brickmakers, housebuilders and the Conservative government had comprehended the affective pull of brick's association with homeownership, individuality, nostalgia and family values. Just as concrete and brick are physically not one thing but an assemblage of many things, their implications are materially and ideologically malleable. Concrete tower blocks were a source of pride for Conservative as well Labour councillors during the 1950s and 1960s, whereas outwardly similar low-rise brick houses later serviced the disparate politics of Liberal-backed co-operatives, left-wing Militants and free-market Thatcherites.

Politicking of this sort persists today. In July 2021, Robert Jenrick – the Conservative Secretary of State for Housing, Communities and Local Government – announced design codes instructing local authorities to mandate that newbuild architecture uses materials that 'fit the history of their area'. Adding that 'urban planning since the war has at times been a disaster', Jenrick (2021) hoped that the new codes would encourage 'northern towns to reflect their redbrick heritage' – a roundabout allusion, maybe, to the 'red wall' of traditionally Labour-voting constituencies penetrated by the Tories in the 2019 General Election (Grylls 2021, 17). While the latter conflation remains speculative, Jenrick's comments nonetheless underline the enduring *discursive* utility of materials – something that can act as a substitute for substantive action. This matters because ignorance of materiality can be lethal. The fire at Grenfell Tower in 2017, for instance, was caused not by the building's concrete skeleton or the brick façade of its original 1974 design, but the flammability of aluminium cladding added in later renovations (Grenfell Tower Inquiry 2019). If the durability of historic tropes about concrete and brick exaggerates the difficulty of letting materials 'speak for themselves' (Drazin 2015a, xx), incidents like the Grenfell fire confirm the efficacy of new materialisms scholars' calls to rethink humanity's relationship with the material world.

References

Abrams, L., Fleming L., Hazley, B., Wright V., and Kearns, A., 2019. 'Isolated and dependent: Women and children in high-rise social housing in post-war Glasgow', *Women's History Review*, 28(5), 794–813.

Alaimo, S., 2018. 'Trans-corporeality', in *The Posthuman Glossary*, ed. R. Braidotti and M. Hlavajova. London: Bloomsbury, pp. 435–38.

Allen, F., 2015. 'Introduction: Concrete', *Parallax*, 21(3), 237–40.

Anderson, H., 1984. 'Appraisal: Hesketh Street', *Architects' Journal*, 18 July 1984, 45–57.

Andrews, G., 1985. 'The greening of Liverpool', *Guardian*, 2 December 1985, 17.

Architects' Journal, 1989. 'Britain's Pruitt-Igoe?', *Architects' Journal*, 1 March 1989, 5.

Attala, L., and Steel, L., 2019a. 'Preface', in *Body Matters: Exploring the Materiality of the Human Body*, ed. L. Attala and L. Steel. Cardiff: University of Wales Press, pp. xvii–xviii.

Attala, L., and Steel, L., 2019b. 'Introduction', in *Body Matters: Exploring the Materiality of the Human Body*, ed. L. Attala and L. Steel. Cardiff: University of Wales Press, pp. 1–8.

BBC, 1979. 'New town, new home', *Where We Live Now*. *www.bbc.co.uk/iplayer/episodes/p01q1kwg/where-we-live-now* (accessed 24 January 2022).

BBC Radio 2, 1981. Margaret Thatcher interview for BBC Radio 2, *Jimmy Young Programme*, 9 September 1981. *www.margaretthatcher.org/document/104529* (accessed 24 January 2022).

BDA, 1973. Policy statement, *Times*, 27 February 1973, Architecture and Environment supplement, i.

BDA, 1976. Advertisement. *Sunday Times Magazine*, 24 October 1976, 77.

BDA, 1977. Advertisement. *Sunday Times Magazine*, 13 February 1977, 39.

BDA, 1978a. Advertisement. *Sunday Times Magazine*, 2 July 1978, 6.

BDA, 1978b. Advertisement. *Sunday Telegraph Magazine*, 8 October 1978, 111.

BDA, 1980. Advertisement. *Daily Mirror*, 13 October 1980, 16.

Bennett, J., 2010. *Vibrant Matter: Toward a Political Ecology of Things*. Durham NC and London: Duke University Press.

Bradbury, R., 1956. 'Housing a hundred years from now', *The Journal of the Royal Society for the Promotion of Health*, 75(9), 535–40.

Bradbury, R., 1967. *Liverpool Builds, 1945–65*. Liverpool: Liverpool City Council.

Brick Bulletin, 1988a. 'Brickwork and urban regeneration on Merseyside', *Brick Bulletin*, 3–5.

Brick Bulletin, 1988b. 'New life for the Albert Dock', *Brick Bulletin*, 17–18.

Broadhurst, F., 2006. 'Geology and building stones', in *Lancashire: Liverpool and the South-West*, ed. N. Pevsner, R. Pollard and J. Sharples. London: Yale University Press, pp. 3–8.

Brodie, J. A., 1905. *Concrete Dwellings, Eldon Street: Report of the City Engineer*. Liverpool: C. Tinling. Liverpool Record Office [LRO] 352 COU.

Campbell, J. W. P., and Pryce, W., 2003. *Brick: A World History*. London: Thames and Hudson.

Carr, C., 1967. 'Liberal pitch for local elections', *Liverpool Echo*, 10 May 1967, 8.

Concrete, 1967. 'Concrete redevelopment in Liverpool', *Concrete*, 229–35.

Cowell, R. W., 2006. 'Prehistoric South-West Lancashire', in *Lancashire: Liverpool and the South-West*, ed. N. Pevsner, R. Pollard and J. Sharples. London: Yale University Press, pp. 9–14.

Crinson, M., 2006. 'The uses of nostalgia: Stirling and Gowan's Preston housing', *Journal of the Society of Architectural Historians*, 65(2), 216–37.

Cruickshank, D., 2015. 'Preface: The First Cities', in W. Hall, *Brick*. London: Phaidon, pp. 8–13.

Darke, J., 1996. 'The man-shaped city', in *Changing Places: Women's Lives in the City*, ed. C. Booth, J. Darke and S. Yeandle. London: Sage, pp. 88–99.

David, R., 1985. 'Urban renewal: The role of brick', *Financial Times*, 8 October 1985, section U, vii.

de Figueiredo, P., 2003. 'Symbols of empire: The buildings of the Liverpool waterfront', *Architectural History*, 46, 229–54.

Drazin, A., 2015a. 'Preface: Materials transformations', in *The Social Life of Materials: Studies in Materials and Society*, ed. A. Drazin and S. Küchler. London: Bloomsbury, pp. xvi–xxviii.

Drazin, A., 2015b. 'To live in a materials world', in *The Social Life of Materials: Studies in Materials and Society*, ed. A. Drazin and S. Küchler. London: Bloomsbury, pp. 3–28.

Echo, 1950. 'Bricks scarce in Liverpool', *Liverpool Echo*, 4 May 1950, 5.

Echo, 1955. 'New type of bathroom in city flats', *Liverpool Echo*, 15 February 1955, 15.

Echo, 1957. 'Up go mammoth blocks of flats', *Liverpool Echo*, 24 September 1957, 6.

Echo, 1959a. 'Minister attacked by Mrs Braddock', *Liverpool Echo*, 8 January 1959, 7

Echo, 1959b. 'Skyscrapers, snobs and savings', *Liverpool Echo*, 12 October 1959, 8.

Echo, 1962a. 'Liverpool to study ready-made homes', *Liverpool Echo*, 30 May 1962, 3.

Echo, 1962b. 'Pre-cast concrete homebuilding may be answer to Liverpool slums', *Liverpool Echo*, 22 June 1962, 9.

Echo, 1963. 'The Man behind the Liverpool estates', *Liverpool Echo*, 8 November 1963, 9.

Echo, 1967. 'A Liverpudlian's Lament', *Liverpool Echo*, 29 April 1967, 8.

Echo, 1970. 'This is the housing of the future', *Liverpool Echo*, 11 September 1970, 3.

Echo, 1979. 'Ten Men and the Challenge they Face', *Liverpool Echo*, 24 September 1979, Homes Extra section, 1.

Echo, 1981. [No Headline] *Liverpool Echo*, 23 September 1981, 3.

Edwards, B., 1992. *London Docklands: Urban Design in an Age of Deregulation*. Oxford: Butterworth-Heinemann.

Ellis, E., and Neild, L., 1979. 'Guilty! Netherley rap for council', *Liverpool Echo*, 8 August 1979, 7.

Finnimore, B., 1989. *Houses from the Factory: System Building and the Welfare State*. London: Rivers Oram Press.

Flowers, M., 1977. 'Netherley United', *Spare Rib*, March 1977, 10–14.

Forty, A., 2019. *Concrete and Culture: A Material History*. London: Reaktion Books.

Gandy, M., 2014. *The Fabric of Space: Water, Modernity, and the Urban Imagination*. Cambridge MA and London: MIT Press.

Glendinning, M., and Muthesius, S., 1993. *Tower Block: Modern Public Housing in England, Scotland, Wales and Northern Ireland*. New Haven CT: Yale University Press.

Govier, E., 2019. 'Bodies that co-create: The residues and intimacies of vital materials', in *Body Matters: Exploring the Materiality of the Human Body*, ed. L. Attala and L. Steel. Cardiff: University of Wales Press, pp. 19–37.

Granada Television, 1986. *Interview with Margaret Thatcher for Granada Television*, 21 April 1986. *www.margaretthatcher.org/document/106368* (accessed January 2022).

Grenfell Tower Inquiry, 2019. *Grenfell Tower Inquiry: Phase 1 Report Overview*, October 2019. *https://assets.grenfelltowerinquiry.org.uk/GTI%20-%20Phase%201%20report%20Executive%20Summary.pdf* (accessed January 2022).

Grindrod, J., 2013. *Concretopia: A Journey around the Rebuilding of Postwar Britain*. Brecon: Old Street Publishing.

Grylls, G., 2021. 'Jenrick wants beautiful new housing on leafy streets', *Times*, 20 July 2021, 17.

Hall, W., 2015. *Brick*. London: Phaidon.

Harrabin, R., 2021. 'Construction companies told to stop knocking down buildings', BBC News, 21 September 2021. *www.bbc.co.uk/news/science-environment-58667328* (accessed 22 January 2022).

Hennebury, D. L. C., 2014. 'An Investigation of the Architectural, Urban, and Exhibit Designs of the Tate Museums' (Unpublished PhD thesis, University of Michigan).

Hetherington, P., 1984. 'Liverpool's political bulldozers take aim on the slums', *Guardian*, 7 August 1984, 4.

Hertford, H., 1956. 'The home of 2056 AD', *Liverpool Echo*, 9 July 1956, 6.

Huppatz, D. J., 2019. 'Brutalism: How to love a concrete beast', *The Conversation*, 2 September 2019. *https://theconversation.com/brutalism-how-to-love-a-concrete-beast-122469* (accessed 9 May 2022).

Hynes, C., 2019. *Brick: A Social History*. Cheltenham: History Press.

Imperial War Museum, n.d. *The Liverpool Blitz*. *www.iwm.org.uk/history/the-liverpool-blitz* (accessed 29 May 2022).

Ingold, T., 2007. 'Materials against materiality', *Archaeological Dialogues*, 14(1), 1–16.

Ingold, T., 2013. *Making: Anthropology, Archaeology, Art and Architecture*. London: Routledge.

Jankovic, L., 2022. 'Radical overhaul of construction needed', *The Conversation*, 20 January 2022. *https://theconversation.com/radical-*

overhaul-of-construction-industry-needed-if-uk-to-have-any-chance-of-net-zero-by-2050-new-research-171280 (accessed 22 January 2022).

Jencks, C. A., 1984. *The Language of Post-Modern Architecture*. New York NY: Rizzoli.

Jenkins, S., 1987. 'Art makes a return to architecture', *Sunday Times*, 15 November 1987, 33.

Jenrick, R., 2021. 'Vision of planning policy that puts communities in the driving seat', *Times*, 20 July 2021. *www.thetimes.co.uk/article/vision-of-planning-policy-that-puts-communities-in-the-driving-seat-sgnqql9zl* (accessed 23 January 2022).

Keay, L. H., 1935a. 'Housing by the Local Authority', in *Liverpool and the Housing Problem*. Liverpool: Liverpool Council of Social Service, pp. 28–9.

Keay, L. H., 1935b. 'Working-class flats', *The Builder*, April 1935, 628–49.

Kern, L., 2020. *Feminist City: Claiming Space in a Man-Made World*. London: Verso.

Latour, B., 2004. 'Why has critique run out of steam? From matters of fact to matters of concern', *Critical Inquiry*, 30(2), 225–48.

Latour, B., 2005. *Reassembling the Social: An Introduction to Actor-Network-Theory*. Oxford: Oxford University Press.

Lawrence, J., and Sutcliffe-Braithwaite, F., 2012. 'Margaret Thatcher and the decline of class politics', in *Making Thatcher's Britain*, ed. B. Jackson and R. Saunders. Cambridge: Cambridge University Press, pp. 132–47.

LCC, 1954. *Multistorey Housing in the USA: Report of City of Liverpool Housing Deputation*. LRO 728.22 HOU.

LCC, 1958. *Everton Heights Redevelopment Areas: Report of the City Architect and Director of Housing*, 27 June 1958, p. 7 LRO 711 HOU

LCC, 1962. *The Construction of Dwellings by Industrial Methods: Report on a Visit by a Deputation of the City Council to Paris and Environs*. LRO 728.22 HOU.

LCC, 1985. 'Homes for the people', *Liverpool News*, February 1985, 8. Militant Collection, Modern Record Centre, University of Warwick, 601/P/2/2/1.

LCC, c.1987. *Urban Regeneration Strategy*. LRO 711.40942753 COU.

McDonald, A., 1986. *The Weller Way: The Story of the Weller Street Housing Cooperative*. London: Faber and Faber.

Mirror, 1975. 'Homes that tell on your sex life', *Daily Mirror*, 4 August 1975, 7.

Moran, J., 2004. 'Housing, memory and everyday life in contemporary Britain', *Cultural Studies*, 18(4), 607–27.

Nettleton, S., Martin, D., Buse, C., and Prior, L., 2020. 'Materializing architecture for social care: Brick walls and compromises in design for later life', *British Journal of Sociology*, 71(1), 153–67.

Newby, F., 2001. 'The innovative uses of concrete by engineers and architects', in *Historic Concrete: Background to Appraisal*, ed. J. Sutherland, D. Humm and M. Chrimes. London: Thomas Telford, pp. 11–44.

Ortolano, G., 2019. *Thatcher's Progress: From Social Democracy to Market Liberalism through an English New Town*. Cambridge: Cambridge University Press.

Pevsner, N., Pollard, R., and Sharples. J. (eds), 2006. *Lancashire: Liverpool and the South-West*. London: Yale University Press.

Pooley, C. G., and Irish, S., 1987. 'Access to housing on Merseyside, 1919–39', *Transactions of the Institute of British Geographers*, 12(2), 177–90.

Post, 1945. 'Liverpool housing experiments', *Liverpool Daily Post*, 2 February 1945, 3.

Powers, A., 2007. *Modern Architectures in History: Britain*. London: Reaktion Books.

Proctor, R., 2014. 'Uncertainty and the modern church: Two Roman cathedrals in Britain', in *Sanctioning Modernism: Architecture and the Making of Postwar Identities*, ed. V. Kuli, T. Parker and M. Penick. Austin TX: University of Texas Press, pp. 113–38.

Reas, P., 1993. 'Flogging a dead horse'. *www.paulreas.com/portfolio-1/project-two-pa8ag* (accessed 24 December 2021).

Richmond, P., 2001. *Marketing Modernisms: The Architecture and Influence of Charles Reilly*. Liverpool: Liverpool University Press.

Samuel, R., 1996. *Theatres of Memory 1: Past and Present in Contemporary Society*. London: Verso.

Saumarez Smith, O., 2019. *Boom Cities: Architect-Planners and the Politics of Radical Urban Renewal in 1960s Britain*. Oxford: Oxford University Press.

Scott, P., 2020. 'Friends in high places: Government-Industry relations in public sector house-building during Britain's tower block era', *Business History*, 62(4), 545–65.

Shankland, G., 1964. 'The central area of Liverpool: Extracts from the report on the draft city centre map', *Town Planning Review*, 35(2), 105 L.32.

Simon, E. D., 1945. *Rebuilding Britain: A Twenty-Year Plan*. London: Victor Gollancz.

Sofian, T., Sudradjat I., and Tedj, B., 2020. 'Materiality and sensibility: Phenomenological studies of brick as architectural material', *Nakhara: Journal of Environmental Design and Planning*, 18, 1–10.

Spence, P., 1974. *Report on Work with Liverpool Personal Service Society with the Citizens Advice Bureau Van at Netherley, September 1973–June 1974*. LRO 352 NET/1/1.

Stirling, J., 1960. '"The functional tradition" and expression', *Perspecta*, 88–97.

Sugg Ryan, D., 2018. *Ideal Homes: Uncovering the History and Design of the Interwar House*. Manchester: Manchester University Press.

Taaffe, P., and Mulhearn, T., 1988. *Liverpool: A City That Dared to Fight*. London: Fortress Books.

Tbsubaki, T., 2000. 'Planners and the public: British popular opinion on housing during the Second World War', *Contemporary British History*, 14(1), 81–98.

Thompson, M., 2020. *Reconstructing Public Housing: Liverpool's Hidden History of Collective Alternatives*. Liverpool: Liverpool University Press.

Unwin, S., 2014. *Analysing Architecture: The Universal Language of Place-Making*. Abingdon: Routledge.

Urban, F., 2012. *Tower and Slab: Histories of Global Mass Housing*. Abingdon: Routledge.

Vale, B., 2005. *Prefabs: A History of the UK Temporary Housing Programme*. London: E. and F. Spon.

Wall, C., 2013. *An Architecture of Parts: Architects, Building Workers and Industrialisation, 1940–1970*. Abingdon: Routledge.

Walsh, K., 1996. *The Representation of the Past: Museums and Heritage in a Post-Modern World*. London: Routledge.

Wates, N., 1982. 'Community architecture: The Liverpool breakthrough', *Architects' Journal*, 8 September 1982, 57.

Watts, J., 2019. 'Concrete: The most destructive material on Earth', *Guardian*, 25 February 2019. *www.theguardian.com/cities/2019/feb/25/concrete-the-most-destructive-material-on-earth* (accessed 23 January 2022).

Weston, A., and Bona, E., 2021. 'Legoland estate which went from dream to nightmare', *Liverpool Echo*, 30 August 2021. *www.liverpoolecho.co.uk/news/liverpool-news/legoland-estate-went-dream-nightmare-21423036* (accessed 24 January 2022).

Whittington-Egan, R., 1976. 'How they turned the city of my dreams into a concrete nightmare,' *Liverpool Echo*, 2 August 1976, 6.

Whyte, W., 2015. *Redbrick: A Social and Architectural History of Britain's Civic Universities*. Oxford: Oxford University Press.

Williams, R., 2004. *The Anxious City: English Urbanism in the Late Twentieth Century*. London: Routledge.

Young, J., 1993. 'Community spirit conquers despair', *Times*, 29 December 1993, 14.

Zukin, S., 1989. *Loft Living: Culture and Capital in Urban Change*. New Brunswick NJ: Rutgers University Press.

7 PLASTIC EARTH

Somatic Correspondences with Legacy Contaminants in Archaeology and Anthropology

Eloise Govier

To correspond with things we must carry on in their midst.
(Ingold 2017b, 116)

Introduction

Anthropologist Tim Ingold describes how landscapes 'emerge as condensations or crystallizations of activity within a relational field'; the landscape is not simply a passive form fashioned by human cognition and movement, but 'woven into life, and lives are woven into landscape' (2004, 333). The ideas outlined in this chapter are inspired by a litter-picking trip to the Sea Mills floodplain (Bristol),[1] a landscape that reveals the lives entwined in its emergence. From a 'vital materialist' perspective (Bennett 2010a; 2010b), the floodplain is riddled with intra-actions and evidences potent 'waste' movements; every seasonal rise in the river and every human who litters, mounds of plastics (like molehills) appear across the floodplain. Alarmingly, the plastic layer of strata forming on the floodplain is emerging and becoming earth (cf. Ingold 2013, 77). This chapter explores the capacities of plastics in earthy contexts and the legacies that these intra-actions create. By thinking through agential realism theory and contemporary archaeological events, I unpack somatic correspondences between humans – as 'multi-celled prokaryotes' (see Reno 2014) – and plastics, to explore anthropological and archaeological approaches to the sensuous and evocative experiences of these contemporary phenomena. I propose that somatic correspondence focuses on mapping the emerging relationship between bodies as they interact, this contrasts with forms of analysis that examine embodied or incorporated practices where the human body is the locus of the analyst's attention (see Connerton 1989; Tilley 1994). Somatic correspondence offers a post-human starting point to account for bodily engagement, and these bodies can be animal, human, mineral, inorganic, geological and so on. Our co-existing, co-beings are bodies that engage and interact with the phenomenal world with or without us human beings. I will begin my chapter by outlining my autoethnographic experience of a litter-picking walk at Sea Mills, Bristol.

Walking the Floodplain

Setting out to walk the floodplain the pace of the group of walkers split; dynamics in the group shifted as individuals and groups of walkers headed out across the long grass. Some abided by frequented walkways, others bravely headed to the riverbank edge. The experience recalled Ingold and Vergunst's distinction between the act of 'setting out' as different from the rhythmic activity of walking; the latter takes many steps and a loss of self-conscious footing before the open-stride of a walk is achieved (2008, 3). Due to the potential presence of hidden entities in the floodplain grass and the various intra-activities scattered across the floodplain, my walk did not move beyond the first 'tentative steps' of those 'setting out'; the macro-lens that enables the appreciation of the 'expansive vista' came fleetingly into focus, but it was the immediacy of the abandoned (and potentially dangerous) things afoot that kept my pace and tread slow, methodical, self-aware (Ingold and Vergunst 2008, 3).

While walking along the grassy floodplain the material remains and activities of the different floodplain dwellers and inhabitants emerged into view; a can of cider lay abandoned on a flattened area of grass; a lump of burnt wood with matted grass circling it signified the human agents who had warmed themselves by an open-air fire. Elsewhere, two snails, defying gravity, clung to the glossy surface of a faded and graffitied road sign. The rear of a television protruded from a tangle of grass; a basket sat embedded in the restrictive grip of organic matter that entangled the plastic entity in its grasp. Clearly, the floodplain housed several different user groups and evidenced the abandoned surplus of their activities along with other entities entangled with the flow of the river. Unlike the lost ball of a distracted dog (and human), cumbersome materials (such as televisions and house piping) also emerged on the floodplain; the abandonment of these displaced entities created intrigue among the litter pickers who were curious of the stories that led to their appearance on the floodplain.

Despite the floodplain being a green space of scenic viridescent beauty, with river life thriving in many places along the Avon, the material activities evident at the place resonated with Tim Edensor's (2005) discussion of debris found at sites of industrial ruin. Edensor argues that an integral part of the movement of 'waste' is its subsequent invisibility and that this is why many rubbish dumps and recycling units are off limits to the public (Edensor 2005, 316). He argues that waste removal needs to be a 'seamless' movement in order to keep consumerist desires burning (Edensor 2005, 316); Bennett (2010a, 5) describes this movement as a 'hyperconsumptive necessity' to junk commodities. Sites of urban ruins invert these processes as they are places where 'rubbish lingers on' (Edensor 2005, 316). This seems also true of the Sea Mills floodplain and indeed other places where litter often acts as a magnet to other waste. These emergent ruins puncture bridal paths, footpaths and other areas of 'natural' beauty.

On the litter walk, I found myself guided by the trails of flattened grass that delineated useful, well-trod paths; weary of ticks and sharp objects, my hyper-attentive focus was on finding litter and remaining unscathed. At one point, I rejoined a small group of the litter pickers who had halted their activities around a plastic bottle that was embedded in the ground. A parting in the grass and repeated footfall had caused a muddy patch in-among the grass, revealing the earthy matter that anchored the grassy blanket that surrounded us. I pulled my phone out of my pocket and filmed a researcher's booted foot that was placed halfway across the body of a clear plastic drink bottle that lay on its side, embedded firmly in the soil. The researcher rocked their foot across the surface of the bottle demonstrating to the group the unnerving squeaking and crackling sound it caused. On this occasion, the worn-away grass had permitted clear visibility of the entity responsible for the noise. The prospect of knowing the layer of litter forming and becoming the floodplain beneath us through sound and feel-under-foot rather than sight became a pressing observation. The idea that the plastic bottle somatically corresponded with the unsuspecting moving human body in this fashion altered my perception of the body of earth that lay beneath me. Ingold problematises the division between the earth and mound; the mound, he argues, 'does not rest on the earth' (Ingold 2013, 76), it is 'on and of' the earth (Ingold 2013, 82). He reminds us '[t]oday's deposit becomes tomorrow's substrate, buried under later sediment. Like the compost heap or ant's nest, the mound, we could say, is becoming earth' (Ingold 2013, 77). In the context of the floodplain, the rambler often becomes aware of the plastic from the sound and feel of the plastic crunching underfoot. Not all will excavate the plastic and recycle it, as we did. Those who fail to release the plastic from the earthy grip of the floodplain play their small role in the formation of the landscape; their footsteps further root the plastic into the earth ensuring its fixture in the formation of the landscape. On this matter, archaeologist Matt Edgeworth (2018) notes that in some contexts:

> plastic objects stand a good chance of being fossilised – a process whereby the hard material may decay or dissolve, but its exterior form survives as a mould which then gets filled with other minerals and becomes a cast of the original object [becoming] traces in the ground not just for a few hundred years, but for millions of years.

The prospect of the 'Pompeii plastic' phenomenon is an insight too troublesome to ignore. In the next section, I explore research focused on the legacy contaminant and how plastic archaeology provides further light on the deposition practices that inform the emergence of plastic earth.

Legacy Contaminants: Plastic Archaeology

Plastic contaminants, particularly in the context of the water as marine and riverine waste, are a 'legacy contaminant' with an emerging (and potent) vital materialism with a developing impact that is amassing with time (Thompson quoted in Katsnelson 2015, 5548; see Rathje and Murphy 2001; Thompson et al. 2004, Woodall et al. 2014). Jambeck et al. (2015) carried out a study of 192 coastal countries in the world to estimate the amount of plastic entering the water in 2010 and to anticipate figures for 2025 if no adaptations to current practices are carried out. The researchers took into account population figures of those living within the coastline (50 kilometres in range of the sea) in relation to the mass of waste generated per capita, the percentage of this waste that was plastic, and the percentage of plastic waste that is mismanaged (therefore has the potential to enter the sea due to location in the coastline); these figures were collated to anticipate the percentage of plastic waste entering the sea (2015, 768). According to their study, the United Kingdom generated 9,253,293 kilograms (kg) of plastic waste per day with 185,066kg of plastic waste littered per day (Jambeck et al. 2015). The United Kingdom contributed an estimated 67,549 tonnes of mismanaged plastic waste into the water in 2010 (Jambeck et al. 2015). How the plastic moves from land to sea is an important area of research; Lechner et al. (2014) criticised the lack of figures for plastic in rivers and conducted a two-year study into the flow of plastic down the Danube. In the study rivers are simultaneously presented as 'pathways' (Lechner et al. 2014, 176) that enable 'plastic flow from rivers to oceans' but also (more agentively) as transporters (2014, 176).

From a pathway to a transporter; how we envisage the role of the river is integral to how we formulate strategic interventions with the entity. As a transporter, the river is conceptualised as an agent moving waste regardless of human intention. Equally, the river interacts with plastic; welcoming, encasing and moving the material across borders. Plastic and water have a special relationship; one that evolves with time and is influenced by the presence of other somatic correspondents (such as light). Initially the plastic is carried by the water, it is an agent whose momentum is in direct correspondence with the power of the water; after some time the plastic breaks down (due to correspondence with sunlight) and the physical changes in the plastic formulate new correspondences offering different modes of engagement (see Zhu et al. 2020). Some microplastics, for example, enter the fleshy body of the oyster or mussel (van Cauwenberghe and Janssen 2014, 65); in doing so the microplastics can enter the food-chain and re-emerge on land. Disconcertingly, Lechner et al. (2014, 180) found that 'plastic is the dominant debris in the Black Sea', and in both years of study (2010, 2012) 'more plastic items than fish larvae were drifting in the Danube' (Lechner et al. 2014, 179). However, there is a spectrum of plastics in circulation, and all are in different states of decomposition; the hard-to-see microplastics entering the food-chain are not the only means by which plastics become land-dwelling entities again.

Ingold notes how the sea '[swallows up] things of human manufacture and – after varying lengths of time – [spits] them up again' (Ingold 2017b, 17). Similarly, Schofield et al. (2021) spotlight the necropsy of a green sea turtle recovered from the Queensland coast, Australia, by Smith and Townsend and show how edible-sized plastics, partially decomposed, were found in the belly of the turtle (Schofield et al. 2021, 443). Plastics have a habit of resurfacing, perhaps this is due to the sheer abundance of the stuff that has been unleashed into the world (see Geyer et al. 2017; Schofield et al. 2021). Thus, as legacy contaminants, plastics move between earth and water, causing pollution – they are 'signatures' and intra-acting agents of the 'Plastic Age' (Mytum and Meek 2021).

The floodplain evidences different waste movement streams: waste that may be purposefully dumped by human agents (fly-tipped, litter) and waste whose trajectory is guided by the agency of the river (to name but two channels). Archaeological studies that attend to plastic litter invariably account for cultural and natural agencies; Carpenter and Wolverton (2017, 95) utilised behavioural archaeology and distinctions between cultural transforms and natural transforms to infer the waste movements and different types of littering behaviour. The study allowed the researchers to identify areas that were particularly 'vulnerable' to directly enacted litter-dropping and sites that become sources for stream pollution (Carpenter and Wolverton 2017, 99). Typologies of plastics have been utilised in the study of the substance, one study categorised plastic via function (e.g., beverage container, bag, etc.) to develop 'litter profiles' for various sites (Carpenter and Wolverton 2017, 96). Another study organised wrappers by colour, and assemblages were subdivided to artefact types where possible (e.g., tags, containers, bottle caps and rings, straws, straw wrappers, apple stickers, other food-related items, and so on) (Mytum and Meek 2021, 205). One study utilised 'object narratives' in connection to plastic artefacts collected from local beaches in Galápagos (Schofield et al. 2020, 230); another focused specifically on single-use PPE connected to the COVID-19 pandemic, highlighting how social media can be used as a *source* of archaeological data to chart flows of single-use gloves (material culture) on beaches and discarded on New York streets via hashtags and social media accounts (Schofield et al. 2021, 440).

While the presence of plastics in sedimentary deposits is on the rise (Schofield et al. 2021, 437), there is a keen awareness around the presence of plastics in the earth – actively becoming earth. In a recent excavation in Wales, archaeologists were taken aback by the 2,000 pieces of plastic that emerged from an excavation of two experimentally built roundhouses at Castell Henllys Iron Age fort (Mytum and Meek 2021). The study offered insight into how contemporary archaeologists apply their methodologies to the analysis of plastic litter. One issue being the inevitability of identifying plastics as fragments rather than whole artefacts, the difficulty being that subtypes of plastics, such as clingfilm, plastic sheeting and sweet and straw wrappers, are difficult to re-assemble in terms of original plastic or plasticised items (Mytum and Meek 2021, 204).

Archaeological studies tell us, therefore, that plastic is resilient (Schofield et al. 2021, 436), that visibility conditions and witnessing litter deposition correlates directly to littering (the harder it is to see the act the more likely it is to happen) (Mytum and Meek 2021), and that once litter enters riverine and marine contexts deposition activities become harder to define (Carpenter and Wolverton 2017, 100). Inevitably, plastics are entwined with human behaviours. However, the binary style of analysis presented by cultural and natural transforms is perhaps unhelpful. Similarly problematic, is research that focuses on the agencies of human and environmental forces such as rivers and wind, primarily because they isolate humans from the environment. Therefore, my contribution to the methodologies currently in circulation that address plastic archaeology is to suggest a Baradian approach to causality and agency (Barad 2007). Barad's concept challenges thingification and analyses entities in-phenomena, thus breaching the binary presented by cultural/natural transform analysis (see Govier and Steel 2021). Barad (2007, 214) writes:

> [c]auses are not forces that act on the phenomenon from outside. Nor should causes be construed as a unilateral movement from cause to effect. Rather, the 'causes' and 'effects' emerge through intra-action.

Intra-action is a term used by Barad to denote a primary unit of reality; she argues that things emerge in-phenomena and that the articulation of individual entities is a form of dissection, one that arbitrarily cuts the entity from the context of its emergence. She places the analyst in relation to the emergence of the phenomena – that being an enactment where agency (and causality) is produced relationally (Barad 2007). Therefore, by recognising agency and causality in-phenomena, Barad's agential realism offers a theoretical position that has the potential to take archaeological concepts beyond the issue of representationalism and anthropocentrism (in addition to Cartesian bifurcation), because the theory recognises the role of the analyst – and the vitality of matter – in the production of knowledge (Barad 2003; 2007, 214; see Marshall and Alberti 2014). Thus, while plastic is a human-made problem, the agencies that emerge and influence the story of the plastics tend to emerge in relationship; like the grassy grip on the plastic basket: causality and agency emerge from the entanglement of basket-grass-earth-human rather than held by an individual agent (see Barad 2007), and these 'somatic correspondences' are singular iterations in the emergence of the plastic basket. In an attempt to reimagine the types of relationships formed between plastics and humans, in the next section I will outline somatic correspondences for the reader.

Somatic Correspondences and Archaeology

I use the term 'correspondence' in the Ingoldian sense of the concept (2017a; 2017b); he prefers the term over 'interaction' and uses it to describe being 'with' (Ingold 2013, 105). Ingold (2017b, 41) argues that correspondence is about 'togethering' and focuses on the 'in-betweenness' rather than 'between-ness'. He writes:

> In correspondence, movement and relating are effectively the same thing, insofar as the movement is responsive to other movements with which it goes along (as in musical polyphony). They are the same precisely because movement is not embodied but animate. (2017b, 118)

> A correspondence is rather like a relay, in which each participant takes it in turns to pick up the baton and carry it forward, while others remain temporarily quiescent, awaiting their turn … It

> simply carries on ... the lines of correspondence are lines of feeling, of sentience. (Ingold 2013, 105)

Artists, archaeologists, anthropologists and other practitioners who actively engage with materials, tend to be the thinking folk that actively correspond with materials through sensuous engagement. Artists take the time to get to know the material, to work with the material, to train with the material (on craft practices, see Marchand 2016); nonetheless, historically their endeavours are often framed under the allusion of human exceptionalism (in relation to other species see Haraway 2003; 2008); from Brunelleschi to Francis Bacon, careers are built and celebrated on the basis of the artist's mastery of the material.

Archaeologists also correspond with materials and build theoretical and methodological frameworks in order to analyse and interpret the materials they unveil from the earth, they understand the touch and smell of the material, and have developed methods to 'read' and understand the material (such as changes in soil colour) through sensuous engagement. Archaeologists are sensitive to changes in the material. Tilley (1994, 10) writes:

> A centred and meaningful space involves specific sets of linkages between the physical space of the non-humanly created world, somatic states of the body, the mental space of cognition and representation and the space of movement, encounter and interaction between persons and between persons and the human and non-human environment. Socially produced space combines the cognitive, the physical and the emotional into something that may be reproduced but is always open to transformation and change.

Within archaeology, post-processualists are interested in the 'embodied subject'; the 'social subjects, thinking and plotting agents who work their way through society and history seeking goals, constantly sending out signals and signs, constantly interpreting the cultural signification around them' (Shanks 2008, 136). Tilley's phenomenological approach utilises the body as a thinking tool to interact with material culture and the landscape (Thomas 2006, 55). Thomas explains that this is a valuable experience because it produces 'an understanding in the present which stands as an analogy or allegory for those of the past' (Thomas 2006, 55). Thus, the phenomenological position has always fore-fronted the 'experiential dimensions' of material culture, and considered how built environments enable or impede human experience (Thomas 2006, 55).

Ingold, however, notes that movement is animate, not embodied, and argues that '"embodied movement" sounds like a contradiction in terms' (Ingold 2017b, 118). In certain forms of contemporary dance, for example, movement is curated to share specific ideas and feelings, and the practised dance movements are embodied movements. Ingold notes that 'movement and relating are effectively the same thing' in correspondence (Ingold 2017b, 118). Rather than furthering the embodied subject of the phenomenological tradition, here I wish to continue with Ingold's call for correspondence; namely, his observation that correspondence as animate movement that breaks with the causal model of agency as cause and movement as effect. Instead, Ingold recognises that 'the body moves and is moved not because it is driven by some internal agency, wrapped in the package, but because as fast as it is gathering ... it is forever unravelling' (Ingold 2017b, 39).

Archaeological phenomenologists have utilised the body as a starting point for engaging with past experiences. It is the somatic quality of this correspondence that I specifically respond to in this chapter, hence my use of the term 'somatic correspondence' to explore the legacy contaminants becoming earth on a Bristol floodplain. Arts and crafts, like dance, are practices that are often built on a refined form of somatic correspondence with materials (to the degree that the actions are embodied); nonetheless, physically engaging with materials through walking, looking, smelling and hearing could also be considered types of somatic correspondence, these moments are when bodies collide and get to know each other. 'Somatic' relates to the body and is used to differentiate from soul, spirit and mind. Therefore, the focus on somatic correspondence is on the physicality of bodily engagement. Importantly, this need not be human-focused. Elsewhere, theoretical techniques such as the object biography, ethnoarchaeology, cognitive archaeology and material agency have formatted analyses to incorporate materials in line with ontologies that engage with materials in terms of the cognitive processes embedded in their emergence or even the spatio-temporality of human consciousness (see Gell 1998; Gosden and Marshall 1999; Malafouris 2008; Wendrich 2013). Somatic correspondences are focused on bodily engagement, and as moving bodies include animals, things and so on, humans need not form part of every equation; therefore, it is a style of analysis that accommodates post-human contexts.

Within the riverine and marine context, 'biofouling' (described as the occurrence of 'colonies of marine life on the object's surface') is a time signature for the potential length of time that somatic correspondence has occurred between the plastics and the marine environment (Schofield et al. 2020, 237). The presence of biofouling on plastics is an iteration that could only occur in the Plastic Age. The movement of plastics in aquatic environments, both vertically and horizontally through the water, is informed by environmental conditions and the properties of the plastic (Schwarz et al. 2019, 95). The higher the exposed surface area, the higher the rate of biofouling; therefore, biofouling increases the density of plastics (Schwarz et al. 2019, 95). High temperatures and rich levels of nutrients will also encourage a higher rate of biofouling (Schwarz et al. 2019, 95). A higher rate of sedimentation is found in plastics with a high surface area (Schwarz et al. 2019, 95); nonetheless, biofouling will also change the density of low-density plastics and also ensure their presence in ocean sediments (Schwarz et al. 2019, 97). Conversely, in deep water conditions, increases in acidity could have an impact on the carbonates and opal causing the accumulation of organisms to dissolve; similarly, the lack of irradiance in deep water might negatively impact on the epiphytic organisms causing a decline in their numbers (Kaiser et al. 2017, 8). Both these shifts could cause 'defouling', leading to a shift in density and causing the microplastics (specifically low-density plastics) to re-submerge from the sediment – even float to the surface (Kaiser et al. 2017, 8; Schwarz et al. 2019, 95). Thus, we see the potential for a cycle of movement along the vertical column, where microplastics oscillate between sediment and water surface (Kaiser et al. 2017, 8). This movement recalls Ingold's (2017b) correspondence as a 'gathering' and 'unravelling' of bodies and captures the somatic correspondences that are at the heart of this chapter. In river contexts, plastic can be retained in the sediment (Schwarz et al. 2019, 97).

Biofouling and defouling are of archaeological concern, the attachment of micro-organisms to historic buildings, for example, can create 'stains' and 'patinas' that deteriorate the 'aesthetic' and mechanical aspects of historic and archaeological buildings and artefacts (Graziani and Quagliarini 2018, 1). Studies have addressed the nuances between materiality, such as stone, brick, concrete, mortar, and have made correlations between properties such as porosity and roughness and the adhesion of micro-organisms (Graziani and Quagliarini 2018, 1; Quagliarini et al. 2022). However, there is a distinction to be made between bodies of microplastics that are hard to see, bodies of archaeological buildings, artefacts and sites that have the hyper-focus of the archaeological discipline and heritage sector, and bodies of litter, and how these bodies uniquely trigger human concern.

Edensor (2005) describes the power of abandoned things lying in an industrial ruin to trigger responses in human agents who bend down to pick up and examine. Edensor notes '[t]he differently performing body, acting contingently in these unfamiliar surroundings, is not merely reactive to the effusion of sensory affordances but also actively engages with the things it beholds' (Edensor 2005, 326). This point resonated with my experience at the floodplain when the litter pickers gathered around a wooden human-made form evidently removed from a panelled room. Isolated, abandoned, and set among the green matter, the painted wooden plinth encouraged discussion among the litter pickers. While we debated the potential use of the thing, the body of the rotten wood slowly became alive with movement; an army of small insects scurrying among the wooden fibre indicated that it had already been colonised and housed an ecological system in full swing. Bennett cites Sullivan's evocative description of the 'black ooze trickling down the slopes' of a New Jersey rubbish site (2010a, 6) to emphasise the vitality of waste. Sullivan reminds us of the 'billions of microscopic organisms' inhabiting the garbage mounds; the waste mounds are nothing less than 'alive' (Sullivan 1998 cited in Bennett 2010a, 6). Reading with Ingold, we could envisage the insects, wood and humans as a gathering of threads – an entanglement of life: 'a knot whose constituent threads, far from being contained within it, trail beyond, only to become caught with other threads in other knots' (Ingold 2010, 3). Removed from the domestic environment, the wooden entity had formed alliances with other materials and insects, the phenomena would be difficult for human agents to compromise. The object had become heavy as it had soaked-up rain and river water and parts of the wood were splintering and rotten from the changes in temperature and humidity. Paint had peeled in areas, and other areas had turned black as it transformed from treated to rotten wood. Splinters protruded, nails were rusted and dislodged. Areas of the artefact revealed the interior structure of the body of wood; through somatic correspondence with the piece, its fragility became heightened, breaking-apart in places.

The transition from thing to object to artefact correlated directly with the researchers' increasing engagement with the thing (see Knappett 2010). Somatic correspondence with the entity through haptic channels was stalled and eventually abandoned; fleshy human hands would yield to splinters, and human bodies could become compromised by rusty nails and unseemly bacterial agents. These elements made it a challenging thing for the human agents to colonise. Edensor (2005, 311) explores 'non-human intervention' and argues that: '[as c]o-participants in the making of the world, animals and plants are always waiting in the wings, ready to transform familiar material environments at the slightest opportunity' (Edensor 2005, 319). This statement resonated with the material trails created by the floodplain dwellers. However, as the previous discussion of the wooden plinth revealed, the floodplain animals and plants did not discriminate between on stage and off stage, irrespective of human presence – grass, snails, ticks, mice, fungi, water, cider can, ants and so on, as co-participants, form worlds with or without us humans. Bennett argues:

> [I]f environmentalism leads to the call for the protection and wise management of an ecosystem that surrounds us, a vital materialism suggests that the task is to engage more strategically with a trenchant materiality that is us as it vies with us. (2010a, 111)

At the floodplain, the (sliced-open) cider can, with its metallic interior on display, rocked gently in the wind, somatically corresponding with the sun, re-iterating spasmodic light. Like the 'Glove, pollen, rat, cap, stick' assemblage that Bennett notices in a storm-drain grate in Baltimore, the cider can similarly 'stopped me in my tracks' (Bennett 2010a, 6) and issued 'a call' (Bennett 2010a, 4). In the context of the floodplain, the cider can was a vital materialism that I somatically corresponded with, I interrupted its existence on the floodplain, rehousing it in my litter-picking bag, and shifted its trajectory to a recycling facility. The River Avon lay as a constant backdrop to our walk; unwatched, the microplastics continued to somatically correspond in the riverine context, some actively contributing to sedimentation others moving out to sea. Their anticipated presence remains an earthy matter of concern.

Conclusion

Jambeck et al. (2015) argue that the rise in synthetic plastics warrants a 'paradigm shift'. The aim of this chapter was to reveal the 'vitality of materials' (Bennett 2010a, 5) on the floodplain and consider how these somatic correspondences play out between floodplain, ocean, household and bodies (be it snail and road sign, oyster or human). While vital materialists are attuned to the power of things, they are also keen to blur the boundary between themselves and those things (Bennett 2010a, 112). Reno (2014, 25) argues that as we are:

> multi-celled prokaryotes we have the ability to fully digest the other life forms ... This digestion is complete not because we completely break these pieces down, but because we retain our integrity as consumer, something that the thing we've swallowed gradually loses.

This biology lesson may reaffirm the power of being a consumer, but it also raises questions. How powerful is the consumer when somatically corresponding with gases, viruses and microplastics? How much integrity do humans have if the things they consume, like the Danube, are riddled with microplastics? How unimpaired and uncorrupted do human bodies emerge from such consumption? Archaeology is making critical steps in the field of plastic pollution by developing innovative, multidisciplinary methodologies to deal with the legacy contaminant in a bid to alter the troubling trajectory that our unwavering relationship with plastics appears to have committed us to. In this chapter, I have argued the case for understanding the relationship between plastics and humans in terms of phenomena and considered the agency and causality that emerges from somatic correspondences between the two entities, in order to reimagine the contemporary reality of plastics becoming earth.

Acknowledgements

I would like to thank Dr Jill Payne for reading an early draft of this chapter and offering insightful feedback. I would also like to thank the Arts and Humanities Research Council (AHRC) *Power and the Water Connecting Pasts and Futures* research team for welcoming me onto project activities. This chapter is the result of my own research, all errors are my own.

Note

1. The litter pick was co-ordinated by the AHRC Power and the Water Connecting Pasts and Futures research group.

References

Barad, K., 2003. 'Posthumanist performativity: Toward an understanding of how matter comes to matter', *Signs: Journal of Women in Culture and Society*, 28(3), 801–31.

Barad, K., 2007. *Meeting the Universe Halfway: Quantum Physics and the Entanglement of Matter and Meaning*. Durham NC and London: Duke University Press.

Bennett, J., 2010a. *Vibrant Matter: Toward a Political Ecology of Things*. Durham NC and London: Duke University Press.

Bennett, J., 2010b. 'A vitalist stopover on the way to a new materialism', in *New Materialisms: Ontology, Agency, and Politics*, ed. D. Coole and S. Frost. Durham NC and London: Duke University Press, pp. 47–69.

Carpenter, E., and Wolverton, S., 2017. 'Plastic litter in streams: The behavioral archaeology of a pervasive environmental problem', *Applied Geography*, 84, 93–101.

Connerton, P., 1989. *How Societies Remember*. Cambridge: Cambridge University Press.

Edensor, T., 2005. 'Waste matter: The debris of industrial ruins and the disordering of the material world', *Journal of Material Culture*, 10(3), 311–32.

Edgeworth, M., 2018. 'Plastic is now part of our planet's fabric – a scientist and archaeologist discuss what happens next'.

https://theconversation.com/plastic-is-now-part-of-our-planets-fabric-a-scientist-and-archaeologist-discuss-what-happens-next-106019 (accessed 7 June 2021).

Gell, A., 1998. *Art and Agency: An Anthropological Theory*. Oxford: Clarendon Press.

Geyer, R., Jambeck, J., and Law, K., 2017. 'Production, use, and fate of all plastics ever made', *Science Advances*, 3(7), 11015.

Gosden, C., and Marshall, Y., 1999. 'The cultural biography of objects', *World Archaeology*, 31(2), 169–78.

Govier, E., and Steel, L., 2021. 'Beyond the "thingification" of worlds: Archaeology and the New Materialisms', *Journal of Material Culture*, 26(3), 298–317. *https://doi.org/10.1177/13591835211025559*.

Graziani, L., and Quagliarini, E., 2018. 'On the modelling of algal biofouling growth on nano-TiO2 coated and uncoated limestones and sandstones', *Coatings*, 8(54), 1–13.

Haraway, D., 2003. *The Companion Species Manifesto – Dogs, People, and Significant Otherness*. Chicago IL: Prickly Paradigm Press.

Haraway, D., 2008. *When Species Meet*. Minneapolis MN and London: University of Minnesota Press.

Ingold, T., 2004. 'Culture on the ground. The world perceived through the feet', *Journal of Material Culture*, 9(3), 315–40.

Ingold, T., 2010. 'Bringing Things to Life: Creative Entanglements in a World of Materials'. *ESRC National Centre for Research Methods NCRM Working Paper Series 05/10*. *https://hummedia.manchester.ac.uk/schools/soss/morgancentre/research/wps/15-2010-07-realities-bringing-things-to-life.pdf* (accessed 21 May 2022).

Ingold. T., 2013. *Making: Anthropology, Archaeology, Art and Architecture*. Oxford: Routledge.

Ingold, T., 2017a. 'On human correspondence', *The Journal of the Royal Anthropological Institute*, 23(1), 9–27.

Ingold, T., 2017b. *Correspondences*. Aberdeen: University of Aberdeen.

Ingold, T., and Vergunst, J., 2008. 'Introduction', in *Ways of Walking: Ethnography and Practice on Foot: Anthropological Studies of Creativity and Perception*, ed. T. Ingold and J. Vergunst. Aldershot: Ashgate, pp. 1–19.

Jambeck, J., Geyer, R., Wilcox, C., Siegler, T., Perryman, M., Andrady, A., Narayan, R., and Law, K., 2015. 'Plastic waste inputs from land into the ocean', *Science*, 347(6223), 768–71.

Kaiser, D., Kowalski, N., and Waniek, J. J., 2017. 'Effects of biofouling on the sinking behaviour of microplastics', *Environmental Research Letters*, 12, 1–10.

Katsnelson, A., 2015. 'News Feature: Microplastics present pollution puzzle. Tiny particles of plastic are awash in the oceans – but how are they affecting marine life?', *PNAS*, 112(18), 5547–9.

Knappett, C., 2010. 'Communities of things and objects: A spatial perspective', in *The Cognitive Life of Things Recasting the Boundaries of the Mind*, ed. L. Malafouris and C. Renfrew. Cambridge: McDonald Institute for Archaeological Research, pp. 81–9.

Lechner, A., Keckeis, H., Lumesberger-Loisl, F., Zens, B., Krusch, R., Tritthart, M., Glas, M., and Schludermann, E., 2014. 'The Danube so colourful: A potpourri of plastic litter outnumbers fish larvae in Europe's second largest river', *Environmental Pollution*, 188(100), 177–81.

Marchand, T., 2016. 'Introduction: Craftwork as problem solving', in *Craftwork as Problem Solving: Ethnographic Studies of Design and Making*, ed. T. Marchand. Farnham, Surrey: Ashgate, pp. 1–29.

Marshall, Y., and Alberti, B., 2014. 'A matter of difference: Karen Barad, ontology, and archaeological bodies', *Cambridge Archaeological Journal*, 24(1), 19–36.

Malafouris, L., 2008. 'Is it "me" or is it "mine"? The Mycenaean sword as a body-part', in *Past Bodies*, ed. J. Robb and D. Boric. Oxford: Oxbow Books, pp. 115–23.

Mytum, H., and Meek, J., 2021. 'The Iron Age in the Plastic Age: Anthropocene signatures at Castell Henllys', *Antiquity*, 95(379), 198–214.

Quagliarini, E., Gregorini, B., and D'Orazio, M., 2022. 'Modelling microalgae biofouling on porous buildings materials: a novel approach', *Materials and Structures*, 55(158), 1–18.

Rathje, W., and Murphy, C., 2001. *Rubbish! The Archaeology of Garbage*. Tucson AZ: University of Arizona Press.

Reno, J., 2014. 'Toward a new theory of waste: From "matter out of place" to signs of life', *Theory, Culture and Society*, 31(6), 3–27.

Schofield, J., Wyles, K. J., Doherty, S., Donnelly, A., Jones, J., and Porter, A., 2020. 'Object narratives as a methodology for mitigating marine plastic pollution: Multidisciplinary investigations in Galápagos', *Antiquity*, 94(373), 228–44.

Schofield, J., Praet, E., Townsend, K., and Vince, J., 2021. '"COVID waste" and social media as method: An archaeology of personal protective equipment and its contribution to policy', *Antiquity*, 95(380), 435–49.

Schwarz, A. E., Ligthart, T. N., Boukris, E., and van Harmelen, T., 2019. 'Sources, transport, and accumulation of different types of plastic litter in aquatic environments: A review study', *Marine Pollution Bulletin*, 143, 92–100.

Shanks, M., 2008. 'Post-processual archaeology and after', in *Handbook of Archaeological Theories*, ed. H. D. G. Maschner, C. Chippindale and R. A. Bentley. Lanham MD and Plymouth MA: AltaMira Press, pp. 133–44.

Sullivan, R., 1998. *The Meadowlands: Wilderness Adventures on the Edge of a City*. New York NY: Doubleday.

Thomas, J., 2006. 'Phenomenology and material culture', in *Handbook of Material Culture*, ed. C. Tilley, W. Keane, S. Küchler, M. Rowlands and P. Spyer. London: Sage, pp. 43–59.

Thompson, R., Olsen, Y., Mitchell, R., Davis, A., Rowland, S., John, A., McGonigle, D., and Russell, A., 2004. 'Lost at sea: Where is all the plastic?', *Science*, 204, 838.

Tilley, C., 1994. *A Phenomenology of Landscape: Paths, Places and Monuments*. Oxford: Berg.

van Cauwenberghe, L. and Janssen, C. R., 2014. 'Microplastics in bivalves cultured for human consumption', *Environmental Pollution*, 193: 65–70. doi: 10.1016/j.envpol.2014.06.010. Epub 2014 Jul 5. PMID: 25005888.

Wendrich, W. (ed.), 2013. *Archaeology and Apprenticeship: Body Knowledge, Identity, and Communities of Practice*. Tucson AZ: University of Arizona Press.

Woodall, L., Sanchez-Vidal, A., Canals, M., Paterson, G. Coppoch, R. Sleight, V., Calafat, A., Rogers, A., Naayanaswamy, B., and Thompson, R., 2014. 'The deep sea is a major sink for microplastic debris', *Royal Society Open Science*, 1(140317), 1–8.

Zhu, L., Zhao, S., Bittar, T., Stubbins, A., and Li, D., 2020. 'Photochemical dissolution of buoyant microplastics to dissolved organic carbon: Rates and microbial impacts', *Journal of Hazardous Materials*, 383, 1–10.

8 BIOMORPHIC CERAMICS

Benjamin Alberti

La Candelaria Ceramics

> Human nature is an interspecies relationship.
> (Tsing 2012, 141)

> [H]umanity is less a predicate of all beings than a constitutive uncertainty concerning the predicates of any being.
> (Viveiros de Castro 2012, 32)

Ceramics from the Candelaria culture of first millennium north-west Argentina present fantastic forms of anthropomorphic and zoomorphic beings: humanoid and peccary heads, appliques of batrachian bodies, and limbs or tendrils of indiscernible creatures. Among the clear humanoid and animal themes appear biomorphs – ubiquitous, multi-scalar bulges that takes the place of bodies or limbs – and phytomorphs – a tendril form, often applied to bulges. The question that this chapter addresses is, how are we to understand plant-like forms on the Candelaria ceramics? There is something significant, I claim, about the human-plant relationship and the interpenetration of clay and plant morphologies and agency that makes this kind of ceramic copying make sense.

Multispecies histories are beginning to make a mark in archaeology (Overton and Hamilakis 2013; Pilaar Birch 2018; Živaljević 2021). The relevancy of such work given climate crises and the urgency and poignancy of the concept of the Anthropocene is unquestionable. In archaeological accounts, extra-human agencies, always present, are now increasingly visible and uncomfortably absent when not. This follows on the heels of the first corrective to humancentric archaeology, a concern with the agency of things and materials in general (Ingold 2007; Olsen 2003). Archaeologists have challenged the inadequacies of recent anthropological turns on this account. The theory of perspectivism (Viveiros de Castro 2004), for example, incorporates animals fully into human sociality but fails to treat artefactual life in the same way (with notable exceptions, see Santos-Granero 2009a), much less matter, which if it appears at all does so as a prosaic backdrop to human action or artefactual agency (Alberti 2014a). Archaeology, ironically, has been accused of just the opposite, taking things and their agency very seriously, but less so other forms of life (Overton and Hamilakis 2013; Živaljević 2021, 662). There is now, however, a robust literature on human-animal relations that includes serious attention paid to the agency of animals, such as their role in their own domestication (Pilaar Birch 2018).

Plant-life appears to be a hold out in thinking about non-humans as active agents in human-plant co-histories (see, however, Attala and Steel 2023). In a recent volume on multispecies approaches to archaeology (Pilaar Birch 2018) there is a surprising lack of attention given to plants. When plants do figure the focus is on economic or ecological relations. Archaeobotany identifies plant species and their possible uses; the analysis of plant imagery serves those same ends, where the taxonomic identification of species is simply another means for understanding plant exploitation. The imagery itself is not taken as a clue to human-plant relations, even when the plant is understood to be a cause of the imagery. Specific rock-art motifs, for example, are taken as evidence of the consumption of hallucinogens, but the nature of the relationship between psychoactive plant and human is not explored.

I argue that a multispecies approach to plant imagery must explore the role and ontology of plants, imagery and medium together. Humans, animals and plants are in a constant state of both material and semiotic 'becoming with' (Haraway 2008; Kohn 2013). Ceramic making is part of these same natural processes of growth becoming, not apart from them. Images, in this sense, grow and are grown too. Feminist physicist Karen Barad (2007) provides both a critique of representationalism and a useful conceptual language that brings into focus the relations drawn together by ceramic making that might otherwise remain obscure. Barad's concept of 'entanglement' sheds light on the role of plants and clay in Candelaria ceramic image-making. Her concept of 'intra-action' usefully describes how separate agencies are separated out in any given encounter through making physical marks. Barad's work sets the stage for the ontological difference inherent in

Amazonian theories of bodies and plant agency, or 'phytophilosophies' (Daly 2021). I argue that the phytomorphs on Candelaria vessels are 'copies' of the seedpods of the psychoactive seeds of the cebil tree. The ceramics harness the affectual power of cebil through the experience of making. The imagery on the Candelaria ceramics acts as a conceptual magnet, an 'entanglement' that pulls together and sorts out significant agencies, including humans, plants and ceramics, among others (see also Boyd, this volume). Copying, it turns out, is less about faithfully replicating appearances and more about mimesis, instantiating affective behaviours and capacities marked by the ceramic growth of the seedpods and other figurative elements. The answer to why Candelaria ceramics copy biomorphic forms is that these are not copies at all. My argument is that while 'copying' of some kind is going on, the ceramics are neither copy nor medium for other agencies. Rather, they are themselves fully agentive ceramic emissaries, beings with intentions, agency and multiple, adaptive perspectives, sent to intercede on the behalf of the Candelaria people.

'La Candelaria' is the name given to a stylistically similar set of material culture from Salta and Tucumán provinces in north-west Argentina (Heredia 1974; Franco 2021). La Candelaria occupies the intermediate *yungas* ('tropical forests') zone that lies between the lowlands of the Gran Chaco and the Andean mountains. The Candelaria ceramics share stylistic elements and themes in common with both lowlands and highlands. Vast pre-Columbian exchange networks connected both regions, through which feathers, shells, stones and other privileged items were caravanned, including cebil seeds. Candelaria ceramics often display humanoid, animals, biomorphic and other ambiguous features on a range of vessels, from miniature to large urns. It is often difficult to make out what a given plastic element is intended to depict, and there is a tendency to mix elements of different origin on the same pot. There are, though, several recurring 'base' forms, most notably the *mamelón* or bulge, a globular or sub-globular shape (see Figure 8.1). The bulge often replaces the lower 'limbs' of a vessel or is added to the main body, and then further figurative attributes are added, often that of a batrachian or fox/peccary/bat-like mammal, and very occasionally a human (see Figure 8.2). The entire body of a vessel can also take on a globular, bulge-like shape (see Figure 8.1). The overall effect is that of fantastical, hybrid creatures. Although

Figure 8.1 A relatively simple Candelaria vessel showing the globular-shaped body and a bulge on its back on which a simple batrachian has been modelled. The front legs show the tuberous form.

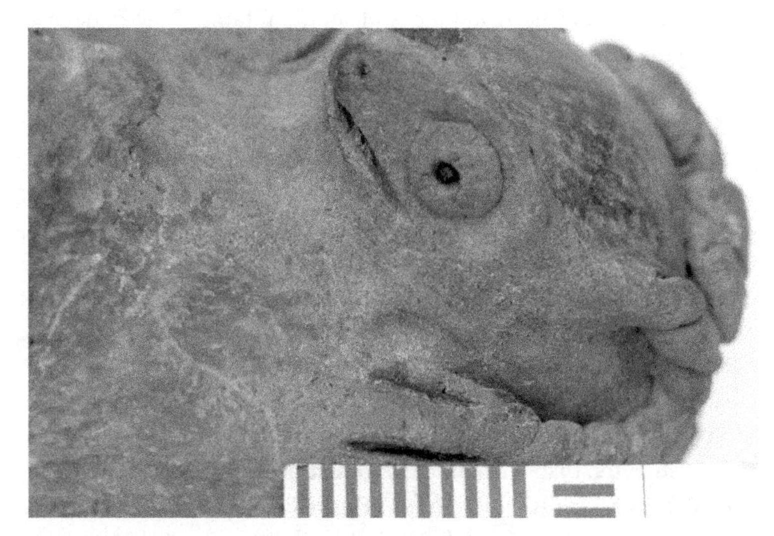

Figure 8.2 A batrachian addition to a bulge form. One of a pair found on the back of a vessel of the type seen in Figure 8.1.

there is resemblance to specific species, the question of what creature is being copied is not easy to answer. It seems that the iconicity of the elements of the bodies applied to the ceramic vessels is not intended to rely on faithful reproduction of the overall organism of the original but rather some specific characteristics. This is less a problem of ambiguous or inaccurate representation, I argue, than a positive aspect of the imagery.

Copying Nature

The Candelaria ceramic forms are conventionally understood to be copying natural forms. Here, I make the broadly ecological claim that it is the processes of nature, and not its external forms, that are being copied (Ingold 2015). Image making is often taken as the hallmark of behaviourally modern humans. An important developmental stage – the ability to symbolise through imitating natural forms – launched our species from its place in natural history into cultural histories. In the US south-west, the earliest extensive rock art tradition is the hunter gatherer archaic (c.8000 BCE–500 CE) (Alberti and Fowles 2018). It is known principally for abstract designs – wiggly lines, circles, dots and grid-like patterns. The conventional model has it that humans arrived and imprinted their imaginations on the blank canvas of a pristine landscape, enacting the separation between natural and cultural histories of place in the process. However, far from beginning an art tradition *ex nihilo*, the artists were actually carrying on a history that they perceived going on all around them. The rock surfaces are home to multiple non-human agencies that have left their traces – lichen, microbes, sun and rain. Copying is occurring: the forms of the abstractions at times bear close resemblance to lichen patterns and the shadows that they leave. It is difficult for an unpractised eye to distinguish between them. The abstract designs, it seems, respond to the local conditions in the same way that the inhabitants of those surfaces were already doing (Alberti and Fowles 2018).

If iconicity does not necessarily entail representation, then what are we doing when we copy? In *Mimesis and Alterity*, Michael Taussig (1993) claims that imitation is one of the most basic forms of learning. In the case of the Archaic south-west, people subsisted from gathering and hunting and were thus acutely sensitised to seeing and sensing in particular ways. The copying that takes place is part of participating in and learning the life that is going on around them, not representing something 'beyond'. I suggest we think of the Candelaria ceramics as 'ecological' in this way that dissolves the distinction between natural and human processes. Copying entails resemblance and art might imitate nature, but not by 'the reproduction of its forms', rather 'in the exploration of its processes' (Ingold 2015, 123).

Barad's Entanglement

Conventionally understood, a ceramic Candelaria pot is an inanimate product of human action. The plastic imagery is the outcome of thought imprinted on matter. The agential arrow moves steadily from human idea to human action to finished product. Meaning, then, is an idea that is attached to a medium. This kind of representationalist thinking – the belief in an ontological distinction between a representation and what is being represented – makes it impossible to conceptualise the plastic forms as anything other than representations of something separate from themselves. No matter how many 'agents' are added – clay, water, heat, spirits, etc. – the result is externally interacting items or artificially animated things. An ontological gap remains between image and support. Karen Barad (2007) offers a cogent critique of representationalism and provides us with language that avoids the pitfalls of thinking non-ontologically, which would be to succumb to representationalism (see also Govier). The issue with representationalism is that it assumes a separation between words and things, so humans cannot escape our own language constructions and therefore cannot get any closer to solving the problem that representationalism poses (Barad 2007, 137). Barad (2007, 46–9) describes how both scientific realism and social constructivism fail to suture the ontological gap. A correspondence theory of truth in which scientific language is deemed to be capable of representing accurately the properties of the external world (nature) results in physical referents that exist independently of our descriptions of them. The challenge is simply to find the correct language to describe what really exists (independently of that language). This form of realism has been thoroughly critiqued as it ignores the social or performative construction of knowledge; how we know is heavily mediated or constructed by historical, social and political conditions. There is no direct access to a value-free external world. What Barad shows, however, is that strong social constructivism also suffers from an inability to overcome the ontological divide between matter and meaning. In the latter case, matter is left intact as such; it is just that we have no direct access to it. Similarly, matter may influence discourse and practice, but the inverse is not true (see Marshall and Alberti 2014, 25–6). Furthermore, how are we to know this external world in any unambiguous sense if it is always mediated by discourse or practice? That is, our only options in defining matter have seemed to be either 'naïve empiricism' or 'narcissistic bedtime stories', in which matter subsumed by discourse takes on our own image (Barad 2007, 183).

In response, Barad (2007) proposes her post-humanist performative theory 'agential realism' in which matter and meaning, ontology and epistemology are never separate. Her neologism 'intra-action' enables us to speak of the various agencies involved – including that of the imagery – in the same breath without assuming the existence of *a priori* separate things. The goal of the concept is to provide a means of describing how determinate things and concepts are brought into being together within 'entanglements' out of a background indeterminacy. Barad, therefore, provides a conceptual language that enables us to imagine how ceramic images can be a magnet for and locus of agencies, without predetermining their ontological status. Intra-action posits that agencies, or the division between subject and object, occurs within an entity, an entanglement. That division (or 'cut') resolves the indeterminacy for that specific set of material-discursive conditions. The intra-action produces, then, the boundaries – both physical and conceptual – of the separate things within the entanglement, while it also produces the entanglement itself. Concepts are very specifically embodied, tied to their material conditions, as they are formed simultaneously (Barad 2007, 139–40). Crucially, things do not 'come into' relation; rather, relations 'bring' things into being (see Steel, this volume). Relations and not relata are ontologically primitive. That is why there are no interactions between predetermined entities, but intra-actions within entanglements that produce the bounded things that relate within that entanglement. Famously, Barad (2007, 123) provides the example of the apparent paradox that light and matter can be either a wave or a particle, which are mutually exclusive states.

The ontological status of an electron (wave or particle) depends on the apparatus used to measure its existence. The 'agencies of observation' are the measuring device plus all other relations in its vicinity (i.e., the scientist, the weather, cigar smoke, etc.), and the object is the electron. The electron marks the plate used to measure it, establishing a causal structure including the boundaries and status of all components of this entanglement. There is no contradiction in the two opposing states of matter, therefore, as the properties or meanings of things and concepts belong to the relationships that constitute them, not to the individual objects and subjects themselves (see Marshall and Alberti 2014; Fowler and Harris 2015, for archaeological examples).

Barad's theory of agential realism provides a way to think about both how to use the tools of non-mainstream Western intellectual traditions to critique our common-sense lens for understanding an image and its medium, and how to conceptualise that relationship so that we do not presume an *a priori* ontological separation. Her account is realist because it demonstrates that rigorous, unambiguous knowledge of a real (albeit locally determinate) world is possible (see Marshall and Alberti 2014). While Barad therefore provides a framework for the analysis of the ceramics, it remains abstract. Moreover, for all its innovation, agential realism is an indigenous, Western theory, and must describe the world in the terms it sets out. That is, while Barad provides an intellectual bridge and one element in a new understanding of how a body of decorated ceramics might be conceived using non-representationalist language, it does not by itself allow us to do the work of analysis. For that, I turn to other resources for understanding the inseparability of image and thing – to Amazonian theories of nature.

Amazonian Natures

In Amazonian 'eco-cosmologies' (Århem 2001), sociality is the model for relations among all beings; all relations are social relations. 'The human' is the model for agency and intentionality and all things, at bottom, have the potential to manifest their humanity. In classical anthropological categorisation, this is animism, which refers to 'the capacity to appraise plants, spirits, objects and animals as other-than-human persons, that is, as volitional, sentient, sensitive, aware, and intelligent' beings who communicate as social persons (Rival 2012, 139). In what follows, I draw on the theory of perspectivism, which works on similar principles to animism but presented as a generalised, Amerindian metaphysics. Perspectivism helps explain why it is that ceramic forms may copy natural forms but not resemble them exactly. I draw on two aspects of the theory in particular, the commitment to a multinatural world in which anything can be a subject, and a concept of body as primarily an assemblage of affects and only secondarily as a biological outer shell.

The theory of perspectivism rests on a metaphysics of multinaturalism in which culture – as a way of knowing – is singular, while nature – the way the world is – is multiple (Viveiros de Castro 2010). The world from a given species' point of view aligns with that species' capacities, needs and behaviours, in short, with its affects. One's perspective depends on one's body, because different bodies count on different bundles of affects, 'what it eats, how it moves, how it communicates, where it lives, whether it is gregarious or solitary' (Viveiros de Castro 2015, 257). Different bodies therefore presume different natures or worlds. The differences that perspectives presume are not superficial but ontological, as '[a]nimals see in the *same* way as we do *different* things because their bodies are different to ours' (Viveiros de Castro 2015, 257). To cite a well-worn example, what a human sees as blood, the jaguar will see as manioc beer. Similarly, the jaguar sees itself and its kin as 'human' and the human as prey. Malicious spirits may also see humans as prey. In the words of Davi Kopenawa Yanomami (Kopenawa and Albert 2013, 116), who anticipates our incredulity, such spirits 'see us as spider monkeys and our children as parrots. It is true!'

In multinaturalism, your world is an unstable place, material things are inherently untrustworthy, and appearances can deceive the senses. Because all species see in the same way, anxiety lies around the smallest signs that one is now seeing another creature as kin, which implies that one is seeing from another species' perspective and therefore one's body has transformed. Importantly, while a basic, physiological uniformity of bodies is recognised by Amerindians, it is appropriate affect that makes the body of each species unique. The visible shape of the body is, nonetheless, 'a powerful sign of these affectual differences', though 'it can be deceptive, since a human appearance could, for example, be concealing a jaguar-affect' (Viveiros de Castro 2015, 257). It is a continual struggle to maintain one's body in its specific form (through species-appropriate behaviours) and therefore safeguard one's point of view.

Plants play an important role in perspectivism, though they have been sidelined in comparison to studies of human-animal relations even as multispecies ethnographies gain popularity (Rival 2012; Daly and Shepard 2019). In fact, one way to counter the dangers of transformation is by anchoring society within the cycles of growth of the forest ecosystem (Rival 2012, 137). Plant life is generally understood to be agentive, with all or most plants capable of adopting a subject position in relation to humans and other beings (Daly 2021). Success in gardening for horticulturists, for example, is predicated on maintaining appropriate relationships with plants. Among the Carib-speaking Makushi people of Guyana, for example, kin terminology is used; cassava plants are 'children' to human gardeners and their tutelary spirit (Daly 2021, 1). The intimacy of relationships with certain plants overtime creates a human-plant consubstantiality via substance transfers, enhancing the subject status of such plants (Daly 2021, 8). Powerful plants tend be those with 'potent sensory properties', such as bitterness and toxicity (Daly 2021, 2), including the wide range of psychoactive plants.

Artefacts, too, can be persons. As Laura Rival (2012, 128) puts it, in Amazonia 'there are no "things", for "something" is always also "someone"'. There is no reason why anything cannot be a subject; to 'know' something is to endow it with the maximum degree of subjectivity (Viveiros de Castro 2007). Artefacts can be agents capable of a point of view, though this varies considerably by group. Artefacts can have varying degrees of agency, depending on the need to manage relations with them. These can be relations of domination and subjugation or predatory ones in which powerful objects are to be feared (Santos-Granero 2009b; Schien and Halbmayer 2014).

Pots that Resemble but Do Not Represent

There is no real canon to Candelaria ceramics, though three salient features support my analysis: first, an overall concern with growth; second, the ubiquitous multi-scaler bulge form; and third, the addition of solid zoomorphic, anthromorphic and phytomorphic plastic forms and incised marks. The growth theme is connected to the bulge, which takes on the form of a tuberous biomorph on many pieces. Bulges appear at many scales and in different positions on the vessels (see Figures 8.1, 8.2 and 8.3). They are always hollow, despite sometimes being very small, and are usually free of further modelling. However, on several examples there is a striking ambiguity achieved by the bulge, which can appear as a leg, breast or fleshy root, by subtle sculpting and the addition of a small 'teat'-like feature (see Figures 8.1, 8.3 and 8.5a).

As root, the bulge can appear as a conspicuous protuberance on the inferior part of vessels, both large and small. The larger vessels are amphora-like in form, with strongly pointed bottoms (see Figure 8.3). Each is equipped with two tuberous forms, projecting downwards from the front of the lowest part of the vessel body. These recall tubers, legs or breasts, though they are often incapable of supporting the vessel in an upright position. The effect generated by the inferior part of the pots is of an uprooted tuberous plant, such as cassava. It is likely that the pots were partially buried, as is common in the area, the bulges submerged under the earth. The same tuberous bulge form appears on many smaller, quadrupedal vessels as legs or feet (see Figure 8.1).

Figure 8.3 Tuberous forms on the inferior part of Candelaria ceramic vessel.

It may also take the place of legs on anthropomorphic ceramic vessels among the Candelaria and neighbouring cultures, the 'teat' transformed into an ambiguous foot or paw.

The second salient feature is the ubiquity of the bulge form. The plain bulge appears in a similar position as the tuberous form on many vessels. Many vessels also exhibit a globular body shape, some of the smaller vessels very obviously so (see Figure 8.1). Moreover, the bulge frequently appears added to the main body of a pot, either singularly or, often, in multiples. The size can differ from barely an inch across to many times that. They are always hollow and communicate directly with the main body of the vessel; they frequently appear on the backs of smaller, asymmetric vessels, either unadorned or supporting other applied elements.

The third feature of the ceramics are the plastic additions made to the basic bulge shape or body of the pot. These often resemble creatures, batrachian forms being particularly common, as well as fox/peccary/bat, and in two cases, human (see Figure 8.2). The whole body can be modelled, just the head, or the smallest detail, such as the end of the nose of a frog. Further details are added to the main body of the pot, including relief humanoid or zoomorphic faces on the neck of the vessel, many of which have pierced ears and noses, and incised markings on the face and body. The body of the pot may also feature small, subtle 'wings' and a 'tail' (see Figure 8.4).

It is possible to identify many of the species that are depicted on Candelaria ceramics through resemblance, though expertise is required. There is an easy argument to be made, therefore, that the Candelaria people represented the most significant or powerful species precisely because they are potent creatures. To make this argument, however, would be to assume a modern ontology, not an Amerindian one. The inherent subjectivity of things means that the 'copy' is not so much a stand in for the original but an example of it, much as Gell (1998) argued for the *etua* motif in Polynesia. Gell (1998, 191) writes: 'a *etua* motif [tattooed] on the body was not a matter of representing an *etua* which existed ... somewhere else. The tattooed *etua* was protective of the person because it was an *etua*, right there on the body, not because it "looked like" an *etua* somewhere else.' I have argued elsewhere that the practice of engraving, piercing and painting markings on ceramics is ontologically equivalent to that applied to human

Figure 8.4 Small orniform Candelaria vessel with phytoform eyebrows. The inside of the rim shows heavy use.

bodies (Alberti 2007, 2014b). The practice was designed to stabilise a body, whether clay or flesh and bone.

The visible body in Amazonian is a powerful sign, Viveiros de Castro (2015, 257 n. 5) writes, but the proof of identity is how the body behaves, because the body is 'behavior rather than visible shape'. There is a likeness in the ceramics, but one drawn from the fullness of experience rather than exclusively visual contemplation from a distance. That is why they look fantastical to us; we expect likenesses to be faithful copies of appearances and our materials to be static. Not so on these ceramics. The Candelaria, I suggest, are not trying to 'copy' an animal or plant; rather, they are 'copying' behaviours and capacities, that is, affects.

Ceramic Cebil

One applied motif that recurs on a group of orniform Candelaria ceramics resembles a seedpod (see Figures 8.4, 8.5a and 8.5b). That resemblance provides the opening for an analysis of Candelaria ceramics in the light of Amazonian theories of bodies and plant agency. I argue that it is the affective potential of the plant and not the physical likeness that is being captured. I take up the theme from perspectivism of the two different notions of bodies – as physiological shell and bundles of affects. The bulge form and the added adornments, I argue, correspond to these two kinds of body. The bulge form is the physical or exterior body, or envelope (Viveiros de Castro 2004, 465). The true body, infused with the human 'soul', is the assemblage of

Figures 8.5a and 8.5b Two orniform Candelaria Ceramic vessels with incised and modelled 'affects', including seedpod phytoform eyebrows and 'wings'. The smaller of the two would appear to be more potent given the density of affects on the body shell.

affects that identify that body through its specific perceptual apparatus as a differentiated being. In the case of the ceramics, this true body corresponds to the assemblage of attributes indexed by the anthropomorphic, zoomorphic or phytomorphic reliefs, additions and incisions. The bodies are not fantastical hybrid beings; rather they are sensible conglomerates of necessary perceptual tools – eyes, noses, eyebrows, fangs, limbs, roots, breasts and many other elements (see Figure 8.5a).

But it is more complicated than that. The bulge forms 'sprout' from the shell of the pot, itself a bulge form; and the smaller figures, incisions and other added elements sprout from the smaller bulges, echoing the theme of growth that has pots literally rooted to the earth. The whole ceramic pot can be understood as a shell to which affective elements are added. But many of those elements themselves are shells; the bulges frequently feature small creatures or parts of creatures (see Figures 8.1 and 8.2). The body shell of those creatures is the bulge, to which are added the affective elements, limbs, eyes and so on. These smaller, added bodies, though often stylised or deliberately incomplete, appear as a single body form. But that is only apparent. There are many examples of doubling. For example, the method of shaping a frog's face and forelegs on a bulge is identical to that used to shape the nose and brows of a humanoid face on the neck of a pot (see Alberti 2016, 142, fig. 3).

The ambiguity and doubling of body parts is clearly intentional. According to Fausto (2020), the ambition of Amazonian art was never verisimilitude nor the imitation of the body. To the contrary, its 'generative impulse is to figure transformation, imaging the transformational flux characteristic of other-than-human beings [by] generating the most complex and paradoxical images possible, images with multiple referents … built on the firm soil of ambiguity and instability, not truth' (Fausto 2020, 21). An example of a deliberate strategy of superposition and doubles involving anthropomorphic and orniform shapes can be found in Amazonia in the archaeological Konduri ceramics (Alves 2020; Gomes 2022). Many of the Candelaria ceramic bodies (shells and assemblages of affects) refuse an easy identification as one or the other kind of body. The bodies as wholes are complex compositions of affects; and affects are often ambiguous in their form. The relationship between the body-as-shell and body-as-affects is fractal, that is, self-similar at different scales (Gell 1998, 137). The doubling and fractality recalls the Amazonian mythic time when beings were undifferentiated into distinct molar forms, all being human. 'A fractal person', Wagner (1991, 163) writes, 'is never a unit standing in … relation to an aggregate but always an entity with relationship integrally implied'. Powerful beings, such as spirits and shamans, are versions of this undifferentiated humanity, out of which specific species forms developed. Each contains all possibilities of being within their bodies as an 'intensive multiplicity' (Viveiros de Castro 2012).

The relief phytomorph 'tendrils' play a particularly significant role, reinforcing the status of the pots as special kinds of being that manifest a multitude of affective possibilities. The appendage appears on several pots of various sizes and complexity and, on examination, can be resolved into a seedpod (see Figures 8.4, 8.5a and 8.5b). The curve of the form suggests a seedpod and the chambers of individual seeds are marked by flattening the applied clay and/or marking it with short incisions. The incised marks connect visually to other incised patterns that appear on faces, bodies and bulges (see Figures 8.5a and 8.5b). Incised marks often appear on the orniform pots, either in the place of eyebrows or on the sides and back of a vessel (see Figures 8.4, 8.5a and 8.5b). They can also be used to emphasise arms on anthropomorphic pots (see Alberti 2016, 139) (see Figure 8.1). The location becomes significant once we explore which plant these phytomorphs resemble, as they bear a strong likeness to the seedpods of the psychoactive seeds of the cebil tree (*Anadenanthera colubrina* var. *Cebil*). Admittedly, there are other seedpods similar in form, but there is a strong case to be made that, logically, they are intended to resemble cebil.

The use of cebil (the name for both tree and powdered seeds) as a hallucinogen was widespread in pre-Columbian north-west Argentina and north-central Chile. In north-west Argentina, the tree grows at altitudes between 350 metres and 800 metres in the *yungas*, the tropical rainforest home to the Candelaria culture (Pérez Gollán 2000; de Viana et al. 2014, 757). Cebil seeds have been found associated with smoking pipes in archaeological contexts in north-west Argentina dating back to at least 3600 BP and possibly earlier, representing the oldest use of psychoactive plants in the Americas (Torres and Repke 1996; Lema et al. 2015). Finds of stone, ceramic and bone pipes, and in the dryer *quebradas* and puna, wooden snuff trays and tubes are evidence of the widespread use of cebil and other psychoactive substances (Pérez Gollán 2000). Numerous seeds have been found in San Pedro de Atacama, Chile, and the Quebrada de Humahuaca, north-west Argentina, where dry conditions aid conservation. One study estimates that 20 per cent of the adult population were ingesting cebil in the period between 200 CE and 900 CE (Torres and Repke 1996, 43). Spanish colonial documents report shamanic practices, including the use of cebil, by Wichi shamans of the Gran Chaco, a lowland area contiguous with *yungas* (Torres and Repke 1996). It was also frequently added to drinks such as the alcoholic *chicha* (Pérez Gollán and Gordillo 1993; Lema et al 2015).

Psychoactive plants are prevalent throughout lowland South America, more than 250 species having been identified (Daly and Shepard 2019). Their use is widespread among Indigenous groups, associated in particular with shamanic practices, as psychoactive plants are particularly effective mediators of inter-species communication. They may also empower or enable their user to master the means necessary to cause harm. Psychoactive *bina* plants are sometimes referred to as 'teachers' by the Makushi; their powerful spirits inhabit 'fleshy storage organs such as bulbs, tubers and roots' (Daly 2021, 10). Use is not limited to human persons. For example, Runa dogs are given ayahuasca (*Banisteriopsis caapi*, Malpighiaceae) to understand fully the speech of their human and spirit masters. Humans, in turn, take it to understand fully animal spirit masters (Kohn 2013, 157).

Psychoactive plants are the 'archetypal "plant-persons"' (Daly 2021, 10). The most salient plants – and certainly those with powerful spirits or souls – tend to be those with potent sensory properties (Daly 2021, 2). For the Makushi, 'soul' (*ekaton*) is composed of multiple ancillary souls that together form the true soul (Daly 2021, 9). Each property can be associated with a part of the 'soul' of the plant. Plant children with 'strong souls' may be enlisted by a shaman to help rescue imprisoned souls (Maizza 2017, 215). Not only are they persons – psychoactive plants can also be teachers or shamans in their own right, 'specialist[s] in cross-species mediation' (Daly 2021, 2). They often have 'masters', as do other significant species. Among the Yanomami, for example, the father of the psychoactive powder *yãkoana* (*Virola elongata*) is *Yãkoanari*, 'a true elder, a very powerful spirit' (Kopenawa and Albert 2013, 79). The effects of the powder are attributed to *Yãkoanari*. If he does not know you, he will knock you violently to the ground when you ingest it. Plant shamans can also steal souls or be 'de-souled' by another shaman leading to 'soul-blindness', an inability to see beyond oneself or one's kind. For example, Runa shamans can steal the souls of the *ayahuasca* plants that belong to rivals – 'ingesting them no longer permits privileged awareness of the actions of other souls' (Kohn 2013, 117). That is, as shamans, psychoactive plants both enable shamanic activity through substance transference with human shamans and can mediate and communicate or travel across worlds themselves.

The location of the cebil pods on the Candelaria ceramics is not incidental. They do not so much replace body parts – such as eyebrows, wings or arms – as form a seedpod version of them. The addition changes the capacities of the body part. Podded eyebrows and eyes may enable different capacities of sight. Curving down to connect with the nose may reference the site of substance transfer between plant and human shaman, the powdered cebil entering through insufflation. The ceramic nose is being prepared to accept transformative substance. Furthermore, the podded wings are clear references to the ability of shamans to travel between worlds. In fact, bird-bone enema syringes have been found in Atacama from as early as 2130 BCE, used for the ingestion of alkaloids from the genus *Anadenanthera* (Horta-Tricallotis et al. 2019).

The ceramic pots have been supplied with an imposing array of affective parts. Seedpods in the place of limbs and facial features indicates a harnessing of the affective potential of cebil to the generalised shell body of the pot – eyebrow, nose and wing, being important organic-ceramic technologies of communication between worlds. Potency was enhanced, no doubt, by the aggregation of multiple affective parts present in the other reliefs and incised marks: fangs, coffee-grain eyes, incised faces, pierced noses and ears, roots, breasts, genitals, and more. Each brings, perhaps, an 'ancillary soul' that adds to the completeness of a very specific type of body, an 'affectual singularity' with its own 'perceptual apparatus' (Viveiros de Castro 2015, 257). Conneller (2011) provides an example that illustrates how such transferable affects might work on an artefact. The donning of red deer masks by the inhabitants of the Mesolithic site of Star Carr, Conneller argues, provided the wearer with the skills or capacities associated with that specific anatomical part, not the animal. The mask was an adaptive tool, allowing people 'to act in a "deerish" way' (Conneller 2011, 62). Similarly, the Candelaria ceramics hint at a being with a broad set of adaptive and transformative tools, whether apotropaic, predatory or protective.

Most Candelaria vessels for which we have provenance were found in burials. No chemical analyses to determine content have been conducted to date, though some seem to be purposively made to be interred as they are hurriedly made and show no signs of use (Alberti 2013). Other examples have horizontal striations around the lip and inner neck, indicating heavy usage (see Figure 8.4). Whatever their use in life, Candelaria ceramics were afforded a suit of affects, many of them fractal or doubles, that ensured they were highly adaptable beings. The absence or presence of eyes, for example, indicates potential relationships with spirits and the dead that the defunct or ghost may be incapable of (Alberti 2013). The vessels can be thought of as ceramic shamanic emissaries with a multitude of bodies – and therefore perspectives – that are placed in the grave to establish relationships with or guard against other beings.

Why Make *Ceramic* Images?

In perspectivism, no clear ontological differences are drawn between humans, animals and plants (Descola 2013, 9). From reading the perspectivist accounts, it is not at all clear what the ontological status is of materials such as clay, temper and water. As a general theoretical proposition, though, any part of the world is capable of subjectivity. I suggest, therefore, that these ambiguously bodied ceramics are neither copy of nor medium for other agencies but are agentive in their own right. Subjectivity is not something added to the material by the maker – what hubris that would suppose! – but is inherent to the materials. It is in the making that this begins to make sense.

Ingold (2015) has stressed that making is a special case of growing: artefacts, as humans, grow through care and attention. Slight anthropomorphic details are common on other Candelaria ceramics used in the intimate acts of preparation of food and other substances, evidence that the latent subjectivity of ceramic pots was attended to daily, whether to enable or control it (Alberti 2014b; Laguens 2024). It is a small experiential step from working daily with clay, plants, animals and human bodies to an understanding that the same processes of growth and intentionality abide in all things. Growth is never a given in any circumstances but requires intention and care from multiple participants. For example, plants play an important part in the growth of male and female bodies (Santos-Granero 2012). Pots too, through food storage, transfer and preparation. Relationships with plant-persons are experienced in a physical, sensorial way, not as abstractions (Daly 2021). Clay, water and temper are collected and mixed, and through the intimacy of touch forms are shaped that resemble other living things. As Taussig (1993) suggests, mimesis is about both copying and sensuous contact. The sensorial experience of the cebil plant is what is being captured or imitated in the ceramic. Is this process of forming – growing – the pot experienced as any different, then, from the cebil tree adding a seedpod to its branch? Or an adult encouraging the growth of knowledge and body of a child through massaging, painting, piercing or feeding? The clay vessel that the potter forms – with all its affectual potential – is another instance of growth, not apart from it.

The Ontological Status of a Plant Pot

Barad argues that the operation of an apparatus, understood broadly, is always a boundary making process – cuts are made. We cannot know what the agencies are, she writes (Barad 2007, 449 n. 11), 'in advance of engaging in the always messy projects of description, narration, intervention, inhabiting, conversing, exchanging, and building. The point is to get at how worlds are made and unmade, to participate in the process, to foster some forms of life and not others', a point that stands as much for how the people of the Candelaria conceptualised their ceramics as it does for our study of them. Barad's cut separates out subject from object on the basis of prior relations; so too in perspectivism subject and object are relational positions that depend on a 'cut', a cut that determines their boundaries from a sea of uncertainty, of indeterminate forms. The ceramic images operate as apparatuses or loci for multiple agencies that are both gathered together in the image and brought into determinacy by it. In this process, there is no appreciable difference between clay bodies, human bodies and plant bodies. Working on clay enacts the same cuts that are experienced in other domains of life – marks are left on bodies. The properties of agency and personhood that result belong to the entire entanglement, not to an external, animating power.

Candelaria ceramics copy biomorphic forms, but they are not 'copies' or duplicates. They are homologues, resemblances that indicate a shared origin. That resemblance, it turns out, is to bodies understood as assemblages of affects – behaviours and capacities – rather than to a biologically complete body. In Candelaria ceramics, the body as a shell is presented in an indistinct, generalised way, as a bulge form. Affects are added on and refer to specific capacities of bodies, not to 'whole' bodies in a biological sense. Moreover, the ontological status of a Candelaria plant pot was not predetermined. Forms were adapted and experimented with regularly, as experience dictated. The confusion or ambiguity of figures that we see in the ceramics is only apparent, the outcome of an ongoing process of learning and thinking through imitation and imagery responds to worlds in which materials are not static and humans learn and grow alongside the other creatures of the world. Forests think in images, Kohn has argued (2013, 222). The Candelaria thought in multispecies ceramic images. The cebil plant – in both its ceramic and organic form – played a pivotal role. 'Once he knows you', Davi Kopenawa says of the *Yãkoanari* spirit, 'he will help you "think right"' (Kopenawa and Albert 2013, 79).

Acknowledgements

I am grateful to Louise Steel and Luci Attala for the invitation to contribute to this volume. The chapter benefited enormously from comments by Louise and an anonymous reviewer, though I was unable to do full justice to all suggestions. Staff at the Museo Arqueológico El Cadillal, Tucumán, and the archaeological archive, Universidad Nacional de Córdoba, Argentina, facilitated access to their collections, for which I am also grateful.

References

Alberti, B., 2007. 'Destabilizing meaning in anthropomorphic forms from Northwest Argentina', *Journal of Iberian Archaeology*, 9(10), 209–29.

Alberti, B., 2013. 'Archaeology and ontologies of scale: The case of miniaturization in first millennium northwest Argentina', in *Archaeology After Interpretation*, ed. B. Alberti, A. Jones and J. Pollard. Walnut Creek CA: Left Coast Press, pp. 43–58.

Alberti, B., 2014a. 'Archaeology, risk, and the alter-politics of materiality', *Fieldsights: Theorizing the Contemporary – Cultural Anthropology Online*. *https://culanth.org/fieldsights/archaeology-risk-and-the-alter-politics-of-materiality* (accessed 3 December 2023).

Alberti, B., 2014b. 'Designing body-pots in the Early Formative La Candelaria Culture, Northwest Argentina', in *Making and Growing: Anthropological Studies of Organisms and Artefacts*, ed. E. Hallam and T. Ingold. Aldershot: Ashgate, pp. 107–25.

Alberti, B., 2016. 'Archaeologies of risk and wonder', *Archaeological Dialogues*, 23(2), 138–45.

Alberti, B., and Fowles, S., 2018. 'Ecologies of rock and art in northern New Mexico', in *Multispecies Archaeology*, ed. S. E. Pilaar Birch. London and New York NY: Routledge, pp. 133–53.

Alves, M. L., 2020. 'Revisitando os alter egos: Figuras sobrepostas na iconografia Konduri e sua relação com o xamanismo', *Boletim do Museu Paraense Emílio Goeldi, Ciências Humanas*, 15(3). *https://doi.org/10.1590/2178-2547-BGOELDI-2019-0105* (accessed 3 December 2023).

Århem, K., 2001. 'Ecocosmología y chamanismo en el Amazonas: Variaciones sobre un tema', *Revista Colombiana de Antropología*, 37, 268–8.

Attala, L., and Steel, L. (eds), 2023. *Plant Matters: Exploring the Becomings of Plants and People*. Cardiff: University of Wales Press.

Barad, K., 2007. *Meeting the Universe Halfway: Quantum Physics and the Entanglement of Matter and Meaning*. Durham NC and London: Duke University Press.

Conneller, C., 2011. *An Archaeology of Materials: Substantial Transformations in Early Prehistoric Europe*. London: Routledge.

Daly, L., 2021. 'Cassava Spirit and the seed of history: On garden cosmology in northern Amazonia', *Anthropological Forum*, 1–19. *https://doi.org/10.1080/00664677.2021.1994918*.

Daly, L., and Shepard Jr, G. H., 2019. 'Magic darts and messenger molecules: Toward a phytoethnography of indigenous Amazonia', *Anthropology Today (Special Issue: Ethnography of Plants)*, 35(2), 13–18.

Descola, P., 2013. *Beyond Nature and Culture*. Chicago IL: University of Chicago Press.
Fausto, C., 2020. *Art Effects: Image, Agency, and Ritual in Amazonia*. Lincoln NE: University of Nebraska Press.
Fowler, C., and Harris, O. J. T., 2015. 'Enduring relations: Exploring a paradox of New Materialism', *Journal of Material Culture*, 20(2), 127–48.
Franco, F., 2021. 'Reinterpretando narrativas selváticas: Una arqueología conceptual de "Candelaria" (Noroeste argentino)', *Relaciones*, 46(1), 113–43.
Gell, A., 1998. *Art and Agency: Towards and Anthropological Theory*. Oxford: Oxford University Press.
Gomes, D. M. C., 2022. 'Images of transformation in the Lower Amazon and the performativity of Santarém and Konduri pottery', *Journal of Social Archaeology*, 22(1), 82–103. *https://doi.org/10.1177%2F14696053211029759*.
Haraway, D. J., 2008. *When Species Meet*. Minneapolis MN: University of Minnesota Press.
Heredia, O., 1974. 'Investigaciones arqueológicas en el sector meridional de las selvas occidentales', *Revista del Instituto de Antropología de Córdoba*, 5, 73–132.
Horta-Tricallotis, H., Echeverría, J., Lema, V., Quirgas, A., and Vidal, A., 2019. 'Enema syringes in South Andean hallucinogenic paraphernalia. Evidence of their use in funerary contexts of the Atacama and neighboring zones (ca. AD 500–1500)', *Archaeological and Anthropological Sciences*, 11(11), 6197–219.
Ingold, T., 2007. 'Materials against materiality', *Archaeological Dialogues*, 14(1), 1–16.
Ingold, T., 2015. *The Life of Lines*. London: Routledge.
Kohn, E., 2013. *How Forest Think: Toward an Anthropology Beyond the Human*. Berkeley CA and Los Angeles CA: University of California Press.
Kopenawa, D., and Albert, B., 2013. *The Falling Sky: Words of a Yanomami Shaman*. Cambridge MA: Harvard University Press.
Laguens, A., 2024. *Archaeology and Perspectivism*. Cambridge: Cambridge University Press.
Lema, V. S., Andreoni, D., Capparelli, A., Ortiz, G., Spano, R., Quesada, M., and Zorzi, F., 2015. 'Protocolos y avances en el estudio

de residuos de pipas arqueológicas de Argentina. Aportes para el entendimiento de metodologías actuales y prácticas pasadas', *Estudios Atacameños*, 51, 77–97.

Maizza, F., 2017. 'Persuasive kinship: human–plant relations in southwest Amazonia', *Tipití: Journal of the Society for the Anthropology of Lowland South America*, 15(2), 206–20.

Marshall, Y., and Alberti, B., 2014. 'A matter of difference: Karen Barad, ontology and archaeological bodies', *Cambridge Archaeological Journal*, 24, 19–36.

Olsen, B., 2003. 'Material culture after text: Re-membering things', *Norwegian Archaeological Review*, 36(3), 87–104.

Overton, N. J., and Hamilakis, Y., 2013. 'A manifesto for a social zooarchaeology. Swans and other beings in the Mesolithic', *Archaeological Dialogues*, 20(2), 111–36.

Pérez Gollán, J. A., 2000. 'El Jaguar en Llamas (la Religión en el Antiguo Noroeste Argentino)', in *Nueva Historia Argentina, Tomo I: Los Pueblos Originarios y La Conquista*, ed. N. M. Tarragó. Buenos Aires: Editorial Suramericana, pp. 229–57.

Pérez Gollán, J. A., and Gordillo, I., 1993. 'Religión y alucinogenos en el Antiguo Noroeste Argentino', *Ciencia Hoy*, 4, 50–63.

Pilaar Birch, S. (ed.), 2018. *Multispecies Archaeology*. London and New York NY: Routledge.

Rival, L., 2012. 'The materiality of life: Revisiting the anthropology of nature in Amazonia', *Indiana*, 29, 127–43.

Santos-Granero, F. (ed.), 2009a. *The Occult Life of Things: Native Amazonian Theories of Materiality and Personhood*. Tucson AZ: University of Arizona Press.

Santos-Granero, F., 2009b. 'From baby slings to feather bibles and from star utensils to jaguar stones: The multiple ways of being a thing in the Yanesha lived world', in *The Occult Life of Things: Native Amazonian Theories of Materiality and Personhood*, ed. F. Santos-Granero. Tucson AZ: University of Arizona Press, pp. 105–27.

Santos-Granero, F., 2012. 'Beinghood and people-making in native Amazonia: A constructional approach with a perspectival coda', *HAU: Journal of Ethnographic Theory*, 2(1), 181–211.

Schien, S., and E. Halbmayer, 2014. 'The return of things to Amazonian anthropology: A review', *Indiana*, 31, 421–37.

Taussig, M., 1993. *Mimesis and Alterity: A Particular History of The Senses*. London and New York NY: Routledge.

Torres, C. M., and Repke, D., 1996. 'The use of *Anadenanthera colubrina* var. *Cebil* by Wichi (Mataco) shamans of the Chaco Central, Argentina', *Yearbook for Ethnomedicine and the Study of Consciousness*, 5, 41–58.

Tsing, A., 2012. 'Unruly edges: Mushrooms as companion species', *Environmental Humanities*, 1, 141–54.

de Viana, M. L., Giamminola, E. Russo, R., and Ciaccio, M., 2014. 'Morphology and genetics of *Anadenanthera colubrina* var. *cebil* (Fabaceae) tree from Salta (Northwestern Argentina)', *Revista de Biología Tropical*, 62(2), 757–67.

Viveiros de Castro, E., 2004. 'Exchanging perspectives. The transformation of objects into subjects in Amerindian ontologies', *Common Knowledge*, 10(3), 463–84.

Viveiros de Castro, E., 2007. 'The crystal forest: Notes on the ontology of Amazonian spirits', *Inner Asia*, 9(2), 153–72.

Viveiros de Castro, E., 2010. *Metafísicas Caníbales. Líneas de Antropología Posestructural*. Buenos Aires: Katz Editores.

Viveiros de Castro, E., 2012. 'Immanence and fear: Stranger-events and subjects in Amazonia', *HAU: Journal of Ethnographic Theory*, 2, 27–43.

Viveiros de Castro, E., 2015. *The Relative Native: Essays on Indigenous Conceptual Worlds*. Chicago IL: University of Chicago Press.

Wagner, R., 1991. 'The fractal person', in *Big Men and Great Men*, ed. M. Godelier and M. Strathern. Cambridge: Cambridge University Press, pp. 159–73.

Živaljević, I., 2021. 'Multispecies pasts and the possibilities of multispecies futures in the age of the Anthropocene', *Etnoantropološki problemi*, 16(3), 659–76.

9 OUR BODIES AND SOILS

The Art of Making Compost and Becoming Places

Luci Attala

> Something... must be wrong somewhere, if the only way to understand our own creative involvement in the world is by first taking ourselves out of it.
>
> (Ingold 1995, 58)

'Soil' is the term given to the result of an infinite array of interactions achieved over enormous stretches of time. Soil appears to be steady and silent. It lies underfoot, with the potency to redesign the earth's surface – to transform and disguise the past. Soil combines temporality, place and motion into material striations that wraparound and embrace the globe. According to Macfarlane (2020, 89), soil is a resource bank for the understorey and a 'black box' of writhing lives that confound biologists. For Tsing (2015) it is a social space and a relational complexity that she likens to a city. For this chapter, soil is also recognised as a magic, teeming underworld – as a shifting, moving, post-human shimmering (Rose 2017) vibrancy (following Bennett 2010), where the ancestors assemble and where our collective material origin story can be read like a book – but I also consider how soil is known as what Augé described as a 'non-place' (1995); a transitory zone that people imagine they walk over (rather than ultimately settle into), and how this characterisation supports and perpetuates the intellectual separation that upholds human exceptionalism. By drawing this to your attention, my aim is to foreground the shared unity of materials and provoke an ethic of care for soils, rather than attend to place-making. This is a call to actively encourage people back into conscious relationship with the materials that form the ground rather than associate it with ideologies that contentiously tie nationalities and ownership to geographies. Consequently, this chapter is interested in how people and soil materially co-create each other, and therefore works to tie your brute physicality – your flesh, hair, nails, teeth and bones – to the multiplicity of entities that collectively comprise soil so that we can all be a matter of the past and the future simultaneously, and that instead of imagining you are using soil or passing by, you know you are physically ingrained and inseparable. In doing so, I hope to stimulate a discussion on the politics of matters that does not position humanity above matter – and encourages a way of approaching life that grasps the brute material connections between bodies and soils (rather than souls) which reminds the reader that how lives live (and die) can directly contribute to the cultivation and nurturing of more-than-humanity. Using a mixture of autoethnography, microbiology, history, and quantum and particle physics, this chapter rethinks position, perspective and place using the material behaviours of compost as a medium and as an activity. By playing with the ghostly paradox of superposition – the quantum mechanics that demonstrates particles can be in two locations at once – I note that whether one is alive or dead, one is endlessly materially present and contributing in extra and ordinary ways.

Soils tend to be described through the lens of plant growth and agriculture; portrayed as loosely cohered media that provide structural and nutritional support for plant life. Made up of multiple ingredients, soils composition and function are explained through the language of yields and plant health. Using these foci, soil is the farmer and gardener's base and agriculture's production line, and any lack of fertility is framed as production value lost. This rendering establishes the value of soil in terms of harvests, a perspective that 'cuts' (following Barad's Cartesian cut, 2003; 2007, 333) a distance between human (and other) bodies and the range of matters that collectively assemble to create the ground or the pedosphere.[1] To diminish this distance, I am focusing on compost and the process of composting to draw people and soils together and amplify the shared materiality and dependency between people and the earth. To begin moving people and the earth more obviously together, it helps to look at what the roots of the word 'compost'. 'Compost' is derived from the Latin words *composita/compositum* and *com-ponere*. *Composita/compositum* means 'composed with' or 'put together in combination' and the word, *com-ponere* describes 'putting together and placing', or to settle, to be at home (from *ponere*, meaning to place). Composting, therefore, refers to a process of rehoming or re-placing by combining ingredients in such a way that they settle, joined in new forms and combinations. A process that effortlessly illustrates what we all know; namely, that the materials and substances of the Earth constantly decompose, return to the ground and recycle into new forms. The role of people in this process is assumed to be the composter, to compost other items, not to *be* the compost and as such demonstrates the intellectual and linguistic disconnect that generates notions of otherness, the ability to detach, and the almost-squeamishness associated with imagining any connection with the ground. I am making the argument that it is another product of the damaging illusion that represents people as walking *on and using*, rather than living *as*, the earth. Therefore, to challenge the habit of presuming that earthy matters are materially divorced from human matters, this piece thinks about how to place you 'into' the Earth – how to implant you back into the ground, to bury your thinking deep into the darkness of the land, where you can meditate on accepting that you are as much soil as you are human (see Sambento, this volume).

In this case, the word 're-placed' describes a cycle, rather than substitution, and is used to highlight the links between lives above ground and underfoot. Adapting Latour's (2018) call to shift sideways, this is a shift downwards to inhabit the soil and become what he terms 'terrestrial' and asks an urgent question about what 'belonging to a territory' might describe. The notion of becoming-with (Haraway 2008) and re-placing both fundamentally 'challenge delusions of separation' (Wright 2014, 278) that prioritise and rely on xenophobia and hierarchies, and, therefore, is invoked here to think again critically about the terms of attachments that people use to associate with places (Aucoin 2017). Consequently, this is not about making *my* place but is the matter of how bodies and soils perfuse and equip each other, regardless of location. Following Puig de la Bellacasa's (2017) it also provides a new form of ecological care, whereby making compost sits within a circular economy of caring, at a time when innovation is required to avoid soil collapse. Re-placing also offers an alternative to the increasingly popular rewilding that encourages separation because it requires that humanity move away from 'nature' for it to replenish. Re-placing, in contrast, allows people to actively, and thoughtfully, contribute to the wellbeing of places physically, and with the more-than-human entities that create the shifting fabric or fields of soils.

Soil: Life's Backdrop

Soil requires multiple ingredients to form; it needs a combination of minerals, gases and organic matters. The mineral components of soils are derived from the bedrock of the area that, through the forces of weathering, the action of water and the power of vegetation growth, have been modified, cracked, split and pulverised into a composite of microscopic rocks. These miniscule pieces hold gases (where there is no water) – mainly nitrogen, oxygen and carbon dioxide – in the little pockets formed between larger particles. Add to this any organic matter that you can think of in various stages of growth or decay, some water and a host of living creatures (i.e., worms, insects, protozoa, bacteria, fungi, moles, etc.) and you have the energetic, shifting concord of ingredients that comprise what is typically termed 'soil'. Soils tend to settle in most people's minds as inert, as a layer or basic earthly covering to walk over. However, as advances in genome technology have enabled microbiological DNA to be recorded, the extent to which soil is alive is now better appreciated.

Today, during the time that Haraway (2015, 161; 2016, 144) calls 'the Great Dithering' and others call the Anthropocene, it is increasingly obvious how human actions are threatening the many ways that lives currently live. Not stopping at organic life, anthropogenic activities have also put soils, the air and water, under threat. Now, as the recognised habitat of multiple species, including billions of microbes, soil's role in maintaining global biodiversity is better understood, as are the concomitant raft of ecosystem services that their presence provides. Exponentially distressed by the application of artificial fertilisers, pesticides, fungicides and other chemicals such as those associated with the use of cement, concrete and microplastics (Sen 2015; see Govier, Scott, this volume), soils are not just altered, they are troubled and degrading, unable to function as previously – for example, as a carbon sink[2] to alleviate the tangle of consequences associated with climate change.[3] Quite simply, as the creatures that live in the soil are culled *en masse*, soil biodiversity declines and so does soil fertility and, in parallel, aboveground biodiversity and fertility inevitably suffer (Bach and Wall 2018). As the Earth's soils degrade, it is possible to treat and regenerate it. To *re-create*, *re-place* and *re-wild* the soil, or to place again, what is and has been (re)moved. There are several ways to achieve bioremediation. For example, planting certain species such as legumes allow pollutants to be removed through incorporation into the plants' bodies. Similarly, fungi disintegrate pollutants using modifying enzymes (Winquist et al. 1990; Tsing 2015), and the soil bacteria that support the plant biome are also able to decontaminate land of certain substances, such as arsenic and lead (Gonzales Tenao and Ghneim-Herrera 2021). In addition, *Geobacter sulfurreducens* is now shown to be able to neutralise nuclear radiation (Cologgi et al. 2011) (fun fact: *Geobacter* is also able to conduct electricity (Bond and Lovley 2003) and may be used to generate electricity from waste while repairing the soil (Franks 2011; Lovley and Walker 2019)). Another way to improve topsoil is by adding organic matter.

The importance of soil biodiversity has been brought to the attention of the human world through the United Nations' *International Year of Soils* in 2015, and the *Global Soil Biodiversity Atlas* (Orgiazzi et al. 2016) the following year. Similarly, Bach and Wall's (2018) chapter on soil in the biodiversity section of the *Encyclopedia of the Anthropocene* illustrates the significant role that soils play with regard to restoring ecosystem biodiversity. But for most people, any clear associations between our lives and that of the soil are fuzzy, academic and notional rather than embodied and actual. The soil is simply an untidy constant that requires attention from farmers and gardeners, it can be bought in bags from the garden centre but it should be kept off feet and out of houses. However, as the liveliness of soil continues to vitiate through contamination, a cascade of detrimental environmental, ecological, social and economic consequences is following, and, as the methods that life uses to perpetuate and flourish are being forced to adapt to this new anthropogenic normal, any previously established ways of thinking about soil must similarly respond and alter. In short, imaginings, or conceptions, of what (and who) soil *is* must be reconsidered so that lives can be lived with awareness of the fundamental ongoing connection that we have with these matters, and that the difference between what is imagined and what *is*, is attended to (Ingold 2021).

To quickly provide an example of how representations can disconnect from material realities, let us explore how soil is often presented in discussions around germination. Soil is displayed as the setting or the inert, unresponsive location that plants use to anchor their roots. Cast your mind back to those time-lapse educational videos of seeds germinating on social media or YouTube. Without exception, the films present soil as a lifeless, dark medium – a place in which to demonstrate where the tiny seed miraculously shapeshifts. These short clips allow us to marvel at how the seed alters, almost bursting with some mysterious aliveness that permits it to first open and then tentatively begin to reach out. Our attention is enticed to notice how the seed develops pale snaking fingers with delicate hair-like feelers that penetrate and cling to the soil, while simultaneously it twists, dancing or meandering up towards the light. The soil is nothing more than the stage on which this performance is acted out.

This kind of beautiful imagery easily enchants. Playing with temporality it certainly demonstrates how embryonic life is mystifyingly dynamic, propelled into action in ways that appear intelligent and are still not fully grasped. But these representations also importantly fail to account for the symbiotic relationship that the seed has with the soil or how the soil is instrumentally active in the support of the seed's transformation. From the footage, it would be easy to assume that plants do this alone, perhaps with a bit of water – but this is simply not the case. Seeds require a multitude of entities that inhabit what is called 'the rhizosphere' – the thin region around the budding roots – to gather and help seeds establish. As the tiny root readies to emerge, a throng of busy micro-organisms act furiously to produce what is called a biofilm, which covers the budding root (Nelson 2018). This coating, comprising bacteria, fungi and protists (unicellular organisms), assists the baby plant to join with the soil at this critical time. Without a film forming, plants would inadequately attach or secure themselves, could fail to benefit from improved nutrient uptake and would have reduced tolerance to environmental stress (Pandit et al. 2020). Simultaneously, the new plant's root starts to exude substances (amino acids and sugars) in response. This exudate helps cohere soil particles together, but also feeds the organisms that are actively assisting the plant (Jacoby et al. 2017). This series of activities provides an interesting picture of partnership and symbiotic engagement (Oldroyd et al. 2011). As the plethora of lively organisms vigorously jostle to welcome the penetrating roots, the plant reciprocates to the hospitality by providing encouraging gifts (Attala 2017).

Using this knowledge, the boundary between what is materially plant and what is materially soil becomes less clear cut and shows that soils should not be conceived of as merely the ground on which life exists, nor should it be assumed to be basic, nondescript dead, dirty stuff desiccated into a dusty (or sodden into a muddy) Earthly coating. Soils are active, multipurpose complex events that both produce and reflect the character of a location, that establish the personality of a place and that actively contribute to the fashioning of life's forms out of the materiality of multitudes of reformed and reforming ancestors. Soils, therefore, are not just the setting or venue of ecosystems, they are a reorganising consistency that emit and absorb gases, provide a habitat for countless creatures, a purifying and filtering passage for liquids, and a recycling unit where substances 'come home' and where nutrients revert for further reuse. In conjunction with this line of thinking, soil might not be adequately described as an object or even a substance. Following Ingold's (2010) definition, soils might be better defined as things (see also Alberti, Steel this volume).

Things, according to Ingold (2010), are unfinishable, boundaryless, constantly changing and ambiguous. Things are where 'the threads of life' (Ingold 2010, 4) gather and continue. Unsure of what exactly a 'thread' of life is, what I take from this characterisation is that stuff amalgamates with stuff and, in doing so, endures. Matters attract, mix, blend, bind and disintegrate relentlessly forming and reforming, without beginning or end in a vast crucible of activities. Soils, like everything, therefore, are materially lively and vibrant (Bennett 2010). They are mixtures of matters – mineral, gaseous and organic – manifesting in kaleidoscopic combinations and with distinctive characteristics (Fayers-Kerr 2019).

The tendency to reduce study to knowing 'objects' rather than things in relationships is now extensively critiqued (Ingold 2010; Govier and Steel 2021; see Boyd and Steel, this volume), especially when the framework for understanding objects insists on a human exceptionalist perspective to do so. Soils provide us with a noteworthy medium to think with (Puig de la Bellacasa 2017), and offer an easy illustration of the flows, connections, porosity and blendings that collectively craft the world. Approaching seed germination with scant reference to the colonies or communities of micro-organisms, the associations of minerals, gases and liquids that also play active and important roles in the processes, overlook these important connections and perpetuates the erroneous vision of the Earth as populated with independent individuals. Studies across disciplines increasingly cite dependencies and relationships above singularities and are progressively rejecting the naturalisation of competition by revealing the ecological collaborations that living requires (Ereira and Attala 2021; Attala and Steel 2023).

The above has shown that soil is better conceived of as a community or as a collective, a place of symbiotic tangled and dynamic support, where entities work together to perpetuate the collective. It is the first recycling centre, a world comprised of kin (Haraway 2015; 2016), a place where most of life emerges and returns. Soil therefore happens. Moreover, it has been happening with negligible input from humanity for most of the world's existence. Compost, on the other hand, is not soil. It is an exercise that humanity specifically employs to harness worldly processes to affect an outcome. And this is where we are now going to turn our attention.

The Histories and Economies of Compost and Composting

The word 'compost' describes the substance produced by decomposed organic matter – typically achieved by mounding, layering and mixing discarded scraps and plant waste. Producing compost is 'a human practice' (Neimann 2020) and not simply a matter of leaving items to decay, nor should it be mistaken with other processes of transformation such as the production of sewage sludge of fermentation. (Certain fermentation processes are sometimes described as composting. An example of this is the Japanese Bokashi method of dealing with food waste. Composting requires oxygen to break down organic matter, fermentation does not. The Bokashi method activates anaerobic breakdown using inoculated bran. Thus, strictly speaking, it is a fermentation process.) Similarly, fertilisers should not be misunderstood as a form of compost. Fertilisers provides artificial or organic nutrients for plants, while compost feeds and improves the quality of the soil. Making compost requires the action of microbes (and others) to alter any layers of rotting substances until the point where they are described as stabilised. Therefore, making compost requires some ecosystem knowledge that enables one to work-with or enlist and encourage the assistance of micro and larger organisms (e.g., worms). According to definitions, compost should not be mistaken for soil because it does not contain the bedrock – the parent material – that establishes soils' initial character. Compost adds humus[4] and, therefore, something human to the soil. It represents a method by which the liveliness that the soil creates is replaced by humans.

Applying manure to replenish nutrients in the soil is a common worldwide practice. However, in locations where livestock are scarce and 'night soils'[5] are not used, composting has offered an alternative solution to soil infertility and as a practice provides a picture of humanity's long conscious associations with the land. The archaeological record suggests that early Scottish farmers spread the contents of their midden mounds across fields (Guttmann 2005) and there is evidence to show that soil improvement techniques were used widely in ancient Greece and Rome (Montgomery 2007). Similarly, in Ethiopia, organic materials have long been piled up by households to produce *kosi* (the local term for compost) (Mukai and Oyanagi 2019) and the dark earths or *Terra Preta* of the Amazon suggest that soils have been managed by Indigenous groups for thousands of years (Silva et al. 2021). However, composting has not only darkened and enriched soils, it also casts a dark shadow over some people's experiences while generating a different kind of riches – as its use in plantations illustrate.

Records, as far back as the seventeenth century, show that slave owners documented concerns that their yields were in decline (Warde 2018). Decades of non-stop cultivation depleted the infamously fertile fields and solutions were sought. To combat dropping profits, a manure market soon developed (Brunt 2007), with slaves' excreta advocated for use in the fields (Foy 2016) along with off-farm nitrogen-rich soil improvers such as fish scraps and guano, all of which proved costly, thus prompting discussions of developing viable alternatives. From the outset, the business of slavery controlled the trade of important commodities such as sugar, coffee and tea in the growing European markets. However, increasing demands saw diminishing returns and increased prices, which stimulated research into agricultural innovation and the development of artificial fertilisers to ensure profitability.

The slave trade was officially abolished in Britain in 1807, yet it took another twenty-six years – until 1833 – for some British Empire slaves to be emancipated; other British territories had to wait. Troubled by another drop in profits that resulted from these freedoms, plantation owners sought financial compensations and turned their attention to finding fresh forms of cheap labour. India, already an important seat of the British Empire's money-earning power and influence, proved to be the setting where employers could reduce costs and replenish the workforce cheaply. This realisation saw countless Indian workers indentured (a process that binds workers to their employers) with many shipped out to toil on various plantations across the British colonies and the production of compost at scale followed them.[6] Indentured labourers continued to suffer inhumane treatment, including containment, long hours and poor, if any, wages (Tinker 1974), yet any attempts to prohibit indentured contracts failed to get through parliament until as late as 1917.[7]

In 1921, a short section titled *Artificial Farmyard Manure* was published in *Nature*, which, recognising the shortcomings of manure, explained how to improve soil by producing compost at scale. Concerned about depleted soil health on tea plantations, the imperial botanist and Cambridge scholar, Sir Albert Howard, working then for the Indian government, took inspiration from the article and created his own method, which he named 'The Indore Process', and positioned it in competition with the now emerging artificial fertiliser industry. Howard controversially fought the establishment by advocating organic over artificial methods, and, consequently, is often presented benignly as the father of organic agriculture (Heckman 2006). But it was on the colonial plantation economy in tropical zones where Howard's compost established its value in terms of boosted yields, availability of materials and the avoidance of shipping costs associated with transporting artificial fertilisers. As the following illustrates:

> Up to the present the most spectacular applications of the Indore process have taken place in the plantation industries – coffee, tea, sugar, sisal, and so forth. The recent fall in prices has naturally been followed by drastic reductions in overhead expenditure, including the amount spent on fertilisers. (Howard 1935, 29)

Thus, Howard's production of compost at scale allowed plantations to remain profitable and consequently played an important role in preserving the flow of millions towards the merchants and bankers in England, while incalculable others suffered in their millions under their employ (Laurence 1994). Colonial agricultural developments in the overseas territories saw an intensification of techniques of extraction and exploitation that remain embedded, even naturalised, into today's systems. Wolford (2021) theorises the socio-environmental consequences of plantations borrowing the term 'Plantationocene' from Haraway (2015) rather than the Anthropocene to signal the responsibilities of plantation economies in building today's industrialised normal, a method that enabled the white elite to flourish at the expense of enslaved others.

Despite this shadowy legacy, compost is now delivering an alternative kind of potency – one that is inspiring a generation of new, green shoots and healthy growth in association with recent moves to rethink production in the world. Composting effortlessly lends itself to post-human moves such as the new materialities because it easily collapses the established intellectual, disciplinary and material boundaries, and actively breaks down and blends items that once appeared disparate. Jones (2019), for example, makes tremendous use of the notion of composting as an economic ontology in the landscapes of a postcapitalist world where capitalism is imagined decentralised and alternative economies are employed. By drawing in the overarching ideas of the more-than-human, he develops a 'more-than-human economy', which, by attending to the ways that compost 'becomes', Jones (2019) engages a mixture that includes: more-than-human labour, making ends meet, surplus, waste and resilience to find ways to bind various ingredients and advocate for new economic thinking. Similarly, soil and culture are drawn together by Landa and Feller (2010) and a 'how to' of relationships with worms is explored by Abrahamsson and Bertoni (2014) to demonstrate the care involved in supporting compost to form. However, I do not want to simply think-with compost and use it as a metaphor, nor use biomimicry to validate a position on a more 'natural' economy. What I do want to explore is the political order of materials with a view to think about how human activity can feed the future and how everyday taking and using requires replacing:

> The miracle of capitalism is that the more it becomes rotten, the more it decays … But as something decays, it also thrives. (Žižek 2022)

> Death is good for the garden. (Harrison 2022, 74)

Making compost requires 'waste' and signals an end or death of those items as they decay. Rather than a graceful transformation, the term points towards the dirty and the disgusting and insinuates a loss of value. In the closed system of the Earth, it is hard to really throw anything away. Throw it, sure, but it will still be somewhere – like *The Cat in the Hat* (Seuss 1957) trying to remove a spot of dirt and in wiping it realises that it has simply transferred to the cloth that now needs to be cleaned. Compost, however, valorises the product of rotting, and therefore very obviously challenges the ideas of what constitutes waste and dirt (see Reno 2014). Moreover, it demonstrates that consumption is not profligate if there are means or mechanisms to replace what has been used (Raworth 2017). By adopting a new materialities approach to composting, this chapter is cultivating the idea of re-placing as a method to consciously refabricate places. Rather than direct reciprocity (Sahlins 1974), or a debt repaid that relies on twisting value into quantities, the actions associated with composting allow people to deliberately contribute to the flourishing and liveliness of the soil, and, in consequence, the character of a place. By working to replace in this way, one intentionally plays a part in co-creating the fabric and health of places.

To replace means to put back. The 're' prefix is associated with doing 'again', as in to make a place again by putting back. Like rewilding, replacing allows what is characterised as damaged to repair. In association with the Anthropocene and the damage done, composting is a method that allows one to meditate on what one wastes and today is regularly advertised as one of the most useful methods of recycling that a household can contribute. As a home composter, I get excited when, through the alchemy of mixing, I transform kitchen waste, cardboard, leaves and bark into a rich, dark humus that I can then re-place, or turn into my garden. I have been composting for several years but have been more conscious about the process recently. In the past, I would simply chuck everything together and hope for the best. These days I try and organise things more obviously, taking care to provide what the microbes might need from me. Following Žižek's comment about capitalism above, and in association with composting, I have been able to reconsider the meaning of decay and recognise more obviously how dying feeds life.

Composting, therefore, has shown me not only how I can contribute to the creation of healthy soils but also how my life is being slowly, incrementally buried, dug into and forming into a place. In addition, my shed self (following Coard 2019) – the epidermal detritus plus hair and nails that fall from me – allow me to further join with places. Not unlike the ideas of quantum mechanics, our shed selves show how we are both cohered and spread – simultaneously me and not me – slowly becoming soil throughout a lifetime. Thus, from a new materialities perspective, waste is not only redefined, it also illustrates how things can be in different places simultaneously. I began this chapter by stating that I wanted 'to re-place you. To embed you back into the earth, [so that] you can meditate on accepting that you are as much soil as you are human.' Acknowledging that parts of you are constantly shedding and rejoining the world of matter offers a minor insight into the incessant composting process of life. The act of composting bodies provides another, perhaps more obvious, example of how 'Death feeds everything that lives' (Wilson 2008).

Life always comes from somewhere. There is a tendency to imagine 'life' as immaterial, as something distinct from the brutishness of materials, and to assume that whatever life is, it quickens the inertia of matter. Fed by philosophical and spiritual notions that claim life somehow *inhabits* matter and that it begins and ends elsewhere (possibly, in some kind of 'heaven'), life is often characterised as the spark that animates matters. However, there is no consensus on what life is or what it is that allows the apparently torpid to muster into action. Despite this unknowing, it is known that all matters 'return', and that your death, according to Jenkinson (2015) should be thought about if you care about the world coming after you.

There are numerous ways to care about the world (Abbots et al. 2016) and re-placing or replenishing is just one of them. Many Indigenous philosophies describe life as a kind of debt that needs generalised reciprocal action (Sahlins 1974) to maintain existential (and material) flows and balance (Ereira and Attala 2021). To hoard or accumulate, therefore, may block or starve areas in need and following Mauss' assessment of the obligations of giving, failing to give after receiving or holding on to items can cause harm, because – using the Maori notion of the *Hau*, the spirit of a thing 'wishes to return to its birthplace' (Mauss 2001, 12). The obligation to reciprocate and the expectations of reciprocity employ ideas typically associated with kinship; namely, one is obliged through the give and take of existence to recognise the material bonds that endure between entities: 'The dirt is your grandmother' (Slow Buffalo in Neihardt 1984, 212).

Night Soils

The word 'soil' is obviously associated with 'soiled'. 'Soiled' originally associated with being polluted with sin, defiled and foul, is currently used to explain a loss of bowel control, and thus links faeces, dirt and the earth explicitly. Flushing human excrement away and getting it out of homes as soon as it is created is a modern method that not all populations benefit from. Stories of lives in locations prior to the installation of household grey water infrastructure offer a different picture of how bodily waste products can be conceived. Born in the Congo, but settled in Zambia, my father recounted stories of when 'the shit cart' came to town. Living in Ndola, Zambia, in the 1940s and 1950s, saw people constructing outhouses at the end their white walled and green lawned urban gardens. Backing on to what were termed 'service lanes', wide enough that donkey drawn carts could pass through for collection, outhouses had a trap door at the back which allowed the full 'honey buckets' to be whipped out and replaced by the '*banamazayi*'[8] (Mwanyangwi 2022) workers each night before dawn. The contents of the town's buckets were spread on fields and used as *mafundu* or manure. According to Madocks (2022), the shift from slash and burn farming to more intense cropping (*mabala*) meant that fields required the application of fertiliser, which the shit carts provided. Madocks (2022) informed me that when one walks over the fields today one can 'quite often see trouser buttons, clay pipe stems and broken pieces of Victorian medicine bottles mixed into the soil – this is the debris from centuries of night soil dispersal'.

Night soils, or biosolids, have been, and still are, seen as valuable in several locations. For example, up until the 1980s, human faeces were a source of income in Japan. Japanese landlords owned their tenants' waste and sold it, and stealing human excrement was a serious crime. Today, in Haiti, the waste, collected by the 'poopmobile' from the community toilets set up to stop human faeces getting into the water supply, is used to enrich depleted soils (Dell'Amore 2011). Similarly, in Kenya, companies are converting raw sewage into fuel bricks to discourage the devastating deforestation being caused by the voracious charcoal industry. In addition, biogas is also being created and black soldier flies are being used to convert faeces into animal feed. These examples of circular economic thinking (Raworth 2017) demonstrate some of the ways that humanity can replace what it has used and produced.

Using human waste is one thing but seeing the entire human body *as* waste is another, and it remains a contentious subject for many – in part because it uncomfortably bridges the gap between what is human and what is earth. Intentionally composting human bodies for soil enrichment is illegal in most countries currently (presumably for concerns about hygiene and contamination) but, nevertheless, has occurred throughout history regardless of laws. For example, recent archaeological studies of battle sites demonstrate that the bones of dead soldiers were collected, sold and ground up for use as soil improvers in Europe (Pollard 2021).

Ancient mortuary practices show that for at least 78,000 years people have taken the time to carefully organise the dead (Martinón-Torres et al. 2021), but as burial space starts to run out, and the chemicals used in embalming render the soils in graveyards toxic, people are now actively seeking alternative solutions. For example, bodies that have not been embalmed can now be buried in forests set aside for the purpose. The Woodland Burial Trust (2022) claims there are more than 300 woodland burial sites across the United Kingdom. These sites are deemed consecrated land, which guarantees that the space will remain in perpetuity. Similarly, in Japan tree burials (*jumokuso*) are increasingly popular. According to Boret (2014), tree burials vary. For example, the term can describe either pouring cremated remains into a hole near an established tree or planting a tree in a hole that is filled with deposited ashes. First adopted in 1999, tree burials are a relatively new option and are often advertised as a natural choice that allows one to be buried in harmony. However, its growing popularity is not simply associated with ecological thinking in Japan. Burial plots are costly and the annual upkeep charges add to the price, thereby making burial difficult for many families. The reduction in cost offered by tree burials means families have been known to relocate already buried individuals to avoid the recurring graveyard fees (Boret 2014).

Woodland burials add to and produce forests. They adapt the notion of a graveyard, rather than abandon them entirely, thus, allowing death to remain contained and organised into spaces and places designated for the purpose. The freedom to 'be anywhere and everywhere' is made possible by throwing the ashes to the wind or the sea. Or alternatively, by being buried in the garden as one of my neighbour's chose to do with his father's ashes. Jon decided to plant a rose bush in a hole with this father (see Figure 9.1). That rose is now

Figure 9.1 Roger rose.

addressed as Roger (rose), in recognition of how Roger is incorporated into the plant and remains with the family.

Today, there are just two states in the United States where intentionally composting dead people is legal. Katrina Spade designed her composting methods on the principles of livestock mortality composting after recognising some problems in the funeral business. Seeing that nature is good at death, and that current methods tend to restrict and delay decomposition, Spade developed a method that enables the deceased to be turned into three wheelbarrows of organic matter to take home and spread on the garden in a period of just a few weeks – bones and all. Spade's company, 'Recompose', uses an above ground system whereby the corpse is rotated in a steel vessel covered with woodchips, straw and alfalfa. With the addition of oxygen and moisture, microbes then act to transform the ingredients into compost, fast. According to Spade (2017), a 'death care revolution has begun' in which the materiality of human bodies is consciously being supported to transform into a compost that can be added to the soil and then used to knowingly support plant growth. This process not only allows people to be re-placed, but it also avoids using the corrosive chemicals currently required by cremation and burial, reduces the extending need of land for graveyards and provides a mechanism by which people can realise (make real) the way they can materially contribute to the future – an action that Robertson (2014) considers may bring existential comfort.

Macfarlane (2020) reminds us that digging into soil is like digging into life and death simultaneously, and Recomposes' services make this all the more obvious. Archaeology reveals how the past is hidden in layers within the soil, but by composting it becomes possible to walk on and see the influence of our immediate ancestors, just under the surface beginning to nourish the future – as the composted and redistributed plant, and other bodies transform into the leaves and fruits to be eaten and into the dust in the skies that cause the sunsets to paint the fading light red.

Conclusion

According to Macfarlane (2020), there is something disconcerting about reaching into the soil because everyone that has ever been lies down there, waiting for you to join them. The linguistic links between the words '*humo*' (meaning soil), 'humus' (which refers to the organic content of soil) and 'human' are not incidental and illustrate the recognition of fundamental material connections between people and the earth. Moreover, the Latin *humando*, meaning to bury, highlights one of the actions that binds people to the soil. For Pogue-Harrison (2003) burying the dead humanised the landscape and is one of the ways that humans retain a connection with those that have gone. That people physically return to, or are replaced, from whence they came is materially factual. It is only human imaginings that allow the cut between matter and ideas to persist and encourages people to fantasise that they are made of different stuff from the world. Extending Augé's (1995) notion of non-place to include soils, this chapter has used compost and the composting of lives to think about re-placing – the conscious making of places that use the materiality of people's flesh to substantially nourish the future.

Swanson et al. (2017, M1) asked the question, 'what if all organisms, including humans, are tangled up with each other?', while Haraway (2017, M25) in the same book, explains that *sym-poiesis* – a term that challenges the notion that anything can be made or exist alone – is the physical reality that we must use to stay with the trouble and form kin with the worldly critters we live with. This chapter shows that acknowledging and working with the tangle in mind could be a route towards genuine environmental care – a kind of care that recognises the fundamental existential connections that tie humanity to other species and entities. Soil has been shown to be both an active community and the location that bodies of all kinds return to as they decompose and recompose into the next generation, and it has been positioned as a core aspect of what could be understood as the physics or political order of materials. Imagining one stands apart from this order is illusory, futile and probably damaging. Grasping that you are materially integrated might be the beginning of 'being ecological' (Morton 2018).

Sahlins (2021) talks of the immortality of materials in a discussion about differences in belief systems and how they locate power. He identifies a split between those who consider power to be located external to the world, and those who understand forces as immanent – present as worldly substances and materials like the rocks, minerals, trees, water, air, and so on. Using this perspective, power emerges as embedded and material, and all worldly flourishing, including that of the human, is inseparably dependent on what material processes provide or enable. This chapter avoids making 'nature' supernatural, instead preferring to level the playing field between all 'things', but it hopes to demonstrate that the materials that comprise people, rocks, earthworms, plants and microbes are substantially integrated and integral to the way that the recursion forces or powers can act to perpetuate and reproduce. This perspective shares or distributes power across scales and avoids the trap of creating hierarchies or externalising power into a god or a demon. The new materialities is concerned with demonstrating how life is unquestioningly and relentlessly material, despite any cognitive abilities that may represent it otherwise. Remembering that one is material encourages a life lived in association with the other forms that materials together create. The powers that decompose form into re-compostable materials and are the forces that recycle lives and provides the answers to the age-old questions, 'What will become of me and what abides after death?' It realises (makes real) how the materiality that forms flesh persists and is always somewhere. Perhaps more importantly it recognises a kinship with the soil and all the ancestors of all species that lie under foot, which allows one to settle as earth and as *the* Earth knowing that our materiality will feed future generations by replenishing the soils that we become.

Notes

1. Pedosphere: the outermost layer of the earth; the soil.
2. Carbon sink: a carbon sink is a reservoir that can absorb and store atmospheric carbon.
3. Plants ensure that carbon can be stored in the soil; therefore, bare ground inhibits this. In association, farmers must care for the microscopic livestock in the soil to help plants flourish.
4. Latin meaning 'earth' and linked to *humanus* ('human') that joins people with the earth.
5. Night soil refers to spreading human excrement on fields. See the section on 'Night Soils', this chapter, for more detail.
6. Indentured labour is described as a system of slavery by some (Mahoney 2020) and slavery in disguise by others (Chaillou-Atrous 2020).

7. Distressingly, recent reports show that modern-day slavery persists in the tea plantations in some areas.
8. A derogatory term for people only good enough to be toilet cleaners (Mwanyangwi 2022).

References

Abbots, E.-J., Lavis, A., and Attala, L. (eds), 2016. *Careful Eating: Bodies, Food and Care*. London: Ashgate.

Abrahamsson, S., and Bertoni, F., 2014. 'Compost politics: Experimenting with togetherness in vermicomposting', *Environmental Humanities*, 4(1),125–48. *https://doi.org/10.1215/22011919-3614962*.

Attala, L., 2017. '"The Edibility Approach": Using edibility to explore relationships, plant agency and the porosity of species' boundaries', *Advances in Anthropology*, 7(3), 125–45. *https://doi.org/10.4236/aa.2017.73009*.

Attala, L., and Steel, L. (eds), 2023. *Plants Matter: Exploring the Becomings of Plants and People*. Cardiff: University of Wales Press.

Aucoin, P. M., 2017. 'Toward an anthropological understanding of space and place', in *Place, Space and Hermeneutics: Contributions to Hermeneutics*, vol. 5, ed. B. B. Janz. Cham: Springer, pp. 395–412. *https://doi.org/10.1007/978-3-319-52214-2_28*.

Augé, M., 1995. *Non-Places: An Introduction to the Anthropology of Supermodernity*. London and New York NY: Verso.

Bach, E. M., and Wall, D. H., 2018. 'Trends in global biodiversity: Soil biota and processes', in *Encyclopedia of the Anthropocene*, ed. D. A. Dellasala and M. I. Goldstein. Oxford: Elsevier, pp. 125–30.

Barad, K., 2003. 'Posthumanist performativity: Toward an understanding of how matter comes to matter', *Signs: Journal of Women in Culture and Society*, 28(3), 801–31.

Barad, K., 2007. *Meeting the Universe Halfway: Quantum Physics and the Entanglement of Matter and Meaning*. Durham NC and London: Duke University Press.

Bennett, J., 2010. *Vibrant Matter: A Political Ecology of Things*. Durham NC and London: Duke University Press.

Boret, S. P., 2014. 'An anthropological study of Japanese tree burial: Environment, kinship and death', in *Death and Dying in Contemporary Japan*, ed. H. Suzuki. London: Routledge, pp. 177–201.

Bond, D. R., and Lovley, D. R., 2003. 'Electricity production by *Geobacter sulfurreducens* attached to electrodes', *Applied Environmental Microbiology*, 69(3), 1548–55. *https://doi.org/10.1128/AEM.69.3.1548-1555.2003*.

Brunt, L., 2007. 'Where there's muck, there's brass: The market for manure in the Industrial Revolution', *The Economic History Review*, 60(2), 333–72.

Chaillou-Atrous, V., 2020. 'Indentured labour in European colonies during the 19th century', in *EHNE Digital Encyclopedia of European History*. Paris: Sorbonne University. *http://ehne.fr/en/node/12279*.

Coard, R., 2019. 'Done and dusted: Exploring the mutable boundaries of the body', in *Body Matters: Exploring the Materiality of the Human Body*, ed. L. Attala and L. Steel. Cardiff: University of Wales Press, pp. 157–72.

Cologgi, D. L., Lampa-Pastirk, S., Speers, A. M., Kelly, S. D., and Reguera, G., 2011. 'Extracellular reduction of uranium via *Geobacter* conductive pili as a protective cellular mechanism', *PNAS*, 108(37), 15248–52. *https://doi.org/10.1073/pnas.1108616108*.

Dell'Amore, C., 2011. 'Human waste to revive Haitian farmlands? Community toilets can yield nutrient-rich fertilizer', *National Geographic*. *www.nationalgeographic.com/culture/article/111026-haiti-waste-poop-fertilizer-farms-soil-science-environment* (accessed 24 August 2022).

Ereira, A., and Attala, L., 2021. 'Zhigoneshi: A culture of connection', *Ecocene: Cappadocia Journal of Environmental Humanities*, 2(1), 7–22. *https://doi.org/10.46863/ecocene.18*.

Fayers-Kerr, K., 2019. 'Becoming a community of substance: The Mun, the mud and the therapeutic art of body painting', in *Body Matters: Exploring the Materiality of the Human Body*, ed. L. Attala and L. Steel. Cardiff: University of Wales Press, pp. 109–33.

Foy, A. M., 2016. 'The convention of georgic circumlocution and the proper use of human dung in Samuel Martin's "Essay upon Plantership"', *Eighteenth Century Studies*, 49(4), 475–506.

Franks, A., 2011. 'Mud power: How bacteria can turn waste into electricity', *The Conversation*. *https://theconversation.com/mud-power-how-bacteria-can-turn-waste-into-electricity-3677* (accessed 24 August 2022).

Gonzales Tenao, S., and Ghneim-Herrera, T., 2021. 'Heavy metals in soils and the remediation potential of bacteria associated with the plant microbiome', *Frontiers in Environmental Science*, 9. *www.frontiersin.org/articles/10.3389/fenvs.2021.604216*.

Govier, E., and Steel, L., 2021. 'Beyond the "thingification" of worlds: Archaeology and the New Materialisms', *Journal of Material Culture*, 26(3), 298–317. *https://doi.org/10.1177/1359183521102555c*.

Guttmann, E. B. A., 2005. 'Midden cultivation in prehistoric Britain: Arable crops in gardens', *World Archaeology*, 37(2), 224–39. *https://doi.org/10.1080/00438240500094937*.

Haraway, D., 2008. *When Species Meet*. Minneapolis MN: University of Minnesota Press.

Haraway, D., 2015. 'Anthropocene, Capitalocene, Plantationocene, Cthulucene: Making kin', *Environmental Humanities*, 6(1), 159–65.

Haraway, D., 2016. *Staying with the Trouble: Making Kin in the Chthulucene*. Durham NC: Duke University Press.

Haraway, D., 2017. 'Symbiogenesis, sympioesis, and art science activisms for staying with the trouble', in *Arts of Living on a Damaged Planet: Ghosts and Monsters of the Anthropocene*, ed. A. Tsing, H. Swanson, E. Gan and N. Bubandt. Minneapolis MN: University of Minnesota Press, pp. M25–M50.

Harrison, O., 2022. *Came the Lightening: Twenty Poems for George*. Guildford: Genesis Publications.

Heckman, J., 2006. 'A history of organic farming: Transitions from Sir Albert Howard's "War in the Soil" to USDA National Organic Program', *Renewable Agriculture and Food Systems*, 21(3), 143–50.

Howard, A., 1935. 'The manufacture of humus by the indore process', *Journal of the Royal Society of Arts*, 84(4331), 26–59.

Ingold, T., 1995. 'Building, dwelling, living: How animals and people make themselves at home in the world', in *Shifting Contexts: Transformations in Anthropological Knowledge*, ed. M. Strathern. London: Routledge, pp. 57–80.

Ingold, T., 2010. *Bringing Things Back to Life: Creative Entanglements in a World of Materials*. NCRM Working Paper. Realities/Morgan Centre, University of Manchester. *https://hummedia.manchester.ac.uk/schools/soss/morgancentre/research/wps/15-2010-07-realities-bringing-things-to-life.pdf* (accessed 4 December 2023).

Ingold, T., 2021. *Imagining for Real: Essays on Creation, Attention and Correspondence*. London and New York NY: Routledge.

Jacoby, R., Peukert, M., Succurro, A., Koprivova, A., and Kopriva, S., 2017. 'The role of soil microorganisms in plant mineral nutrition: Current knowledge and future directions', *Frontiers in Plant Science*, 8, 1617. *https://doi.org/10.3389/fpls.2017.01617*.

Jenkinson, S., 2015. *Die Wise: A Manifesto for Sanity and Soul*. Berkeley CA: North Atlantic Books.

Jones, B. M., 2019. 'Com(post) capitalism: Cultivating a more-than-human economy on Appalachian anthropology', *Environmental Humanities*, 1(1), 1–26.

Landa, E. R., and Feller, C., 2010. *Soil and Culture*. Dordrecht, Heidelberg, London and New York NY: Springer.

Latour, B., 2018. *Down to Earth: Politics in the New Climatic Regime*, trans. Catherine Porter. Cambridge: Polity Press.

Laurence, K. O., 1994. *A Question of Labour: Indentured Immigration into Trinidad and British Guiana*. New York NY: St Martin's Press.

Lovley, D. R., and Walker D. F. J., 2019. '*Geobacter* protein nanowires', *Frontiers in Microbiology, Section: Microbial Physiology and Metabolism*. *https://doi.org/10.3389/fmicb.2019.02078* (accessed 4 December 2023).

Macfarlane, R., 2020. *Underland: A Deep Time Journey*. London: Penguin Random House.

Martinón-Torres, M., d'Errico, F., Santos, E., et al., 2021. 'Earliest known human burial in Africa', *Nature*, 593, 95–100. *https://doi.org/10.1038/s41586-021-03457-8*.

Montgomery, D. R., 2007. *Dirt: The Erosion of Civilisation*. Berkeley CA and Los Angeles CA: University of California Press.

Morton, T., 2018. *Being Ecological*. London: Penguin Books.

Madocks, R., 2022. *Northern Rhodesia and Zambia Group or (the NRZ) Facebook*, 21 May 2022. *www.facebook.com/groups/nrzofnr/?multi_permalinks=10158488762581817¬if_id=1653123667454663¬if_t=feedback_reaction_generic&ref=notif* (accessed 30 July 2022).

Mahoney, M., 2020. 'A new system of slavery? The British West Indies and the origins of Indian indenture', The National Archives. *https://blog.nationalarchives.gov.uk/a-new-system-of-slavery-the-british-west-indies-and-the-origins-of-indian-indenture/* (accessed 4 December 2023).

Mauss, M., [1925] 2001. *The Gift: Form and Reason for Exchange in Archaic Societies*, trans. W. D. Halls. London: Routledge.

Mukai, S., and Oyanagi, W., 2019. 'Decomposition characteristics of indigenous organic fertilisers and introduced quick compost and their short-term nitrogen availability in the semi-arid Ethiopian Rift Valley', *Scientific Reports*, 9, 16000. *https://doi.org/10.1038/s41598-019-52497-8*.

Mwanyangwi, N., 2022. *Northern Rhodesia and Zambia Group or (the NRZ) Facebook*, 21 May 2022. *www.facebook.com/groups/nrzofnr/?multi_permalinks=10158488762581817¬if_id=1653123667454663¬if_t=feedback_reaction_generic&ref=notif* (accessed 30 July 2022).

Nature, 1921. 'Artificial Farmyard Manure', *Nature*, 107, 828–9. *www.nature.com/articles/107828a0.pdf*.

Neihardt, G. J., 1984. Cited by DeMallie, R. J., (ed.) *The Sixth Grandfather: Black Elk's Teachings Given to John G. Neihardt*. Lincoln NE: University of Nebraska Press.

Neimann, M., 2020. 'Composting's colonial roots and microbial offshoots', *Edge Effects*. *https://edgeeffects.net/composting-colonial-roots/* (accessed 4 December 2023).

Nelson, E. B., 2018. 'The seed microbiome: Origins, interactions, and impacts', *Plant Soil*, 422, 7–34. *https://doi.org/10.1007/s11104-017-3289-7*.

Oldroyd, G. E. D., Murray, J. D., Poole, P. S., and Downie, J. A., 2011. 'The rules of engagement in legume-rhizobial symbiosis', *Annual Review of Genetics*, 45, 119–44.

Orgiazzi, A., Bardgett, R., Barrios, E., Behan-Pelletier, V., Briones, M., Chotte, J. L., Deyn, G. B., Eggleton, P., Fierer, N., Fraser, T. D., Hedlund, K., Jeffery, S., Johnson, N., Jones, A., Kandeler, E., Kaneko, N., Lavelle, P., Lemanceau, P., Miko, L., and Wall, D., 2016. *Global Soil Biodiversity Atlas*. Luxembourg: European Commission, Publications Office of the European Union. *https://esdac.jrc.ec.europa.eu/public_path/shared_folder/Atlases/JRC_global_soilbio_atlas_high_res-2019-06-13.pdf* (accessed 4 December 2023).

Pandit, A., Adholeya, A., Cahill, D., Brau, L., and Kochar, M., 2020. 'Microbial biofilms in nature: Unlocking their potential for agricultural applications', *Journal of Applied Microbiology*, 129, 199–211. *https://doi.org/10.1111/jam.14609*.

Pollard, T., 2021. 'These spots of excavation tell: Using early visitor accounts to map the missing graves of Waterloo', *Journal of Conflict*

Archaeology, 16(2), 75–113. *https://doi.org/10.1080/15740773.2021.2051895*.

Pogue-Harrison, R., 2003. *The Dominion of the Dead*. Chicago IL: University of Chicago Press.

Puig de la Bellacasa, M., 2017. *Matters of Care: Speculative Ethics in More Than Human Worlds*. Minneapolis MN: University of Minnesota Press.

Raworth, K., 2017. *Doughnut Economics: Seven Ways to Think Like a 21st Century Economist*. London: Random House Books.

Reno, J. O., 2014. 'Towards a new theory of waste: From matter out of place to signs of life', *Theory, Culture and Society*, 31(6), 3–27. *https://doi.org/10.1177/0263276413500999*.

Robertson, E., 2014. 'Volcanoes, guts and cosmic collisions: The queer sublime in *Frankenstein* and *Melancholia*', *Green Letters*, 18(1), 63–77. *https://doi.org/10.1080/14688417.2014.890530*.

Rose, D. B., 2017. 'Shimmer when all you love is being trashed', in *Arts of Living on a Damaged Planet: Ghosts and Monsters of the Anthropocene*, ed. A. Tsing, H. Swanson, E. Gan and N. Bubandt. Minneapolis MN: University of Minnesota Press, pp. G51–G64.

Sahlins, M., [1974] 2017. *Stone Age Economics*. London: Routledge.

Sahlins, M., 2021. *The New Science of the Enchanted Universe: An Anthropology of Most of Humanity*. Princeton NJ and Oxford: Princeton University Press.

Sen, R., 2015. 'Micro-organisms, -biomes and -networks of Earth's living soils', *Microbiology Today Magazine*. *https://microbiologysociety.org/publication/past-issues/soil/article/micro-organisms-biomes-and-networks-of-earth-s-living-soils.html* (accessed 24 August 2022).

Dr Seuss, [1957] 1985. *The Cat in the Hat*. New York NY and Toronto: Random House.

Silva, L. C. R., Corrêa, R. S., Wright, J. L., Bromfim, B., Hendricks, L., Gavin, D. G., Westphal Muniz, A., Coimbra Martins, G., Vargas Motta, A. C., de Freitas Melo, V., Young, S. D, Broadley, M. R., and Ventura Santos, R., 2021. 'A new hypothesis for the origin of Amazonian dark earths', *Nature Communications*, 12, 127. *https://doi.org/10.1038/s41467-020-20184-2*.

Spade, K., 2017. 'When I die, recompose me', *TEDxOrcasIsland*. *www.ted.com/talks/katrina_spade_when_i_die_recompose_me/transcript* (accessed 4 December 2023).

Swanson, H., Tsing, A., Bubandt, N., and Gan, E., 2017. 'Introduction: Bodies tumbled into bodies', in *Arts of Living on a Damaged Planet: Ghosts and Monsters of the Anthropocene*, ed. A. Tsing, H. Swanson, E. Gan and N. Bubandt. Minneapolis MN: University of Minnesota Press, pp. M1–M12.

Tinker, H., 1974. *A New System of Slavery: The Export of Indian Labour Overseas, 1830–1920*. Oxford: Oxford University Press.

Tsing, A., 2015. *Mushroom at the End of the World: On the Possibility of Living in Capitalist Ruins*. Princeton NJ: Princeton University Press.

UN International Year of Soils, 2015. '2015 international year of soils: Healthy soils for a healthy life', *Food and Agriculture Organisation of the United Nations*. *www.fao.org/soils-2015/en/* (accessed 24 August 2022).

Warde, P., 2018. *The Invention of Sustainability: Nature and Destiny c.1500–1870*. Cambridge: Cambridge University Press.

Wilson, T., 2008. *Griefwalker* [documentary film]. National Film Board of Canada.

Winquist, E., Tuomela, M., and Steffen, K., 1990. 'Bioremediation of contaminated soil with fungi', *Pollution Solutions Online*. *www.pollutionsolutions-online.com/article/soil-remediation/18/erika_winquist_marja_tuomela_and_kari_steffen/bioremediation_of_contaminated_soil_with_fungi/1649* (accessed 24 August 2022).

Wolford, W., 2021. 'The Plantationocene: A lusotropical contribution to the theory', *Annals of the American Association of Geographers*, 111(6), 1622–39. *https://doi.org/10.1080/24694452.2020.1850231*.

Woodland Burial Trust, 2022. 'Woodland burial sites in the UK', *St Albans Woodland Burial Trust Website*. *http://woodlandburialtrust.com/content/woodland_burial_places.php* (accessed 24 August 2022).

Wright, K., 2014. 'Becoming-With: Living lexicon for the Environmental Humanities', *Environmental Humanities*, 5, 277–81.

Žižek, S., 2022. 'Don't act, just think', *Big Think*. *https://bigthink.com/videos/dont-act-just-think/* (accessed 24 August 2022).

INDEX

N